635.642 STA

Stark, Tim.
Heirloom : notes from an
accidental tomato farmer /
KERMAN 1076271152

D0014607

ECKERTON
HILL FARM

HEIRLOOM

NOTES FROM AN ACCIDENTAL
TOMATO FARMER

TIM STARK

BROADWAY BOOKS
NEW YORK

PUBLISHED BY BROADWAY BOOKS

Copyright © 2008 by Tim Stark

All Rights Reserved

Published in the United States by Broadway,
an imprint of The Doubleday Publishing Group,
a division of Random House, Inc., New York.

www.broadwaybooks.com

BROADWAY BOOKS and its logo, a letter B bisected on the diagonal,
are trademarks of Random House, Inc.

The author and publisher gratefully acknowledge the following for
permission to reprint material in this book:
Excerpt from "Blackberry-Picking" from *Opened Ground: Selected
Poems 1966–1996* by Seamus Heaney. Copyright © 1998 by Seamus
Heaney. Reprinted by permission of Farrar, Straus and Giroux, LLC.

These essays have appeared in slightly different form in the
following publications:
"Groundhog Days" and "The Misunderstood Habenero" in *Gourmet*.
"The Tomato People" in the *Washington Post*.
These essays were read in slightly different form on the following program:
"The Tomato People" and "A Farm Grows in Brooklyn" on
NPR's *This I Believe*.

Book design by Judith Stagnitto Abbate/Abbate Design

Library of Congress Cataloging-in-Publication Data
Stark, Tim.
Heirloom : notes from an accidental tomato farmer /
by Tim Stark. — 1st ed.
p.   cm.
1. Stark, Tim.   2. Tomato growers—
Pennsylvania—Biography.   3. Tomatoes—Heirloom
varieties—Pennsylvania.   I. Title.
SB349.S73 2008
635'.642092—dc22
[B]   2007048075

ISBN 978–0–7679–2706–2

PRINTED IN THE UNITED STATES OF AMERICA

1 3 5 7 9 10 8 6 4 2

First Edition

FOR MY MOTHER AND FATHER

Contents

A Farm Grows in Brooklyn

An unsustainable writer's life—hunkered down at a desk on the top floor of a Brooklyn brownstone—proved to be the soil in which the farmer within me took root. Out in the street one wintry March evening, pacing and frothing over poverty, injustice, and those politely worded impersonal rejection letters quarterlies dispense the way banks hand out toasters, I came upon a trash bin loaded with basement scraps: water pipes, furring strips, two-by-fours studded with nails that could be straightened out and reused. From these scraps, I saw in a flash of insight, I could construct a seed germination rack. In the gardening catalogs, a deluxe seed starting kit, complete with full-spectrum light and soil heating mats, cost about eight hundred dollars. Which I didn't have.

What I did possess—or so I fancied—was a farmer's resourcefulness. Four years earlier, I had started a vegetable garden on the land I had grown up on in Pennsylvania. Road trips in a battered Toyota pickup kept me and my landlord seasonally flush in tomatoes and pesto. I had never given serious thought, until this moment, to expanding into a truck patch. It was an idea so impractical it bordered on fantasy. Most everything I planted—peas, lettuce, carrots, beans, sweet potatoes, beets—got chewed down to nubs by deer and groundhogs. Whether these fur-bearing gourmands were susceptible to primitive superstitions about nightshades, I don't know, but come August, you'd look at my garden and think the only thing I'd planted was tomatoes. The vines strafed the basil and thyme, shaded the sun-loving peppers, and strangled the zucchini, which, only weeks earlier, armed with baseball-bat-sized fruit, had conquered the same ground. As for the tomatoes plumping up on those vines, some looked more like peaches, pears, lemons, or Cinderella pumpkins. There were purple, white, pink, and green orbs of musky softness whose rich, acidic juices colonized the canker sores that throbbed in my mouth until my addiction petered out in September. This jungle of sumptuous, mismatched love apples had its origins in winter days spent poring over the annual yearbook of the Seed Savers Exchange, a phonebooklike compilation of nonhybrid, heirloom seeds offered for a small fee by the gardeners, master and amateur, without whom the tomato would be red for eternity. Cherokee Purple, Green Zebra, Garden Peach, Plum Lemon, Radiator Charlie's Mortgage Lifter. I could not help noticing how these tomatoes responded to me in ways that women, bosses, and literary editors never had.

It took five trips to drag my lumber and water pipes up three flights to my apartment. I already had soil heating mats, seeding trays, soil mix, and seed for some sixty tomato varieties. I bought cheap shop lights and hung them from the water pipes an inch above the seeded trays. A week later, my writer's garret was home to three thousand fledgling tomato plants, tightly organized in labeled rows, stretching toward fluorescent bliss.

Alas, you can't file away three thousand tomato seedlings like another so-so draft. I had always replenished my writer's war chest with freelance consulting gigs, so to support my tomatoes, I took on a consulting job that required frequent trips to Albany. When the seedlings outgrew the four trays in which they were crowded together, I spent a weekend potting them up into individual plugs, which meant I now had to accommodate forty plug trays. I bought more shop lights—enough to satisfy the photosynthetic needs of half my seedlings—and put the tomatoes on two twelve-hour shifts, half the trays soaking up the fluorescent rays while the other half slept. Since a sliver of light will keep a seedling awake until it keels over of insomnia, I went out to the street and hauled home four refrigerator-sized boxes so the slumbering trays could be placed in the pitch dark.

I was keeping farmer's hours now, especially when I had to catch the 6:00 a.m. train to Albany. Up at four thirty in the morning to put my tomato seedlings through the Chinese fire drill, transferring the sleepers from the boxes to the fluorescent lights, bedding down the ones that had been up all night, watering and inspecting, readjusting my circulation fans, and checking on the chile peppers germinating on the heat mats. Another Chinese fire drill when I got home in the evening. My bedroom was a humid microcosm, bugs helicoptering here and there, the damp smell of tomato musk everywhere.

Once, during a meeting in Albany, I convinced myself I had forgotten to insert the thermometer into the soil of my chile peppers that morning. Horrific scenarios preyed on my imagination: with the thermometer exposed to air, the heat mats would grow hotter and hotter, the chile seedlings would fry, the refrigerator boxes would ignite. I left the meeting early and *flew* home to New York City, convinced I would have to rescue my seedlings from a burning brownstone.

As it turned out, the thermometer was lodged snugly in the soil, where it belonged.

City life agreed with my tomatoes. Unharried by the elements, they had their first brush with adversity on an April day when I carried them up to the roof. The real sun was no forty-watt bulb. The seedlings nearly wilted to death. For two weeks, I spent every free moment weaning them from the fluorescent lights, hauling them onto the roof, then back down when the wilting started. Adaptation to the sun brought with it a burst of growth: my seedlings needed larger containers. The rooftop was big enough to hold ninety trays, but I needed to construct cold frames to protect the seedlings from the unstable April weather. My landlord intervened when I found a trash bin full of windows for my cold frames. This was a landlord who, during lean months, had kindly accepted tomatoes and zucchini in lieu of rent. Concerned, and for good reason, that the windows of my cold frames would take flight in the wind, he evicted my tomatoes.

Two trips in my Toyota pickup brought all of the seedlings back to my boyhood home in Pennsylvania, to Eckerton, where I laid claim to a couple of acres of shaley ground and tracked down an old high-school classmate who managed to start up the Ford 8N tractor that had sat unused for fifteen years. The only labor I could afford was pro bono, so I convinced all of my friends who were doctors and lawyers that it would be fun to come out to the country for a weekend and help transplant two acres of seedlings with garden trowels. From there, my first season as a farmer unfolded as if the inverse of Murphy's law was at work. Although I had no irrigation, the clouds delivered almost every week. When buyers at the local produce auction refused to bid on my gangly, multicolored misfits, Greenmarket in New York City offered me space. And so, back to that beautiful mosaic of a city they went, these upstarts with the quirky immigrant names: Black Krim, Extra Eros Zlatolaska, German Johnson, Aunt Ruby's German Green, Zapotec Pleated, Rose de Berne.

The rest of that first season is a frenetic blur of pulling weeds and picking tomatoes and begging for people—my girlfriend, mother, father, friends, neighbors, anyone—to help me pick tomatoes.

And hawking tomatoes. Pulling into Union Square Greenmarket in the morning, always late from having picked until dark, I would brace myself for the relentless questions. Because I was practically subsisting on the tomatoes myself—there was no time for a sit-down meal—the descriptions came literally off the tip of my tongue: Yellow Brandywine's nectarine-rich sweetness, Cherokee Purple's winey acidity, Green Zebra's salty tang, White Wonder's appeasing mildness. Trusting more to their own instincts, the chefs grabbed empty tomato boxes, climbed aboard the truck, and rummaged away in an urban version of pick-your-own. When I was splitting at the seams with abundance, the overloaded Toyota blew a clutch and I had to rent a box truck, which the tomatoes ably filled. The truck buzzed with chefs.

City life agreed with my tomatoes. I sold out every time.

As the season wore on, though, I began to feel toward this lucky crop the way a father might feel toward an onerous brood of children, wearily anticipating the day the last spoiled brat gets hauled off to college. I remember the Friday evening my girlfriend and I came into the city to deliver tomatoes because I wasn't coming to market until Monday, and by then I would have *two* full truckloads. We were muddy and worn out from picking all day and we had not eaten since breakfast. There were the added aggravations you would expect on the most humid evening of summer: a grocer who waited up for me and then groused about how "tomatoes are in the dog house." Two parking tickets. A maître d' who physically blocked my passage when I tried to sneak a delivery through the dining room during peak service. Restaurants had yet to discover how a reputation for seasonal purity might be clinched by having a filthy farmer waltz fifty pounds of just-picked tomatoes between crowded tables and into the kitchen.

On the way uptown with the final delivery, we got snagged in gridlocked traffic, and I felt a tremendous urge to pull a Jackson Pollock with my remaining tomatoes, to yank the stems out like hand-grenade pins and pulp the white van wedged in front of me.

"To the dog house with all of them," I announced. "I will never grow tomatoes again!"

When we finally made it to the last drop-off, at Restaurant Daniel, chef de cuisine Alex Lee helped us carry the tomatoes into the kitchen. When Alex introduced us to Daniel Boulud, Daniel looked us over and promptly said, "Let me give you something to eat."

"A quick bite to eat sounds great," I said. I was thinking of all the tomatoes waiting to be picked at the crack of dawn.

"Here, there is no such thing as a quick bite to eat," Daniel explained as a table was set up in the kitchen for us. We must have been the most bedraggled, bordering-on-homeless specimens on the Upper East Side of Manhattan that night, and here was Daniel Boulud offering us a coveted seat. I sat down and rose again, thinking this time of my truck parked at an expiring meter. "Don't worry," Alex said, heading outside with some quarters.

My farmer's appetite rendered me callous to the task of committing to memory the courses served to us that evening. There were seven in all. Each course featured a paired wine and a kitchen staffer who offered a table-side explanation of the provenance of the ingredients in the dish. And the bread! I mopped up every drop of every sauce until every plate reflected my face with its week's growth of whiskers.

I do remember a clear, lemon-tinted soup made from the freshly squeezed juices of Taxi tomatoes. At the bottom of the bowl, a tiny wild Mexican tomato glimmered like a fathomless ruby.

Hey! Those were my tomatoes!

Never again? I say that every October. And every March, I drag out the Dumpster-inspired germination rack that moved to Pennsylvania with me. For twelve years now, I've made a living from tomatoes. It's not a bad life. I still do not own a farm, but I have my own tractor.

And that landlord who gave my tomatoes the boot? He works for me.

A Brief History of Farming
at Eckerton Hill

The new summer home of Isaac Eckert, President of the Farmers'
bank, was the scene of a pleasant gathering upon the occasion
of the flag presentation by Mr. Eckert's Hamburg friends. The
home, which has been named "Eckerton," is delightfully situ-
ated upon the crest of a hill about a mile and a quarter north
of Lenhartsville.

So begins the article that appears top and center on the front page
of the June 23, 1906, edition of the *Reading (PA) Weekly Eagle*.
The page is formatted like the *Wall Street Journal*, small boldfaced
headlines leading off columns of tinily printed news that is broken
in two places by pencil-type sketches, one of the Eckerton home,
the other of the "garage and stable" constructed a stone's throw
away. ECKERTON AND ITS FLAG RAISING stands preeminent
amid a potpourri of local and national news briefs, listed with no
concern for order of importance, and including, among other
items, two fatal trolley accidents; the fiftieth wedding anniversary
celebration of Mr. and Mrs. Aaron Diefenderfer; Theodore Roo-
sevelt's demands that a vacation-minded Senate decide whether
a lock-and-dam-type canal would be appropriate in Panama; and

the feats of one Theodore Newcomer, who, while cultivating corn in Swope's Valley, came upon and killed a blacksnake measuring seven feet four inches in length and twelve inches in diameter. The snake, according to the news item, was "said to be the largest reptile killed in that valley for many years."

> *The location is one that could not be duplicated. The scenery is wild and picturesque. Surrounding the house are beds of blooming flowers, beyond there is a wide lawn. This is skirted on the one side by a field of waving wheat and on the others by growing timber. Beyond these tower the mountains, dressed in deep green foliage.*

A most amenable gesture on the part of the mountain timber, donning its finest verdure for the christening of a banker's recently cleared acres. Upward of 120 guests, including the twenty-piece Hamburg Band, participated in the Eckerton flag raising. Shuttled to the event in cars belonging to Isaac Eckert and his friends, the guests were served dinner on the wide porch that encircled the Eckerton home. Then an iron flagpole was put into place and, as the band struck up the national anthem, Old Glory was hoisted to the wind.

"We are brought together by feelings of good fellowship," spoke a J. Fred Isett. "We ask [Isaac Eckert] to accept this gift, a token than which no grander can be given to any man."

"You might have presented Mr. Eckert with a diamond or a ruby," said ex-congressman H. D. Green, "but you could not have presented him with a more acceptable gift than this flag."

Once the speeches were concluded, the band led the party on a march around the two buildings. In my imagination, the Hamburg Band is a rousing Bavarian ensemble, sun-spangled brasses mirroring the "deep green foliage," accordion bellowing huskily, the tuba's *BOOM-pah BOOM-pah* thrumming barn walls and silos for miles around. Marching just behind the band is the crowd of earthy Germanic people, some of whose ancestors had set off from points along the Rhine back when there was land to be claimed from Penn's woods. Their preferred tongue is Pfälzisch, a version of Low German that bears as many resemblances to Yiddish as it does to the language of Goethe. The list of attending guests is nearly as long as the article itself—Balthasers, Raubenholds, Millers, and Zettlemoyers. A fair number of them are surely the tillers of the soil without whom a summer retreat could not have been possible for the president of the Farmer's Bank. Coming on top of everything they have to be thankful for at this moment—a promising new century with Old Glory rippling in a hilltop breeze, seed heads forming in tall fields of wheat, the sun-warmed earth giving off damp, fecund odors—the music stirs them to a fever pitch of emotion. Twice around the property they marched. *BOOM-pah, BOOM-pah, BOOM-pah.*

"The remainder of the afternoon," according to the article's final sentence, "was devoted to social intercourse."

Cropped and framed, this page in the history of northern Berks County, Pennsylvania, hung on the living-room wall of the Eckerton summer home when my family moved into it in August of 1969. The Farmer's Bank was still the Farmer's Bank in 1969. And the house still featured a wide wraparound porch. But the property had grown to thirty acres, twelve of them farmland and four planted with fruit trees. Taking advantage of cheap Depression-era labor—skilled men willing to work for beer—the shirt manufacturer who took over Eckerton in the 1930s had undertaken an aggressive building campaign. He converted the "garage and stable" into a guesthouse. On the hillside above the orchard, he dug out a large swimming pool. Enclosing the pool on one side was a looping art deco railing, there to protect post-Prohibition-era revelers from crashing through the windows of the greenhouse jutting out beneath the concrete walkway. A sense of permanency was lent to Eckerton's cleared space by liberal applications of mortar and the pink-streaked mountain stone known locally as "bacon slab." In front of the main house, a walled-in teardrop-shaped garden was lush with roses the day we moved in. Two lofty gazebos sat upon bacon-slab foundations. Between the landscaped property and the bordering wilderness, a retaining wall was twelve feet high in places. The property was in spotless condition, the gardens impeccable, mortar scoured white, the surrounding trees still "dressed in deep green foliage" on the other side of the retaining wall.

The serendipitous interplay of chance events had landed my family at Eckerton. My father was a trial attorney in Allentown when a client came to him with this problem. The client had found his dream house in the secluded hills west of town. Swimming pool, orchard, lush beds of geraniums and petunias and roses. Less than a mile, as the crow flies, from the Appalachian Trail. The price of the property was out of reach for the client, but with two houses situated on the land, he'd managed to secure his dream by finding a partner willing to go in on it with him. After the client put a hefty down payment on the property, however, the partner backed out, his wife having soured to the idea of being cooped up in the middle of nowhere. Lacking the wherewithal to meet the doubled mortgage obligation, the client wanted to know what, if anything, could be done to recoup the down payment.

The client's story threaded its way among my father's preoccupations. A sleepless sort of life-imitating-a-Cheever-story malaise threatened my father's home in the Allentown suburbs. He ached for a change of venue, a fresh start, the cleansing propensities of silence and wide-open country spaces. An Eagle Scout buried beneath barrister flab, my father warbled to himself over the prospects of taking my sister and me on birding expeditions along the

Appalachian Trail. And his sense of righteousness was smitten with the mental picture of my mother pulling up ever-bearing weeds, filling in for the wife who had backed out, doing penance big-time.

"What can I do about the down payment?" the client wanted to know.

"Nothing," my father answered, "but I wouldn't mind having a look at the place." With only one child, the client was more than willing to settle for the smaller converted "garage and stable." His lawyer had hit a grand slam. The client could keep his equity *and* his dream house.

I was six years old when we moved in. It was late August and one of the lasting first impressions I have of the house I grew up in is of the musky aroma of mildew and pine sap that every year becomes suddenly overwhelming in late summer, a bosky over-ripeness as of a bud that requires a full season's buildup of day-in, day-out humidity to burst into full aroma. For our predecessors, that aroma must have been a sign that the fag end of summer was at hand, the pool water temperature dipping down the right side of the season's bell curve, yellow jackets coating the plops of winey fruit. Time to wipe down the Adirondack chairs and put them in storage, shut everything up until summer reappeared, redolent with the blossoms of peony and lilac. But this summer retreat had become our permanent home. For me that mildewy bloom was full of new possibilities. We closed it up in the house with us for winter, a house that was half porch, and it did not go away until the radiators had fully pasteurized it in the dead of January.

Luckily for us, Eckerton came with a full-time caretaker. The day we moved in, Milt Miller was circling the lawn in an old blue-green riding mower, a doubled-up burlap bag over the metal seat, his face lined with greasy creases, a face weathered by a lifetime of obstinacy and squinting and hard work. When he was not in the saddle of his mower, Milt patrolled the grounds with a square-bodied waddle, a retired farmer whose lifelong immersion in toil had made him blocky and squat the way a stone will be rendered smooth and round by a mountain stream.

Round and round Milt went on his Pennsylvania-brand lawn mower. He saw no reason to wave or stop by to introduce himself when we arrived, nor to ask whether we would continue to require his services. When we finally approached him in the orchard, just to find out who he was, Milt allowed that we were welcome to help ourselves to some pears.

Milt Miller's bank barn sat at the bottom of the hill we lived on, next to where our dirt driveway started from the narrow township lane. The barn dated back to the mid-nineteenth century, when the Zettlemoyer family owned all of the land surrounding (and including) Eckerton. In the mid-1920s, Milt had married Jennie Zettlemoyer (pronounced on the thickest of Pennsylvania Dutch tongues as "Chennie Thettle-moyah") and settled into the white farmhouse across the road from the barn. Milt became so embedded in the mythology surrounding *my* Eckerton that I grew up mistakenly believing he had built the barn when he was starting out as a farmer, hauling the trees out of the woods that were being cleared for farmland and slicing them up at the sawmill rigged up next to his house. Milt's sawmill was a tin pan alley of leaning-together rooftops placed there to protect from the elements a variety of oily bladed mechanisms—planers, rip saws, band saws—that were set in motion by a pandemonium of wide, partially flayed crisscrossing belts, each slithering side to side on its pulley ends, the whole network set in motion by the engagement of the hit-and-miss crank-start tractor engine sputtering away in the first ramshackle hut. The engine made a coughing sound as it worked—*Ker-pooch! Ker-pooch!*—puffing and coughing that was drowned out each time a blade screeched through a board, spraying sawdust onto one of four conical piles that sat on the berm of the township road.

The rafter beams inside Milt's barn were whole trees shorn squarely so you could see bark where the straight cut of the blade had missed the inward curve of the tree. The floorboards were three inches thick. No longer in use, the barn was in the early stages of decay the first time I poked around inside. Broken windows. Slats missing on the sides, some of them dangling loosely like dead fish on a line. Amid loamy tufts of composted cow manure, a shiny-leaved generation of sumac trees thrived in the barnyard.

When Milt had started out farming, he would have worked the ground with horses. But even when his operation was at its peak—about a hundred acres of hay, oats, corn, and winter wheat to support his herd of cows—the biggest tractor he ever used was the twenty-eight-horsepower Ford 8N that was housed in our implement shed. The Ford 8N pulled two twelve-inch plows, which meant it took a solid two weeks of cooperative weather and nonstop plowing to get his fields turned under in spring.

Milt's farming career was hampered by the failure of his marriage to produce offspring. It does not pay you to pay somebody to load bales of hay onto the wagon or to stack the hay in the mow of the barn, or to help clean the manure out of the cow stalls or to slosh through knee-high snow to make sure the cows get milked in winter. If you don't have well-fed kids to do it for you, well, you have to do it all yourself.

Milt's soil didn't help much, either. His precipitous acres, soaring high above ours, were slippery underfoot from all the loosely clinging shale. Every time heavy rain fell after spring plowing, rivulets of water meandered through his fields, collecting particles of the loam that held the shale in place, meticulously gathering up tons and tons of precious topsoil and depositing it in sandlike mounds on the edge of the woods or down in our fields, leaving behind cairns of scree and hummocks of orange-brown subsoil that were as yielding to the plow as concrete.

We did not purchase Eckerton from the shirt manufacturer. The property had passed through other hands before ours. To my knowledge, the only notable addition wrought by our predecessors was an inscribed granite tombstone placed over the poolside grave of a beloved pet:

BOOTS: HE WAS A FINE GERMAN SHEPHERD. 1936–1949
If Humans had the Sterling Quality of Dogs, their friendship,
forgiveness, faithfulness, trust, and true love,
this would be a better world to live in.

Milt Miller and Boots stood out large as Titans in my imagination. So did the capacious weeping willow tree next to the swimming pool, its droopy plume of golden branches fuzzy with sunlight, its fat roots buckling the driveway surface like the veins of an overworked horse, pulsing to explode.

So, too, did the ambitious shirt manufacturer. His name was Williams, and he combined a nose for business with a Gatsbyesque flair for extravagance and impulse. The only detailed first-person account I have of the man came from Roy Hein, who ran the old red-brick gas station in Lenhartsville until a few years ago. In 1934, Williams had commandeered Roy to drive him in his spanking-new Buick Super Six all the way to Ontario, Canada, in order to view that tabloid miracle of Depression-era survival, the Dionne quintuplets. The rest of what I know is the stuff of legend and a few surviving photographs. Williams's shirt company landed big contracts during the Second World War. He adored the company of women and invited the local women's club up every chance he could, to poolside parties, picnics, swing-band dances in the large gazebo, fashion shows at which even the plumpest women's club members were given an opportunity to strut along Eckerton's bacon-slab walkways.

At some point, Williams must have showed up at Milt Miller's sawmill with specifications for boards he needed for one of his building projects. Although Milt was in a position to demand more than beer for his labor, the struggling young farmer was eventually talked into selling Williams twelve acres of his best land, providing a buffer between the swimming pool and Milt's sprawling fields. Not in a million years would Milt have parted with his coveted loam but for the intermittent droughts that every ten years or so bumped him onto the high-risk pile at the Farmer's Bank. Nonetheless, he continued to farm the twelve acres he'd sold to Williams.

When Williams's son was killed—his one and only child, scion of a shirt empire, died in a plane crash—the poolside parties came to an abrupt halt. The gazebo dances were replaced with prayer sessions. In the middle of the undulating field he had purchased from Milt, Williams planted a bed of geraniums in the shape of an enormous cross, a pink and red cross that captured the attention of anyone who chanced to look down from a plane in the skies above Eckerton.

If corn was the farmer's gold, as the local saying goes, it was also his heartbreak. Milt watched his corn curl up and die without a single kernel in the drought of '57. The scorching back-to-back summers of the mid-1960s finished him off. When a developer waved money in his face, the exhausted farmer parted with his land forever. Milt moved with his wife to a smaller house up the road and took his dismantled sawmill with him. The old Zettlemoyer homestead was subdivided and resold. The barn, together with a portion of the land, was bought by Timberlake Camp, a Philadelphia-based outfit that brought inner-city African American children out to the country. Milt's old farmhouse wound up in the hands of Mildred and Jimmy King, who had grown up share-cropping in Mississippi and moved north during the years of civil rights unrest. The only parcel of land Milt had to work with his Ford 8N tractor was the twelve-acre tract he had sold to Williams. He still cut a few boards from time to time, but Milt's livelihood consisted almost exclusively in the upkeep of the grounds and buildings that constituted Williams's only surviving legacy.

The greenhouse, groined out of the side of the earth in concert with the swimming pool project, was Eckerton's crowning engineering achievement. Built so its glassed-over side would take maximum advantage of the low-angled winter sun, the greenhouse abuts the underground wall of the pool on its back side. By one of those action/reaction principles of physics, the process of freezing actually gives off heat. As temperatures plummeted below freezing, the thickening layer of ice on the pool surface transferred warmth into the adjacent greenhouse.

It would be a long time, however, before the greenhouse would appear to me as the product of anything resembling progressive thinking. That first fall, we potted up more than a thousand geranium cuttings for the greenhouse so that we could transplant them around the grounds come spring. Heedless of the bugs that made mincemeat of her pale Irish flesh, my mother applied herself to the gardens and orchards with a devotion that hearkened back to her student years at the Sisters of St. Joseph convent. There was no end to the repetitive chores, which I resisted with an energy greater than the chores themselves required. Japanese beetles to pluck from the roses. Cherries to pit. We easily had twenty times more tree fruit than both families together could possibly eat, preserve, bake, or press into cider in any given season. My mother would drag me out to the orchard and I would wander away from the peach tree she had assigned me to pick from, over to a quince tree, where I would start picking unripe quinces and tossing them into the tree my mother was working under. It seemed the only thing the bitter, gnarled, furry quinces were good for, tossing them one after another, just to see how long it would take for my mother to cut through the drowsy miasma of humidity and swarming fruit flies and wonder, Hey! Why are quinces dropping out of a peach tree?

Or when apples were in season and the World Series was in the air, I would shinny up into one of the overgrown Baldwins that stood as tall as Milt's barn and proceed to shake the branches until the sound of apples battering the ground was like the rumble of a thousand hoofbeats. I would fill baskets with the fragrant fallen Baldwins and then, planting myself on a mound some sixty feet from a tree with a good fat trunk, proceed to watch the best fastballs I could muster splat off the mighty bat of some imagined legend. Nothing like disposable baseballs when there wasn't another kid around to play catch with. I am convinced the invention of our national pastime must have come about as the result of ideas stolen from some lonely kid stuck in an orchard.

Milt Miller took note of the apples slaughtered at the base of the tree trunks. And he saw the tree branches I broke when I climbed them, branches he had to cut up with a chain saw and drag into the woods. Then, too, there was the baseball glove I was forever leaving out in the yard, where it inevitably wound up in the path of Milt's riding mower so that he had to stop and get off the mower to move the baseball glove out of the way. My mockingly red baseball glove with its facsimile of Roberto Clemente's autograph. Forcing Milt out of the seat of his riding mower was about the worst sin you could commit at Eckerton. He didn't just move the baseball glove to a safe location. He'd pick it up and throw it down on the ground and stomp on it as if his afternoon had been completely ruined. And the whole time he was attacking the glove, angry, spastic quacking sounds erupted from him, Pennsylvania

Dutch execrations that bubbled up from the acid cauldron of compulsion that was his stomach: "GOTT FER DUMMTA YOUNGA DEI HAENGA." I couldn't understand a word of it. All I knew was he would work himself into a horse lather because even on the hottest days in summer Milt would be wearing a flannel shirt and a layer of long underwear. He bundled up like this because he was convinced his endless battles with indigestion resulted from the infiltration of cold upon his stomach. For this reason, his diet had come to consist almost exclusively of hot, steaming oatmeal. Oatmeal for breakfast, lunch, and dinner.

There were all kinds of unspoken rules we were forever breaking, my sister and I mostly, but my parents, too, taboos we didn't know about until Milt reacted with one of his quacking fits. When we turned on the shower adjacent to the swimming pool, Milt pounced upon our afternoon of leisure, red-faced and quacking: "GOTT FER DUMMTA DU ALTDA SCHDANTD." He did not leave off quacking until he had dismantled the showerhead and permanently turned off the pipe in the greenhouse that fed water to it. We never did figure out what it was about the shower that made it off limits.

In Milt's mind, no doubt, his child, if he had only had one, would not have spent whole afternoons dallying around with his baseball glove or gathering up baskets full of green unripe plums for throwing off the roof of the house at his sister, not when there were bushels of good, ripe fruit to be picked on the trees. We were *auslanders* for sure, descended from Irish and Slovenian stock, my ancestors having collected facefuls of bituminous dust in the mines of western Pennsylvania so that one day we could be taking forbidden showers at some banker's summer retreat. Out of bed for 5:00 a.m. chores, by contrast, many of my schoolmates were being groomed to do the same thing their ancestors had done, those Lenharts and Seidels and Heffners and Raubenholds who'd marched twice around Isaac Eckert's summer retreat before devoting themselves to an afternoon of social intercourse. Farming was to them a grease monkey's concern: the art of buying scrap equipment and fixing it up endlessly—rehabilitating a half-buried-in-mud disc harrow, replacing pistons and oil rings, shimming up reduction gears, dropping the oil pan, rebuilding the transmission. They relished the grease under their fingernails more than they did the dirt. And the things they talked about were incomprehensible to me—muskrat pelts, hay tedders, exhaust manifolds, gravity wagons, Johnny Cash, the Remington thirty-aught-six. From October to March, it seemed, hunting was the only acceptable topic of conversation.

I made a concerted effort to be more like my schoolmates. After talking my father into buying me a BB gun, I headed to the orchard and shot at a rabbit who was nibbling on grass at the edge of the woods. The BB gun made hardly a sound when I pulled the trigger, which convinced me I couldn't possibly have harmed the rabbit. When the rabbit hopped into the woods, I ran in after and found him flopping around on the ground, his fur matted with blood near his tail. As I choked back tears, my father had to finish off the rabbit with a .38 special. I dug a grave for my rabbit and placed a bacon-slab tomb over it. The epitaph I painted on the tomb said, in keeping with an Eckerton tradition, "Here lies a fine American rabbit." My hunting career started and ended with that rabbit. And I never told any of my schoolmates about it.

In the end, though, few of my early rising schoolmates went on to become farmers. And if you asked me to put forth some examples of the kind of resourcefulness to be found in the house that molded the future farmer I was to become, I would have to think long and hard and even then what I would come up with would be little stupid things. The way we always resorted to the trusty butter knife, say, when we needed a screwdriver.

Or maybe I would point to my father's uncanny strategy for enclosing all of the porches of our summer house: his trove of clients willing to offer carpentry skills in lieu of attorney's fees. There was one client named Elmer who went about his porch-enclosure duties with the enthusiasm of a character out of a Samuel Beckett play. Elmer moved in with us and my dad provided him with a company car, which was really the second family car, my mother's car. When we went out during the daytime, Elmer indulged in long naps on the sofa. And in the evenings he argued with me over what we were going to watch on television. Elmer actually looked like Samuel Beckett with his spiked hair and shocked eyes, the raw day-laborer angularity to his jawbone. For all I know, he might have been Samuel Beckett himself, penning *Krapp's Last Tape* on scraps of two-by-four, or curling up on the couch with a volume of Dante when he was supposed to be pounding nails. When my mother caught Elmer napping one too many times, a plate full of picked-clean chicken bones next to him on the sofa, she fired him and he left in the only car available to him, which, of course, was the only car available to my mother.

What taste I got of the kind of farming I would eventually embrace came on the mornings I helped Jimmy and Mildred King, the couple from Mississippi who had moved into Milt's farmhouse, clear a tree-strewn patch of rocky, sloped Eckerton land. With nothing more than a shovel, they had turned every square inch of the half acre their house was situated on into a lush vegetable garden. But before Jimmy could get his shovel to break the surface of the ground we made available to him, he had to clear out hundreds of trees, stumps, and rocks the size of radial tires. It was Mildred and Jimmy who first turned me on to fresh-out-of-the-ground carrots, sweet potatoes in no need of sugar, tender okra, lettuce with identifiable flavor, peas direct from Valhalla. Mildred's basement was full of canned vegetables, too. Pickled garden-fresh beets were my favorite. I would slurp the purple vinegar from the softened nuggets and then devour the tangy earth-flavored flesh. Mildred gave me jars of pickled beets in exchange for my labor, even though I couldn't have been of much use to Jimmy. Mostly, I enjoyed listening to him talk, commonsense talk that showcased a disdain for Nixon and food-stamp programs, a reverence for sweet potato pie and Willie Mays. "Mm-hm, Timmy, that's right," Jimmy would sing out when I said the right thing. Chatter was high-octane fuel. It helped Jimmy loose the stubborn rocks. Nobody but a sharecropper's kid would have gone to the trouble he did of preparing that pitiful scrap of ground for sweet corn. Jimmy was hardly an *auslander*, the way he worked. He eventually turned every square inch of that hillside patch with a shovel, and between the added horse manure and the afternoon shadow cast by Milt's barn, which prevented the paltry ground from drying out, he produced a bumper crop of sweet corn that was the best I'd ever tasted.

As for the man who was responsible for my having to share my sock drawer with a family of flying squirrels every winter, he was home for dinner less often than Elmer during the porch-enclosure years. An avid reciter of Dylan Thomas and Vachel Lindsay, my father could be stirred to emotional heights by the sight of a pileated woodpecker. Once or twice every summer, I would succeed in dragging him outside with a baseball bat so I could shag some fungoes with my Roberto Clemente baseball glove. "Shag" and "fungo" were words he relished, this man who could recognize some crass little pub ditty as the work of Kipling. Reading had furnished my father with a vocabulary that rarely defaulted to the word "thing." "Shamisen," "sporran," "aphid midge," "antimacassar," "epaulette." These are all words that, to this day, trip off my father's tongue in my memory.

In the courtroom, that same tongue was a blessing to my

father's clients, defending them with verbal frissons, walking the overconfident policemen he cross-examined in circles until they contradicted themselves. He went three years straight without losing a case, racking up two murder acquittals along the way. But he was overworked, and his vision of a weeping-willow-shaded, peony-lined rest cure for his marriage had not taken into consideration a few critical details, most notably the neon-blinking watering holes mining the route between Allentown and Eckerton. Whatever had gone wrong back in the suburbs was a wound that refused to scab over in the salubrious country breezes. My father's occasional fits of beer-fueled Irish rage resulted, at least in part, from his pent-up need to return to the wilderness. He eventually started moonlighting in spring as a whitewater rafting guide and in winter as a ski instructor. In the courtroom he took to wearing his hiking boots so that when the boots were sufficiently broken in he could hike the Appalachian Trail from Georgia to Maine and climb mountains like Kilimanjaro and Everest. He began camping out in our thirty-acre yard, too, setting up a three-man dome big enough to accommodate him, a small library, and one plump beagle, Chinka, who whined to be let out of the house at about six o'clock every morning, then rubbed her wet nose against the tent until Dad unzipped the fly for her.

The deal between my father and his client, whereby everything but the two Eckerton houses was to be held in common, could only have been struck by members of a prelitigious society, noble savages in the year of the Woodstock concert. The client was a former college football star who had a natural bent for telling stories. Since he could never square himself with having to share his piece of God's country with another party, he fixed it in his mind that we were his tenants. My usually combative father adopted an affable, palms-up, nolo contendere manner with the drunk who would inevitably sidle up to him at a bar and insist that "No, no.

You're the tenant up there. I know the owner and he told me so." Indeed, our inability to properly care for the property and its contents, which consistently incurred the wrath of Milt Miller, only seemed to confirm our renter status. Needless to say, the client was no longer a client.

The poolside epitaph about "the Sterling Quality of Dogs" must have made a strong impression upon our presumptive landlords, who proceeded to transform Eckerton into a sanctuary for strays of all kinds, chiefly ill-tempered dogs who tore the ear off our Saint Bernard, chased our cats up trees, and surrounded us with barking and snarling every time we stepped outside our house into neutral Eckerton territory. One by one, they appeared on the hill, these pets whose previous owners had subjected them to years of deprivation and beatings before dumping them off at some heavily traveled intersection. People were to blame for their bad behavior. And we were people, I guess. So these dogs declared war on us. In league, they were like a pack of crazed Indians descending upon our wagon train, circling our automobiles rabidly, growling and snapping at the tires, forcing us to stop and start the whole way down the quarter-mile driveway.

These resourceful mutts even formed a navy whose first admiral was one peevish white spitz named Snowflake. Snowflake's favorite tactic was to appear from beneath the weeping willow tree as you were jumping off the low diving board. He would dive in right after you, this fearless patroller of the chlorinated depths, gnashing at your arms and face as you unwittingly came up for air. Every member of my family got bitten at least once by these dogs, whose crimes cried out for extenuation by virtue of the Dickensian struggles they'd been forced to endure before Eckerton, struggles that made any objection we could possibly raise to the chunks they took out of our calves seem like the pettiest of Band-Aid quibbles.

But the dogs never bothered with Milt Miller, perhaps because they sensed that he belonged at Eckerton more than any of us did. In his entire life, the farthest Milt had ever traveled was to the state capital in Harrisburg, fifty-nine miles west. And that trip he made but once, to clear up some bureaucratic snag involving his driver's license. If Milt had never applied for a driver's license, though, I doubt his daily orbit would have raised a single eyebrow from an official of the state. His entire life had been lived within a five-mile perimeter of Eckerton. He would have been three years old when Isaac Eckert showcased his summer estate, but I like to think that, wherever he was at the time, he must have been within earshot of Eckerton's first heartbeat, the *BOOM-pah, BOOM-pah* of the Hamburg Band marching around the two houses. From the beginning, Milt's rhythm had been uncorrupted by the preoccupations of the unfolding century. He was too young for the First World War, too old for the Second. The Depression barely dented a man like him, built hard as brick and willing to work whether or not he got paid.

Once, when my mother asked him what he did to enjoy himself, Milt replied without hesitation: "Plow." The damp sensual pleasure of bringing earth to light. The wormy aroma of satiny upturned clods drying beneath the April sun. That was what turned Milt on. Back when horses were quietly doing the work, there was the reassuring snap of timothy and clover roots, the suck of winter-slogged loam being slowly parted, the oaty balls of barely digested straw giving off steam and fecundity on cool spring mornings. Plowing was an unending chore with horses, the team of two frothing along their harness straps and down at their hindquarters as they slowly turned over another twelve-inch swath of sod. At the end of each long pass, the horses needed ten minutes or so of rest, the unreining during which a young farmer named Abraham Lincoln was known to get in his reading. Milt would have gathered up unearthed rocks while his horses rested. What an endless supply of shale his fields offered.

Anytime the ground was fit, Milt would have brought his horses out to plow. A brief thaw in winter was an opportunity to start on spring plowing, which threatened the lives of the horses if it dragged too far into May, when the heat was too much for this kind of work. But even on the coolest days, the horses needed rest, sometimes as much as fifteen minutes, during which Milt would have gathered up more rocks and talked softly to his horses and applied salve to their collar sores. As lunch approached, Milt had to be careful because his slightest gesture toward the barn would send his voracious team bolting for their oats and water. When the barn was too far away to go in, he removed the bits from their mouths and slipped on a nose bag full of oats and corn. And he sat with his horses and talked some more to them and fed them apples from Williams's orchard and sipped beef bouillon from a thermos and took in deep, satisfying breaths of the moldy, rich, promising upturned earth.

The Dionne quintuplets, beatniks, baby boomers. What did any of these things have to say to Milt Miller? The four-year rotation was everything. Where his wheat and timothy grass had germinated in fall, he walked through and spun clover seed on a fine spring morning when he could count on the thin film of daybreak ice thawing in the afternoon so the clover would sink into muck and eventually germinate. In July, after harvesting his wheat and straw, he brought the cows in to graze the timothy and clover. What didn't get grazed, he mowed down and chopped up into heifer feed so the timothy and clover could get off to a clean, healthy start the following spring, growing into lush hay in time for an ideal cutting round about the longest day of summer. The sixteen daylight hours of the solstice would have been about what was needed to cut everything in the morning and then, provided conditions were right, put all the hay into the mow of the barn in the afternoon and evening. The following spring, he planted corn, which thrived on the nitrogen-rich decomposition of the plowed-under timothy and clover. The spring after corn harvest, as early as possible, the ground was plowed and oats were planted so they could be harvested in time for fall, when the ground was plowed again for wheat and timothy. The same piece of ground was plowed in spring for oats and in fall for wheat and hay.

And the rotation started all over again. The job was never ending with horses. Milt was slow to change over to a tractor, partly because of the poor returns he got on his hardscrabble soil and partly because he was not one to pass up a good thing for something new. *Is the ground fit for plowing?* Milt asked himself this question every morning of his life. There was no use chafing over how long it took the team to turn a couple of acres. Either boil over with impatience or learn to enjoy it. And enjoy it he did.

What Milt claimed he did for recreation was something he had not done for years, though—something, in fact, he was never going to do again in his life. Which is not to say he didn't continue to wake up mornings and ask himself, out of an old habit, whether the ground was fit to plow. What it did mean was that unfulfillment bubbled away like a yeasty brew in his belly. The oatmeal piling up in his cold stomach soured to mash. The riding mower was for him a scaled-down plowing experience, a retired farmer's plodding consolation. He didn't need the money nearly as much as he needed the engine thrumming his aging loins, the day-to-day struggle with uncertainty that wouldn't abandon him because his tractor had completed another loop. Even when the grass did not need to be cut, we began to suspect, his addiction to plowing was such that he went ahead and cut the grass anyhow. Milt was in the saddle so much we hardly noticed he was also responsible for hacking back the poison ivy and oak saplings threatening the perimeter of the lawn, or replacing panes of glass every time the wind sent an evergreen branch through the greenhouse, or pruning the fruit trees, or skimming pine needles off the surface of the swimming pool.

And he still rode his Ford 8N tractor. The tractor belonged to Eckerton but nobody dared lay a finger on Milt's workhorse, which he used for all of one day each summer, hooking up the sickle bar attachment to mow the weed-choked hay growing in the field, sitting proud and upright as a pontiff on parade as he traversed the field he'd long ago sold to Williams. The cut hay was left to decompose, since Milt had no place to store it. Like the tractor, Milt's barn was still Milt's barn, even if he had no title to it. The sight of his barn, which he had to pass by every day on the way to work and on the way home, contributed as much as anything to the havoc in his stomach. Inside it, the city kids from Timberlake Camp had taken to carving their names in hearts with love arrows shot through them. Thieves had begun to pry loose his meaty floorboards. Rain infiltration was turning the roof beams to pulp. It drove Milt crazy that the Timberlake folks didn't have the common sense to put a new roof on his barn. But then, even among the native Pennsylvania Dutch, the Mennonites were about the only ones sure-footed enough anymore to do the requisite balance-beam routine sixty feet up. And the Mennonites had enough barns of their own to keep dry. If he had only had a son or two, Milt could have knocked that barn roof off in a day.

Bindweed, Canadian thistle, quack grass, poison ivy, lambs-quarters, crabgrass. These weeds would overspread Eckerton but for the constant vigilance of one retired septuagenarian. The curculio beetles would team up with crown gall on the plum trees. The water pipes would sputter and choke on the acorns of chipmunks. Day after day, Milt worked at it with two jittery old riding mowers kept in action by his frugal ingenuity. Not that he cursed us for neglecting to modernize his fleet. Hydrostatic shift, a padded seat, eight forward and four reverse gears: these were all unnecessary extravagances that would have upset Milt's stomach even more.

Back when Milt was turning his ground with horses, debris left on the surface at the end of the job was considered a sign of shoddy work, something you would never want your neighbor to feel inclined to comment upon. Walking behind the team, Milt would have snagged any exposed cornstalk and thrown it in the furrow, where the next pass of the plow would be sure to cover it. As the years passed and we never once left our "summer home," Milt began to confront our clutter with a similar eye for debris-free perfection. Our swimming trunks and towels and deflated beach balls turned up in the garbage can. Whiffle-ball bats, footballs, badminton rackets, baseballs, and shuttlecocks disappeared altogether. As did my Roberto Clemente baseball glove. Milt's most memorable action was taken against the yellow inflatable four-man raft that had served so well as a floating fortress whenever Snowflake approached us with paws paddling and jaws snapping. The raft tended to settle in the corner of the pool amid the pine needles that it was Milt's duty to skim off the surface. Rubbery and resilient, the raft played with Milt like a big, reckless, tongue-lolling puppy, splashing water on him and bouncing away from whatever grumpy direction he wanted to toss it in. With his pocket-knife, Milt stabbed the raft so many times there was no chance a patch could save it. Then he slung the deflated carcass over the art deco railing as though it were a piece of laundry he'd dutifully hung out to dry.

If Milt suspected that he might be an agent of mischief, he went about that mischief with an entitled air, as though he were divinely sanctioned, an orchard sprite, the troll under the bridge. He still scolded me as ruthlessly as ever, his mouth a blowtorch fueled by the gases in his stomach. The quacking never let up. "DUNNA VEDER! GOTT FER DUMMTA YUNGA."

And I struck back. I got my BB gun and took it down to Milt's barn and shot out every window that was not already broken. After that, I went into the implement shed and unscrewed the spark plugs from Milt's riding mowers and threw them into the woods.

Milt started to come apart in the late 1970s, after his wife died. He took to indiscriminately hacking away at all impediments to the progress of his lawn mower, leaving the Christmas pines with a trendy miniskirted look. He would wake up on a cold, drizzly November morning and convince himself that, indeed, the ground was fit to plow. And to see Milt out on the riding mower in an icy, driving rain, sopping wet in his burlap-covered seat, cutting grass that didn't need cutting again until spring, you would have to pinch yourself to make sure you weren't dreaming. One day, at the top of the orchard, Milt ambled away from his curved-hooded 1940s GMC truck and the truck took off on its own, somehow weaving in and out of the first four rows of trees, miraculously avoiding chestnuts, sour cherries, Northern Spy apples, and Bartlett pears before knocking flat one of the quinces in the bottom row and coming to rest over the lip of a stone wall, sustaining, amazingly, only a dent in the front fender. The old truck was built like he was.

The Farmer's Bank was still the Farmer's Bank until the 1980s, when it was gobbled up by National Central and subsequently changed hands numerous times before it wound up a branch of Wachovia. About the same time as the Farmer's Bank's demise, the partitioned Zettlemoyer homestead lost its desegregated charm when Mildred and Jimmy King moved back to Mississippi and Camp Timberlake stopped bringing kids up from Philadelphia.

In one of Timberlake's last seasons, state police searching by helicopter for a camp runaway spotted marijuana growing on Eckerton. They landed and pulled out thirty-five plants. While police were searching the brush for more pot plants, my sister's boyfriend zipped up in a sporty little red roadster of the kind no kid just out of high school could possibly afford. He was wearing camouflage duds and the passenger seat of his roadster was full of watering pots. "Hey, what's the deal with the police?" he asked my mom, who told him he better hit the pike and hit the pike fast. My father's golden tongue worked wonders on those state police, none of whom, fortunately for us, had ever been ignominiously skewered by him on the witness stand. No charges were filed, but all attempts at cash cropping on Eckerton Hill were postponed until fifteen years later, when some suspicious seedlings began germinating beneath lights in Brooklyn.

In my personal dictionary, the definition of the word "entropy" would be "what became of Eckerton after Milt Miller died." And next to the definition would be a pencil-type sketch of Virginia creeper climbing over the retaining wall and spiraling up the trunks of the oldest oaks and sycamores and pines. Virginia creeper growing with jungle lushness inside the greenhouse, choking the life out of all but the spears of sumac trees, which grew with such velocity they cracked the windows from the inside as deftly as did the branches falling from the overgrown pines.

Here, at last, was the future that had raked like shattered glass over the lining of Milt Miller's stomach. On every Eckerton boundary, the "deep green foliage" reclaimed cleared space at a pace of two or three feet per year, fencing off each season's gains with a briary tangle of wild berries and poison ivy. A combination of ice storms and heavy wind smote our magnificent weeping willow so many times it was nothing but an enormous black thumb sticking out of the ground. The bacon-slab walls crumbled. The trees in the orchard sprouted Medusa-like tresses, their branches obliquely angled as pick-up sticks, canceling one another out, producing little more than a handful of tiny, wizened fruit. Every plum tree—the sour Italian ones and the syrupy sweet reds—developed tarry contusions and died.

The swimming pool developed a crack, but it was filled up for as long as it could reasonably hold water, mostly because Snowflake needed a place to paddle around in his waning years. My father, the born-again Eagle Scout, was also using the pool to practice his Eskimo rolls with the kayak.

I was away at college when Milt died, so the decay did not tiptoe past me in increments the way it did for my parents. After I graduated, the longest I managed to hold down a job was the year and a half spent teaching at a prep school in New Jersey. In between jobs, I kept coming back to Eckerton, to ride the lawn mower, to paint the outbuildings, to restore the greenhouse, to wrestle with Virginia creeper and poison ivy. My efforts were patchy at best, lacking Milt's oatmeal-fortified tenacity. Milt's absence had created a vacuum that our neighbors, too, much more so than I, tried to fill. But Eckerton fell further behind.

After Snowflake died, the pine needles piling up in the empty swimming pool decomposed into an acid loam that sported Canadian thistle, then sumac saplings, then oak saplings. The pool was redolent of a Cheever story, "The Swimmer," where the ambitious husband, resplendent in his noonday glory, sets out on a Sunday-afternoon impulse to swim home from the backyard pool of a friend. The eight-mile "river" he proposes to swim, dubbed the "river Lucinda" after his wife, is composed entirely of the backyard swimming pools of his social counterparts. By the time he reaches home, though, his own swimming pool is sprouting weeds, his abandoned home is in a shambles.

Once again, my life imitated a Cheever story. In their divorce settlement, my father disburdened himself of the property with the same fluid ease as he'd taken the place on, leaving my mother with the complicated half share of Eckerton and heading to New Hampshire with his kayak and skis. By then I was living in Brooklyn, working as a freelance consultant. "Freelance" meant there were plenty of opportunities for cleaning pine needles and oak-tree saplings out of the swimming pool, for mowing the lawn and painting the small gazebo, for gathering up salvageable fruit from the withered orchard, where a half bushel of peaches in any given year was a blessing. If Eckerton had become organic without Milt Miller, it was a laissez-faire variety of farming I practiced, a hunter-gatherer's potluck that filled my baskets. The same lackadaisical kid who couldn't be bothered to fill a bucket with sour cherries when the trees were rotting with overabundance was now scouring the scarce grounds for every usable specimen of pear or quince or peach to take back to Brooklyn, where it could be baked into pie or cobbler, or boiled into jelly. Every three or four years, though, the weather conditions would be right for a windfall of old apple varieties, enough Grimes Goldens and Northern Spies and Baldwins and Greenings for me to climb into the trees and shake the branches like old times. Only this time the fallen apples were pressed into cider. No matter how poor I was, there was always apple brandy to get drunk on.

Exactly one rose plant was still standing in the rose garden when I started my first vegetable garden there, borrowing a shovel from the neighbors and turning the ground by hand. All of the underground water pipes that had once irrigated Eckerton were cracked and useless, so I made watering containers by using a nail to punch holes in the lids of juice jars. The first clever invention of a Milt Miller wannabe. When I worked in the garden, the dogs from next door circled and barked at me. You'd think they would take the initiative to rip the bejesus out of the groundhogs or rabbits who were eating my lettuce and carrots and sweet potatoes, or at least chase off the deer who grazed my garden in the evenings. These foragers had taste buds that I can only describe as cutting edge. The rabbits were inordinately fond of exotic microgreens—barely germinated sprigs of lettuce and beets and basil and broccoli—long before microgreens were a mainstay in the kitchens of New York City. The deer preferred delicate pea shoots, satiny mesclun greens, the melting cotton-candy sweetness of two-inch-high corn shoots. If the frisée managed to reach full size, it was only because some patient groundhog was holding out for the savory blanched inner leaves. Since I was not up to adding any BB gun trophies to the "fine American rabbit" I had long ago laid to rest at Eckerton, I was left with zucchini and tomatoes, a little bit of basil, and some chiles. Instead of growing a wide variety of vegetables, I decided, out of necessity, to opt for a cornucopia of tomatoes and chiles.

My delusions of farming had started with that first garden. The idea of taking over Milt's field—I still thought of it as Milt's field even though the neighbor had hired it out to another farmer—was a siren call that, from a safe distance, concealed its impracticability in a pristine, faraway logic. Was I not blessed, after all, with all of the basic assets—land, greenhouse, tractor—that would make starting up possible for a cash-strapped writer?

The farmer who had taken over the field was cut from the same cloth as Milt Miller; he was an old Pennsylvania Dutchman who wore a bright orange hunting cap with earflaps and drove a 1950s-era John Deere tractor with a put-putting two-cylinder engine. In Milt's fields, he rotated oats and wheat and corn and hay as he did in numerous other small "throwaway" plots—six- to twenty-acre parcels, all of them within commuting distance of his John Deere, all of them too small to maneuver around for the farmers with two-hundred-horsepower tractors. A year before I took my farming plunge, he had grudgingly given me access to nearly half an acre of my mother's land, even plowing it up for me, convinced as he was that I would find the work so overwhelming I would never ask him to turn the ground for me again.

But I was only thinking of a large garden then, a garden like Mildred and Jimmy King's. As it turned out, I barely came up with enough transplants to fill half of the ground he had plowed, and the whole parcel turned into a weedy, barely harvested mess by the end of the summer. Chaos had found yet another foothold at Eckerton. When I came back the next year—the year I started three thousand tomato seedlings in a Brooklyn brownstone—and told him I was going to try my hand at *two* acres, he shook his head and complained to the neighbor, whose de facto landlord treatment of us had gone uncontested for too many years. Seeing the Pandora's box my farming standards would unleash upon the hill, the neighbor bullied me and informed me that I would have to cough up some big-time rent if I wanted to plant my tomatoes in *his* fields. I pressed ahead nonetheless, refusing to ante up as I transformed Eckerton into a grand showcase for a farmer's first-year follies—my crooked rows of tomatoes socked in with weeds, my potted-up ornamental chiles congesting the driveway. What a mess I was creating. But the clouds were on my side that first year, producing enough rain for the weeds *and* my tomatoes. As food writers and photographers began to visit Eckerton for a look at my crop of otherworldly love apples, our neighbor bellowed and stomped and, in a house-cleaning Milt-like fury, vowed to bulldoze my tomatoes and weeds and potted chile peppers along with my mother's cluttered house into Maiden Creek below. Forced to recognize, nonetheless, that my mother did, indeed, hold a half interest in Eckerton, he hired a surveyor and an aggressive lawyer who initiated a division of the property that promised to be messier than the messiest of divorces.

What ensued was the great struggle of my life. Two struggles, really, one between a pair of ideologically opposed farmers over a scrap of shaley ground and the other over the fate of Eckerton.

I wish I could say it was a heartfelt commitment to noble stewardship of the land that urged me to entangle my mother in a rancorous legal dispute. But I suspect the real reasons were a little trickier to put a finger on. At the age of thirty-three, the ambitious writer I had set out to become stood on the brink of transmogrifying into some quirky, growth-stunted recluse, living off Mom. We fought the good fight and it took a couple of years to fully wrest recognition of my mother's right to half of Milt's twelve acres, the six-acre parcel on which Williams had planted his geranium cross so many years before. But Eckerton is still in joint custody. Indeed, a marriage would have been easier to break up.

I've made some efforts at minimizing my messes, although my fields look shabby come September, especially in comparison to the well-sprayed fields of my seasoned counterpart. For their part, our neighbors muzzled their dogs when I finally got around to hiring some much-needed help. We all get along swell these days, if tenuously, like Protestants and Catholics, like Amish and Mennonites.

But I still had Milt Miller to confront in that first year. I needed a tractor to turn the two acres I had fought so hard to win. So I started snooping around the implement shed, scratching my head over the Ford 8N that had sat untouched since Milt had died almost fifteen years earlier. A state-of-the-art workhorse in Milt's heyday, the Ford 8N is today the kind of tractor a gentleman farmer will buy for a couple thousand dollars at auction, good for cleaning manure out of horse stalls or mowing ten to fifteen acres or plowing snow in the driveway.

I called up Daryl, an old schoolmate, to help me figure out how to get the Ford 8N started. Whoever had rested the tractor, Daryl informed me, had taken good care of it. He'd done all of the basic things, like emptying out the gasoline, topping off the antifreeze reservoir, removing the air filter and battery. As he said this, I could feel Milt's presence, his waddling back and forth in the implement shed for the last time, preparing the tractor for whoever would stumble upon it years after he was gone. With no children to survive him, there was nothing left in this world for him to lavish his fathering instincts upon—his land was gone, his barn, his wife. His sawmill would be sold off for scrap. The riding mowers were junk without him to keep them wired together.

There was nothing but this Ford 8N tractor. We searched all over the shed, retracing Milt's footsteps until we found the air filter that had been stowed away in the back of a small closet. Daryl made a list of things I needed to buy—a new battery, some belts, a can of Marvel Mystery Oil to replace the lead in the gasoline.

"The tractor doesn't have any spark plugs, either," Daryl said.

"Spark plugs?" I said. The word sent a tremor of guilt through me. Milt Miller was so palpable I could hear the angry quacking in his brain as he drained the gas and topped off the antifreeze and then, one by one, unscrewed the spark plugs and dropped them in the deep pockets of his bib overalls. Just so the troublemaker who'd stolen *his* spark plugs would think twice before taking the seat of his Ford 8N. He must have seen, in ways that I was too young to understand, how the land could take hold of a young *nixnutz* like me and never let go.

He never should have sold off those first twelve acres. *You wouldn't believe those Dionne girls, Milt, like five peas in a pod. What do you say, how about ninety-five dollars an acre?* And then that last summer that he farmed, he was in such a rage when the corn dried up for the second year in a row. Two summers of dust-covered lungs, the ground so dry he couldn't get the plow to break through until October. I got no use for it anymore, *sis druka wie shtab*, he spat to the developer, who resold it before he even had a chance to reconsider what he'd done. But by spring, he wanted her back. Lord, did he want his land back.

Within a day, we had the Ford 8N running. After one last scrape with the neighbor, this time over my rights to Milt's tractor,

I hooked up a nine-tine field cultivator and proceeded to claw over the ground. The cultivator left most of the field debris on the surface. Milt would not have approved, but I was working on limited resources, and the cultivator was a giant leap in comparison to the shovel. Back and forth I went over the ground with the cultivator, softening it up for my tomatoes.

There is so much time in the seat of a tractor to stew over things, to dream and calculate and tie your stomach into knots over silly nothings, knots that no amount of oatmeal can ever undo. Buoyed along on the adrenaline rush of my first real tractor ride, I couldn't help thinking of Milt Miller at the age of six, the same age I was when I first laid eyes on Eckerton. Young square-faced Milt looking out the window of the one-room Zettlemoyer schoolhouse that sits next to the house and barn that will one day be his. He is unable to pay attention to Mrs. Druckenmiller's English lessons because Noah Zettlemoyer is outside making *lundt* with Polly and Sadie, his team of dapple grays. Polly is the stronger horse, so Noah coaxes Sadie forth: "*Mach dich no*, Sadie. Gee, girl. Get up there, Sadie. Gee, now." All of a sudden, Mrs. Druckenmiller is leaning over the daydreamer. She has been trying all morning to get Milt to pay attention. And now she waves a folded-up piece of paper in his face and says firmly, "Take this note out to Mr. Zettlemoyer." And as he walks out into the sunlight and waits at the end of the row for Polly and Sadie, Milt is sure Noah Zettlemoyer will read the note and then tell him to fetch a hickory stick.

But all Noah does is laugh. "*Younga, gleisht die schule nett?*" he says, grabbing Milt under the armpits, lifting him off the ground, and setting him down on Polly's broad, damp back, where he waits quietly, his heart thumping with excitement. When the team is rested, Noah taps Polly on the rump and barks, "Get up there, Sadie. Gee, girl." Rocking with the motion of Polly's sturdy haunches, Milt tilts to the right but grabs the *cumit shpay*, which is the only word he knows for collar hames, in the only language worth knowing, the language they speak outside. As Noah coaxes Sadie forth and Milt bounces and grips tighter and breathes in the smell of sweaty bridle leather and newly plowed earth, he thinks of the kids watching him from the classroom, stuck inside with their English lessons while he gets to ride Polly all the way to the end of Noah Zettlemoyer's field and back again.

Lucky me, he thinks. Lucky, lucky me.

TOMATO PEOPLE

IT WAS INEVITABLE that we would come to be labeled "the tomato people." Which is not to say that I
truly deserve inclusion among this unique crew. I am too much the
shill, the one who packaged up a way of life and hauled it off to the
city, where the chefs and then the food writers, the catalogers of
everything from rare grits to Iranian caviar, took notice. To them,
we had something new to dissect, this hodgepodge of multicolored
sun-softened shapes that begged for name tags and descriptions.
How unlike the reception back home in Pennsylvania, where we
were so ass-backward and queer as to merit nary a sentence in the
sixteen-page weekly that still lands with a slap, and often winds
up soggy through and through, on the front stoop. *My opinion is,
any tomato that grows fuzz like a peach goes against the fundamental
grain of nature!*

One of the food writers must have been first to put it down
on paper, the name having scrapped about in the wind to that
point, a blurt issuing from the lips of a bored waitress as I made a
lunchtime delivery, a customer's reaction on arriving at our Greenmarket display: "Hey look . . . tomato people!"

Viewed separately, we seem a miscellany. Surely it was little more than a shared interest in earning a living that first brought us together. What brings us back every spring, I am convinced, is the tomato. I have begun to suspect a genetic link. Let's just say our ancient forebears might have arrived on this planet in the same space capsule, touching down in Mesoamerica at the height of the Aztec empire. And now, after centuries of migration and inter-marriage and internecine conflict, their descendants have reunited, unsuspecting as long-lost siblings in some Shakespearean drama.

Just look at the road the tomato has traveled. When it first enters the Western consciousness, it is anointed the *pomi d'oro*. Golden apple. Shaped like a lumpy baseball, it has been farmed to such girth from its pea-sized origins in the mountains of Peru. If the pea-sized variety is the Eve of tomatoes, then the *pomi d'oro* would be the Cain, after the biblical father of agriculture. When Hernán Cortés enters the picture, the analogy takes a Tower of Babel twist, the *pomi d'oro* destined to spawn varieties as legion as the races of man. The tomato will travel to Spain. To Italy and Russia and China and France and Bulgaria. Everywhere it grows, the tomato puts on weight and picks up local color. Imagine the expression on Montezuma's face if he were to chance upon our market stand in Union Square, New York City, mid-August, early twenty-first century. The albino White Wonder; dusky Black Krim; gargantuan Striped German, yellow with red streaks emanating from the center like bicycle spokes, easily four times the size of the largest *xitomatl* to burst upon Aztec tongue.

So imagine those first tomato people, landing in their space-ship and, crafty as any people capable of navigating the Milky Way, assimilating among one of the great pre-Columbian cultures. Ransacked by the arriving conquistadors, they disburse in small groups, some of them traipsing north, others stowing away in the trinket-laden holds of returning ships. To sustain themselves, they bring, among other things, *xitomatls* that have been dried in the sun. Settling in Lisbon or Barcelona, Genoa or north of the Rio Grande, they have nothing but tomato seeds to remind them of where they have been. They are vectors of the great tomato diaspora. Their progeny will become housecarls and fur trappers and slave traders and charwomen. Some will continue to pass tomato seeds on to their children, but most will lose interest after a few generations. *By God, I refuse to be a peasant!* Peasants nonetheless and fruitfully multiplied over every continent. More than a handful of them embark upon one last great migration, over mountain or sea. To the New World, then, where they start out digging canals or tunneling into bituminous coal or laying railroad track so their grandkids can one day sell insurance or practice law. The years pass quickly. In little more than a century, experts are hailing a postindustrial age, this heyday of "check engine" lights, PIN numbers, and all manner of comforts rendered in the service of those coal miners' and track layers' grandkids.

To what, then, can the grandkids of the insurance salesmen and the lawyers aspire? Why shinny up the status pole when your ancestors have already done it for you?

My grandma was a Marshall, one of twelve children, a wee-bit bundle of doting bird bones, pecking assuredness in her every motion, a great big heart that fluttered like Christopher the canary's, whose cage bathed in the morning light beaming through the wide living-room window. Grandma's rigorous sense of pedigree had been honed in the western Pennsylvania hamlet of New Baltimore. You were either a Marshall, she believed, or you were a pig farmer. So exclusive was the first of these categories that a handful of her brothers and sisters fit into the second. The only way to escape the two tiers of this society was by bushwhacking down the steep embankment to the turnpike (there was no New Baltimore exit) and flagging down the bus. Just back from France, with a snazzy piece of hinged chrome to assist the knee he had injured in an accident involving a captured German Jeep, Grandma's youngest brother Nork (a true Marshall, destined to marry a pig farmer) hobbled onto the berm of the turnpike and hailed an eastbound bus on which every seat was taken. The bus driver sat for a minute before announcing, in a southwest Pennsylvania drawl, "Now which a you'uns is goin' to give this soldier a seat so we can git movin' again?"

Grandma married a man who moved her closer to the confluence of the Stoneycreek and the Little Conemaugh. Johnstown, Pennsylvania. Steeltown, USA. The gaseous, surreal sunsets. The laundry coming off the line with cinders embedded like blackheads. There was a good living to be made in a steel town, so long as you didn't trip and fall into a vat of man-made lava. Or get crushed by a crane like Grandma's twin brother Cyril did. The man Grandma married had a German name, although he was but one-fourth German. Pappap Stark: shoe department manager, scoutmaster, picker of wild berries—blackberries, dewberries, elderberries. Pap said elder-*bury*, like Roxbury, the town just west of Johnstown where my father was raised.

Surrounded by cigar boxes filled with buttons, gum bands, washers, and tongue depressors, the basement nook to which Pappap retired most afternoons, weary from another shelved attempt to make the Marshall grade, was a work of shoelace engineering. Strings dangled from above his swivel chair, each one anchored by a weight whose shape told him what lightbulb or electric gizmo the string controlled. Triangular lead weight for his reading lamp, stainless steel eye screw for the stairway light. A brass cotter pin served up KDKA Pittsburgh, the voice of Bob Prince: "It's a deep fly to right field . . . Clemente is under it and yessir, the game is a can of corn. The Bucs sweep the Giants at Candlestick."

Upstairs, Grandma snickered and whistled into Christopher's cage as Pap rolled his own cigarettes, crumbling into creased tissuey paper the tobacco he pinched from a robin's egg blue pouch that said "Bugler." He dreamed of bugles as he smoked, too, the startling pleasure of morning reveille: *Come and get your beans, boys, come and get your beans.* Cool mornings with mountain ponds expelling dense clouds of rolling fog, the mildewy smell of pup-tent canvas, the dew-moist berries waiting to be picked, his bright son waking next to him.

My sister and I spent two weeks of every summer with Gram and Pap. When I came down to the basement, Pappap would sometimes put down the paper to talk about the ball game or to update me on the family of red-breasted nuthatches who'd taken over the neighbor's bluebird house. Sometimes he'd get up to notch my height on the wall where all eight of his grandchildren's dated lengths were scrupulously recorded. Or he'd sit and quietly rub his rosary beads with his thumbs: *What could be purer, oh Lord, than my unwavering admiration of your elderburies?*

Just as often, though, he feigned sleep, abruptly closing his eyes on me, retreating into those dank pup-tent memories: *Come and get your beans boys, come and get your* . . . Pappap could see in me the same flaws Milt Miller saw. I lacked the preparedness of his law-school-bound son, who had earned the twenty-one mer-its required to become an Eagle Scout; who knew the difference between the Plantagenet Henry IV and Henry IV, progenitor of the French Bourbon line; who had learned, in the event his ship might one day be torpedoed, how to inflate the shirt on his back for buoyancy.

You could not get me to sit still long enough to read anything more than the box scores from the previous day's ball game. Even worse, I slurped the clear, greenish, seed-beady gel sacs out of the kaleidoscopically arrayed cavities of the tomatoes Pappap had nurtured with loving care outside the kitchen door. The way you might slurp an oyster from its shell, the way you might lick the filling from an Oreo cookie. Slurped the best part and left the des-ecrated shell for Grandma to toss out. This wasn't the Depression anymore but, good Lord, such waste. Such beautiful tomatoes, too. Pappap tried to inculcate in me an appreciation for fat, juicy beefsteak slices that could be pinned down with a fork and knifed into triangular, bite-sized portions. Over a musk-fragrant slice of tomato, he would demonstrate the proper handling of cutlery for me. *Eat the whole thing, Bud, just like so.*

Again and again, I punted. "It's okay, Bud," Grandma would say when I'd used up all the tomatoes on the dinner table. "Plenty where that came from, Bud." And out she'd go to the garden, Pappap's garden. In the middle of dinner, Grandma would go outside and pluck another dead-ripe tomato from the vine just so young Bud could slurp the gel out of it and leave the rest for dead. I was the only son of an only son. Up to me whether the Stark name—our Stark name—would remain in the phone book when my number came up.

Sad-eyed, Pap grew gravid with disappointment, the skin leath-ery on his cheekbones. When he was gone, Grandma and Chris-topher the canary and most of the remaining brothers and sisters moved to the same trailer park in Florida—Goat, Pug, Lum, Alice, Mary; Marshalls and pig farmers together again, at last. Call it New New Baltimore—Grandma sharing a trailer with Aunt Mary, Goat moving in by himself, the whole crew strategically reassembled so they could, as my father liked to say, *not* talk to one another.

Pig farmer. Hmm. Luckily, I waited until after Grandma had passed away before stumbling upon my true vocation.

Wait a minute! Just what, you have every right to inquire, distinguishes the so-called tomato person from your Ellis Island–variety limeydagobohunk . . . uh, pig farmer?

Well . . . um . . . let me stand back for just a moment and point out how, even as World War II behemoths like Johnstown acquired rust, the agrarian revolution surged ahead with renewed vigor. Fewer and fewer farmers feeding more and more people. Tractors big as a house. Fertilizer extracted from ammunition. Herbicides proven in Vietnamese jungles and patented by the same conglomerates now in the business of patenting seeds.

Bing! Bang! Boom! Look at that corn grow!

But the tomato continues to be a spoiler. For all their efforts to make the homegrown variety as readily available as Murphy's Oil Soap—from hydroponics to gene manipulation to those non-stop comfort flights from the greenhouses of Holland—the agro-industrialists have succeeded only in stocking the grocery shelves with expensive tomatoes that appear to bear the succulent richness of the fully ripe, just-picked specimen. To fall for them is a bit like talking dirty on the telephone for $3.99 a minute. You pay a lot of money and you still don't get the real thing. The concentrated flavor of a whole box of them couldn't match what I used to slurp from just one of Pappap's seed-gel sacs. At least the "vine ripes" don't pretend to be anything more than a crystalline mush of mealy blandness whose only virtue is a sandbaglike imperviousness to the touchy-feelies of discriminating customers. I know of one food writer who had to be physically removed from his local grocery store after approaching the mountain of tomatoes with a fungo bat to demonstrate the modern love apple's rawhide consistency. Modern love indeed.

Most memorable of all the baby pictures in my arsenal is the one of me grinning through a mask of spattered tomato soup. The photograph earned me, in my pretoddler years, the nickname "Heinz tomato man." Not until decades later did anyone stop to consider how my spatter-faced moment might have been freighted with meaning, historically significant in the way of, say, Jacob's coming out of his mother's womb with his hand clutched to the heel of his brother Esau. Now that's a stretch, for sure. But I'm willing to wager that my best shot at immortality would be to have that snap of the Heinz tomato man lacquered onto my tomb next to these words: *HE GREW GOOD TOMATOES.*

I wish I could say that, all my life, the only thing I ever wanted to be was a tomato farmer. But who, really, could say that? My youthful tractor experience was limited to the time I spent with Ron and Terry, who lived on a farm up the road. Playtime at their house always entailed a bit of work. One afternoon, I was helping them clear rocks out of a field in which they wanted to plant corn. Their dad was driving the tractor, pulling the rock-laden wagon while Ron, oldest of the three of us, tried to keep us focused on the rocks, whose size was partly concealed beneath the soil. This was one of those fields that will yield up new rocks forever. What was the point of the exercise? Terry and I lost interest after an hour, preferring the little game we invented, which involved jumping on and off the rolling rock wagon. When we were moving along at a good clip, Terry slipped off the tongue of the wagon and before Ron and I could stop the tractor with our screams of "STOP! OH MY GOD, STAHHHHHP!" the wagon had bounced twice over him. Front wheel. Then back. Ba-boom. Ba-boom. *Ohmygod, oh God, please, no.* Jounced rocks clacked and spilled off the sides of the wagon with each bounce. *No no no. Please God no!*

Terry's dad cut the tractor engine and raced back to his son, pocketknife in hand, moving with lightning speed, as if quickness could somehow unwind the last fifteen seconds, as if breakneck haste would force the tractor back to where it had been before Terry slipped, without the heart-thumping remorse pouring in, without the huddled far-off crows cawing languorously in the midday sun. He slit both of Terry's pant legs with the pocketknife, slit them open to the hip so you could see the tire marks, the bruises. The tires had missed his head and chest. Terry got up and limped around, and when it was established that, miraculously, he had no broken bones, Ron and his dad fell into the kind of charade grown-ups use to preempt a toddler's hysteria after a wobbly kneed fall. There was work still to be done. Terry sat on the wagon in a state of near shock while Ron and I walked alongside, somberly derocking the field. When we pulled in front of the barn at the end of the job, Terry's mother came out and asked him, "What did you do to your pants there?" Nobody answered right away, and when I finally volunteered, "He got run over," Ron rolled his eyes and said, "Now watch what he does." The mishap was in the hands of a mother, now, and Terry at last cried warm, sacred tears.

Before I could even begin to make the big leap out of the garden, I needed to answer some fundamental questions. Would I need a chisel plow or a moldboard plow? How did one organically manage two acres of weeds without pulling them all by hand? How was I to spread compost on two acres without a manure spreader *or* a front-end loader? Should I use calcitic or dolomitic lime to bring the pH back up? What, pray tell, was a hay tedder?

When I queried the old farmer who had taken over Eckerton's fields after Milt Miller died, he blunted my organic pretensions with real-life aphorisms: "Corn must be sprayed." "Organic means weeds and powdery mildew and not much else." "The deer will eat your sweet potatoes." "The deer will eat your beans." "The deer will eat your peas." He was reminding me, in his not-so-subtle way, of a brisk December morning a decade earlier when I caught him and his sons flushing out a pair of does from the cedar bushes next to the swimming pool. I had heard the first gunshots and ran up toward the pool, where the deer had run for cover. The sound of my footsteps sent the deer racing across the field in front of the hunters, so I screamed at the top of my lungs, "DON'T YOU DARE SHOOT THOSE DEER. DON'T YOU FUCKING DARE PULL THAT FUCKING TRIGGER." Guns dropped. Like illicit lovers caught on the verge of coitus, the hunters hung their heads as the hunted scampered to freedom.

Now you get to see Bambi from the grower's point of view, I could read from the old farmer's thoughts as he smiled and listened to me recite my excited plans. He wanted to be helpful, of course, to a young man who potentially represented the next generation of farmers. When it looked like I had only a passing interest in starting an overblown garden, he was the one who had plowed and disked a section of the field for me and told me where tomatoes would grow best.

Sometimes the farmer's white-haired wife would pick him up and drop him off so he could leave his tractor in the field. One morning, I caught him spreading chemical fertilizer on my mother's half of the field, sneaking out on his tractor while his wife sat and watched from the passenger seat of the pickup truck. It was the deer-hunting episode all over again. When I asked his wife why he was doing something I had expressly asked him not to do, she looked down her nose at me and said, "Because *he's* a farmer."

I had not been prepared for this reaction, my peers refusing to recognize what I was doing as being even remotely in the same ballpark as what they were doing. And it crossed my mind on more than a few occasions that this whole farming enterprise I was embarking upon might just be one futile attempt to win the approval of the roughhousing farm kids I'd gone to school with, the lawyer's kid come back to try his hand at the locals' game.

The individual I needed to lime my field so I could bring the pH back up turned out to be the same Terry who years ago had gotten run over by the rock wagon. My Little League companion. At last, it seemed, I had a foot in the door. I called Terry on the phone, and when I explained what I was doing, he hesitated on the other end. "What would you want to do something like that for?" he finally asked. But he invited me down to C. J. Hummel's in Lenhartsville on a Thursday night so we could catch up on old times and talk business.

C. J. Hummel's. When I was growing up, the same place was called Hummel's Danceland and all the action took place on Saturday nights. A band called The Fairer Sex would alternate sets of square-dancing numbers with popular tunes like "Smoke on the Water" and "Bad, Bad Leroy Brown." I was a big fan of the thin, freshly cut french fries Grandma Hummel pulled from vats of bubbling oil, all dripping with grease, as she stood upon her kitchen perch, which afforded her an unimpeded view of the dining-room counter. They were almost as good as McDonald's, those fries, not quite as salty, crispier, but greasier. "You're using too much KETCHUP!" Grandma Hummel would explode as I spanked a Heinz bottle over my glistening pile of fries. The unbridled excesses of the Heinz tomato man! Once, she even stepped out of the kitchen to physically remove the raped bottle from my grip.

In those days, you were forbidden to wear a wide western-style belt to the Saturday-night hoedowns at Hummel's Danceland. And just in case you got it in your duplicitous head you might sneak into the establishment with a fat band of rawhide about your midriff, Clarence Hummel (Grandpa Hummel) would stand guard at the entry door to monitor adherence to the posted dress code, which included prohibitions against miniskirts and pointy shoes. After Clarence died, they renamed the place C. J. Hummel's, after him, and even put a sketch of him on the fancy new sign out front. Clarence must have had premonitions about the future of Hummel's Danceland, the liquor license the place would one day acquire along with the fern-green venetian blinds, the upscale Tiffany lamps. The grease-dripping french fries endured, but, in keeping with market demand, Saturday-night hoedowns were replaced with Thursday-night country-style line dancing. First thing I did on arriving at C. J. Hummel's was order some fries and marvel at the changes the place had undergone. There was nobody around to scold me for raping the ketchup. And for better or worse, everywhere you looked on line-dancing night, the unabashedly wide western-style belts sported shamelessly brassy buckles.

I was there strictly on business, though, having extricated myself for an evening from my consulting duties and my overcrowded brownstone-sprung tomato seedlings. I had learned enough to know that I wanted calcitic lime for my tomatoes, Blue Ball lime, as they call it, since the high-calcium limestone was mined outside of the Lancaster County town of Blue Ball. But high-calcium lime would mean a longer trip for Terry, since the high-magnesium, or dolomitic, lime could be collected fifteen minutes away. I was prepared to make an impassioned argument in favor of Terry's undertaking the Blue Ball run so I could bestow the tomato-sweetening, blossom-end-rot-fighting calcitic lime upon my first crop.

I wasn't at all prepared for what I encountered when, licking the ketchupy grease from my fingertips, I finally located my man, who was so full of beer he could barely stay on his feet. Terry was engaged in heated debate with a Thursday-night cowboy in a ten-gallon hat who stood, when you added the height of the hat, two heads taller than he did. I don't remember what exactly they were arguing about, whether Ford trucks were better than Chevy trucks or vice versa. Something like that. The debate would probably have remained a good-natured *I know better than you* tête-à-tête but for the fact that every time Terry emphasized a point, he inadvertently spilled beer on his adversary.

"I told you stop throwing fucking beer at me." Terry was shoved backward. His beer went flying. Like a storm cloud, the grayish ten-gallon hat hovered over Terry, who, though in no condition to land a punch, nonetheless stepped manfully forward with fists raised.

Before I could talk business with my man, I had to be his guardian angel, stepping in and ushering him away from the ten-gallon hat, over toward the bar, where he wasted no time ordering two shots of Cuervo with chasers. "I don't understand," Terry said when I brought up the limestone. "I thought you went into law-yering like your old man. Why would you want to be a farmer? You want to stack hay in a barn? Tell you what, hay is the only thing that grows in that shale and hay ain't worth shit."

"I remember some damned good sweet corn," I objected. "Re-member? You had so much corn we took it into Lenhartsville and sold it door-to-door off a red wagon."

"That was the summer it rained nonstop. We never got half as much sweet corn again. One year. Big whoop."

Terry's bafflement over my interest in farming was a wall he could not get past long enough for us to negotiate a deal. He started to drift asleep after the second round of shots. When the DJ put on a slow number, a big red-headed girl came up to him, a girl who I could see must have had a crush on him. With his dark hair and well-defined features, Terry had always been a good-looking fellow whose easygoing nature appealed to the fair sex. He was tugged onto the dance floor, where his admirer wrapped her arms tightly around him and held him up as they slowly turned in a circle.

So much for my Blue Ball lime. I finished my beer and headed for the door as Eric Clapton was singing. Terry was propped up on the dance floor, sound asleep, his head resting safely on the shoulder of one most contented redhead. *Yes, I feel wonderfoo-ool tonight.* In the parking lot, I stopped by the C. J. Hummel's sign. Old Clarence looked like a mortician in his gray suit and sedated half grin. "I knew it," I could almost hear him murmur through clenched teeth. "I knew nothing good would come of those wide western-style belts."

I didn't give up so easily. I persisted until, finally, Terry's father got up at four o'clock one morning and ran down to Blue Ball for my lime. Arriving in my field at sunup, he insisted I ride with him in the truck when he spread the lime. It was scary going, the big diesel truck rattling and bouncing and sliding sideways on the steep hardscrabble shaley face, the long steel arms dispensing thin parallel lines of finely granulated lime that gave off puffs of rising white baby-powder clouds. Terry's father managed the bounces with an easygoing, talkative good humor while I held tight to my door handle so I wouldn't slide down the seat against him. "Don't listen to all the claptrap about chisel plowing," he advised. "If you want to be a weekend farmer, go with the chisel plow and hire Reading Bone to come out and spray your chemicals. But your moldboard plow is the ticket. Turn all those perennials upside down. It's good to see you back here, Timmy." Terry's dad looked like he'd lost a significant amount of weight. I didn't know it at the time but he would be dead in five months of lung cancer. But that morning, with the long shadow of the lime truck creeping across the powder-hazed shalehead that was about to become my truck patch, he had all kinds of spirited advice for me: "Keep a ball of wire handy at all times. Don't take a damned penny from the government, even when times are hard. Get yourself a lime truck route or something if you have to, like I did. But I'll tell you, Timmy, I'm proud to see you back here, farming this ground. One day you'll realize this was the wisest move you ever made."

The advice about the moldboard plow was moot because I had neither a moldboard plow, which takes the ground and flips it upside down, nor a chisel plow, which shatters the ground surface with deep parallel grooves. I went with what was available to me, Milt Miller's old shed-ridden leaded-gas-guzzling Ford 8N tractor and the nine-tine cultivator that went with it. Back and forth I went, pulling the cultivator with Milt's tractor, back and forth, mixing in the lime and the compost my friend Daryl had spread out onto the ground with the bucket of a skid loader. Back and forth, over and again, until I could stick my hand into the softened ground all the way to my wrist.

For the rest of the work, I needed human bodies. Just how many human bodies would not be apparent until the work started piling up. I got off easy at first, harnessing the labor of two doctors and two lawyers from New York City who, in exchange for some garden-fresh meals and a breath of country air, were willing to spend a grueling weekend transplanting thousands of tomatoes and chiles into the ground with garden trowels. The rain fell and, before long, my seedlings needed staking and weeds were sprouting everywhere. I tried doing everything myself, getting down on my knees in one corner of a two-acre field and pulling out overgrown lambsquarters and Canadian thistle by hand. There was no time, it seemed, nor money, to go out and buy myself a pair of gloves for handling Canadian thistle, but after a week or so the calluses performed the same function as a glove. I fell further and further behind. I needed bodies. I needed people willing to work at tomatoes for cheap.

Tomato people. So maybe a few of the descendants of the insurance salesmen and the lawyers have climbed back down the status pole, climbed down and raised a licked finger to the wind. As for those with ancient tomatoes in their blood, let's just say some kind of affinity was felt for places like the shaley hill in Pennsylvania where I grew up. Eckerton Hill, where sanctuary was offered to all manner of unwanted hobo tomatoes. Tomatoes that wanted to be peaches. Tomatoes that preferred to look like pears or bell peppers. Tomatoes that squirted the discriminating customer in the eye. Tomatoes so concentrically scarred and hopelessly half ripened, so incapable of being stacked two high, let alone on a jolly red mountain, the decent man's first impulse might be to take them all out and shoot them. Tomatoes, in short, whose bulges and cat faces proved they were the gangly descendants of the European *pomi d'oro*, the Aztecan *xitomatl*.

And so the tomato people, their twisting, turning genealogies showing similar scars of survival, began to arrive at Eckerton Hill.

Jill was the first comer. A most unlikely farmer, she was one of the lawyers who had helped me transplant seedlings. Two years out of law school, her interests had turned mostly toward knitting sweaters and taking classes at the Fashion Institute. Jill had inherited the boutique aesthetic of her great-grandmother, a trained milliner who had opened a hat shop in Greenwich Village after arriving in the States from Vilna, Lithuania, which she left behind after burying her husband, who had contracted TB in the czar's jail after the suppressed revolution of 1905. Jill was more of a Virgo than I was, never satisfied with how things turned out, how "red in tooth and claw" seethed beneath the proprieties of courtroom etiquette, how every sweater had to be pulled apart and redone three or four times before it could even be called satisfactory. Intrigued by the onerous responsibility I had saddled myself with on the sun-facing slope of Eckerton, Jill brought her knitting down from New York City on weekends and pitched in with weeding. We would spend whole days attacking lush carpets of quack grass, purslane, wild mustard, lambsquarters, Canadian thistle, and crabgrass. Starting at opposite ends of a tomato row, we worked toward each other, down on our knees, gripping the weeds close to the soil line, pulling them out so as to get the whole root system with each yank. The occasional wild carrot, with tap roots anchored deep in the clay subsoil, required a bit more muscle. I was faster than Jill, covering two-thirds of the row to her one-third. But she was more thorough: within a week, you could see how my beaten-back weeds rebounded more exuberantly than hers did. It rained and rained and rained that summer, so the weeds were in pig heaven.

Cho came next. Raised on a rice farm in Korea, Cho had served as an English interpreter during the Korean War before moving on to a distinguished civil service career in Seoul. Forced into retirement and still hungry for work, he had come to the States to be near his son, who was in med school. An old war buddy of his, a lawyer in nearby Reading, brought him out to visit the farm. When it came to pounding tomato stakes in the broiling June sun, there was nobody who could stay with me like this sixty-six-year-old former rice farmer. Sometimes, feeling diminished by the unmitigated drudgery of the work, the sweat burning his eyes, Cho would take pains to point out how, in spite of his sun-toughened farmhand's face, he had worn a tie for most of his working years. "My wife, she find out what I do here," he would remind me, "she make me come home immediately."

Cho would bring along his rice steamer and plug it in at the pavilion next to the empty, cracked swimming pool. He always had a plentiful supply of perfectly done rice to share with me. And he would forage around the edges of the field for weeds I never knew were edible. Cho's favorites were not lambsquarters nor purslane nor dandelion. For dinner, I would go out and splurge on some frozen cod, and we would simmer the cod with onions, garlic, and carrots from the garden and Cho would add his Korean-named weeds and we would eat cheaply and plentifully at night. And we'd have energy in the morning to pound stakes and pull weeds and pound stakes and pull weeds. The rain kept falling that summer, kept falling and falling so the stakes punched through the mud easily enough. Sitting in the pavilion, nibbling on rice and waiting for the showers to end, we had plenty of laughs together, Cho and I. I called I-78, the interstate that connected New York City to Lenhartsville, "the tomato highway."

"Like the Silk Route," Cho would say, shaking his head and giggling. I prayed that his wife would never find out what he was doing in the States.

On weekends, when Jill came down with her knitting, we worked at the weeds if it wasn't raining. "We did this row before," she would remind me. "Look how much better my side looks than yours. Get them by the roots!" If the rain made field work too muddy, we would clear a little space on the porch of the cluttered house I grew up in and she would sit there with needles clicking, knitting a sweater for me, the sweater she would pull apart at night: *The neck is too wide! The elbows lumpy! I'm so stupid!*

And try as I might to read a book out on the porch, I was too invested in tomatoes to concentrate on anything but the *thuck thuck thuck* of plump water drops plopping from the roof, whose twisted, fallen downspouts lay in the overgrown bushes encircling the house. The rain kept falling the way it did the year Terry and I went door-to-door in Lenhartsville with overabundant sweet corn. This should have come as a blessing to a tomato farmer trying to make a go of it on shaley ground without an irrigation system. But I hadn't made any provision for a fungus-spraying system either, so it was only a matter of time before my tomato plants would start to curl up and die. *Do I want it to rain or do I not want it to rain?* Trying to answer this question set my stomach to fits of interminable rumbling. Beside me, Jill's knitting needles kept clicking away as I wrestled with my stomach and fretted over my tomatoes, which remained healthy and green in spite of the rain. Loaded with fruit, too, loaded like I'd never seen my twenty-some-odd garden tomato plants, the cherry tomato vines abundant with little green acorns, the Brandywines and Persimmons monstrously large. Was this beginner's luck or would some shocking fruit-marring blight rear up its head, cobralike, and strike me when it came time for the tomatoes to turn color? *Click, click, click.* How could I possibly pick so many tomatoes if they all ripened? Who would buy so many tomatoes when they were picked? And how many Toyota pickup truck loads would it take to haul so many tomatoes down the tomato highway to their destination?

When the rain stopped, we pulled weeds even as we fell further behind on them. Which raised another troubling question: How would we continue to control the quack grass and the Canadian thistle when all hands were dedicated to picking tomatoes? As the rain started to fall again, we would keep at it for as long as we could, wearing Hefty bags to keep dry, the weeds slipping easily from the mud. But then the rain would come in torrents and we'd retire to the porch again, my hands aching to pull more weeds. It would have been better for my peace of mind if I, too, had had something with which to occupy my hands while it rained. *Click, click, click.* Why oh why had I planted so many tomatoes? *I don't deserve a sweater. I'm so stupid.*

The first ripe tomatoes trickled in for weeks. My experiment with sixty-some-odd varieties enabled me to be one of the first farmers with ripe field-grown tomatoes. There were the varieties I expected to come in early, the Czechoslovakian Stupice (pronounced "stoo-pee-chay") being first, its greenish-orange half-ripened homeliness made even homelier by the cold and the rain. And then there were some I hadn't expected so soon—bright yellow Taxi tomato; orange and gold streaked Tiger Tom; tiny berrylike wild Mexicans; exotically sweet Sun Gold cherry. The first box of assorted tomatoes I took to the local produce auction drew frowns of incomprehension from buyers who would gladly have paid a premium for field-grown red beefsteak tomatoes. They crossed their arms and refused to bid until the auctioneer dropped the price to about what I had paid for the box I had put them in.

But Greenmarket in New York City was another story. When we arrived for the first time with all our pretty little potted pepper plants and fifteen pounds or so of first tomato pickings, the tomato aficionados were combing through the stands, champing at the bit, sniffing around for the real thing, quibbling over the delay wrought by the cool, wet conditions. Jill had done some thinking about how the stand should look, ordering fabric with tomato and chile pepper motifs for the tables, setting up a temporary outdoor boutique for our psychedelic tomatoes. "At last," said our very first tomato customer, reaching into the basket, pulling out some odd-ball specimens, oblivious to the strange shapes and colors, smelling them, feeling them, dropping a few in her bag. "The young man at this stand up here tried to tell me his tomatoes grew outside and I took one look at them. Not a single scar. No marks at all. After all this rain? I said yeah, buddy, just fell off the turnip truck myself. You don't have any more than this?"

"Next week," I promised, but the next week came—another week of overcast skies—and we had maybe twenty pounds of to-matoes, enough to fill a peck basket, no more. Polite but deter-mined, the tomato aficionados descended on that basket en masse, a single many-tentacled organism.

After twelve years of growing vegetables, I have learned to ac-cept that every farming season presents a unique set of conditions that invariably prove to be, on the whole, less than optimal. Bigger and greener my tomatoes grew through the damp chilly nights of that first season, the indeterminate vines shooting up above the stakes Cho and I had pounded in, bigger and greener with only a rare ripe fruit to be found. I liquidated my bank account to pay Cho and cursed my green tomatoes for pushing me closer to insolvency. The only therapy, it seemed, was to squat down and pull weeds. On the way to market at four o'clock in the morning, my hands ached for the quack grass and Canadian thistle growing on the interstate dividers. As my Toyota pickup dodged in and out among sleepy, lane-drifting tractor trailers, it was all I could do to keep my foot on the gas pedal and not pull to the weed-choked berm.

"What's this pink one?"

"Radiator Charlie's Mortgage Lifter."

"The yellow and red?"

"Hillbilly."

"This little orange and gold guy?"

"Tiger Tom."

"You going to have more of these?"

"You bet." When the sun finally did make its long-awaited appearance, pouring it on with an otherworldly dose of humidity, my fickle tomatoes discarded the hard green tease act for an overeager-to-ripen treachery. *You said you couldn't wait for tomatoes, so . . . here we are!* Long unruly vines flumping all over, cherry tomatoes popping underfoot and tapping me on the shoulder. *Don't forget me. I'm as ripe as they come.* Jill would concentrate on the tiny wild Mexican cherry tomatoes, whose fragile skin required a little trick of the wrist so they would disengage from the vine without splitting. Cho and I went after the big tomatoes, working uphill, Cho's breathing growing heavier as the temperature drew well into the nineties. Cho would go and go and go. Hard as we tried to get him to take a break, he would sooner die of a heart attack than lose so many perfect tomatoes. "Waste," Cho would mutter, shaking his head with peasant sagacity when darkness finally reined him in.

In the pitch black, we would fill flats with tomatoes and load the flats on the back of the Toyota and cram the flats wherever they could be crammed in the cab up front with us. We would finish loading the Toyota at midnight, only to discover we'd forgotten to put the tables on. No choice, then, but to unload all of the boxes, place the tables on the floor of the flatbed, and reload, this time with even fewer of the ornamental chile plants, which littered the driveway, making it virtually impassable in front of my mother's house, where the neighbor had to get through on his way to and from work.

In bed after 1:00 a.m. with the alarm clock set for 3:30. No wonder we often slept in until 5:00 a.m., by which time it was too late to beat rush-hour traffic into Manhattan. A crowd would be waiting when we arrived at market, always the last farm to pull in, the notoriously tardy tomato people. The whole day at market

would devolve into a fruitless attempt to set up our little boutique as tomatoes were sold out from under us. There were people
who wouldn't believe us when we told them what we were selling.
"Those don't look like any tomato I've ever seen," they protested.
Whatever they were, they made for a nice picture sprawled out
atop the tomato-motif tablecloth. Japanese tourists, art students,
camera-toting gourmands, food stylists. All day long the cameras
flashed.

As the loads continued to increase, we started packing the
overflow into my mother's Subaru station wagon. Jill drove the
Subaru to market while I took the Toyota. When the Toyota finally
collapsed beneath the weight of the tomatoes, I rented a U-Haul
truck. And still, we found ourselves tight on space. Tomatoes were
running amok on us, turning on the vines faster than we could
ever hope to pick them. I would get to the end of a row and look
back to find another bushel of them had ripened in the time it had
taken me to work my way down. Overripe fruit exploded beneath
the ruthless sun, bequeathing lustrous blobs of seed-bearing gel
sacs that licked my elbows and knees as I passed. Sour with rot,
the part I used to slurp from Pappap's tomatoes clung to me and
dried solid by day's end. There was no choice but to keep moving
forward, though, even as I muttered to myself the exact opposite
of what I had been muttering two weeks earlier: *For one day, for one
lousy day, couldn't you damned tomatoes just stop ripening?*

Cho kept right on picking, picking, picking. Waste traumatized him. Rotting tomatoes were turning up in Cho's nightmares.
Rotting tomatoes amid sodden fields of rancid rice. No doubt,
fewer of the tiny brown grains went unharvested on his father's
farm.

I was singing the sleepless blues for sure, even if on Sundays,
the day before Monday market, I enticed a few friends to help out
so that we managed to pick off and discard some of the split cherry

tomatoes and get the truck and car loaded for market, tables and all, by midnight.

And then my mom and dad started coming around. In the final summer of their marriage, which also happened to be the last year the cracked, leaking swimming pool was filled with water, my father had perfected his Eskimo rolls as my mother looked on from the pavilion. He would intentionally capsize the kayak in which his lower half was encased, then struggle to right himself. The trick involved forceful hip action combined with a decisive downward thrust of the paddle. My father's misty, bearded face would appear momentarily on the swimming pool surface, eyes popping with determination as he drew in a frantic gasp of air. Back under he'd go again. It drove my mother crazy to sit through this repetitive parody of drowning. But she stayed anyhow. "Oooooh, I can't stand it," my mother would protest as my submerged father sat in his upside-down cockpit, soundlessly, contemplating his next move.

When he eventually got the hang of it, my father could pull off a hundred Eskimo rolls in one direction, then a hundred in the other direction. He could flip upside down, pass the paddle from one hand to the other, and go back up the side he'd come down. My mother would have stayed by his side forever. But he bolted for the mountains and streams of New Hampshire.

My mother lost so much weight in the first years after her divorce that her svelte, newly twenty-year-old figure had high-school classmates of mine hitting on her when she tested out the local singles scene. She eventually hooked up with Bill, an Ivy Leaguer and Vietnam War vet with a ponytail and an unkempt beard who ran a small, tidy, overfull used-book store in downtown Allentown, across the street from where my father's law office had been. More important, from my drowning-in-tomatoes perspective, Bill and my mother started coming out into the field. They were noncommittal at first, doubling over their shirts so they could fill the pouches thus formed with plump, perfect tomatoes and then pack the tomatoes out of the field. "You do realize," my mother had a habit of reminding me, "there's no way you are going to get all of this picked before dark."

Just what a thin-skinned thirty-three-year-old reduced to pursuing his livelihood in his mother's backyard needed to hear. "Don't help me if it bothers you," I said, squeezing my eyes shut because of the sweat burning in them. How easy it would be to quit. Back to my apartment in Brooklyn I could go, back to fermenting cider and making quince jelly and frittering away the days contemplating stories I wanted to write about my parents and an orchard and a useless swimming pool, stories nobody would read even if I did get around to writing them. "It's my loss, Mom. Really, you don't have to help."

But my mother couldn't abide the waste any more than Cho could. Back into the field Mom would tromp, she and Bill, mining some vein of ripe fruit the rest of us had overlooked. She called my two-acre patch "the magical garden" because of the Alice's-dreamlike quality of the purple, white, red-streaked, ruffled, spotted, and lopsided wonderflesh that filled her makeshift pouch. As she packed the tomatoes in boxes at the edge of the field, my mother rubbed them until they shimmered voluptuously. Many shirtfuls of tomatoes came out before Mom and Bill took to hauling empty boxes and baskets into the field like the rest of us did. I knew they had crossed over the line when the dark green, tarlike tomato residue stains appeared on their fingers. The difficulty of scrubbing out those stains was good reason in itself to stay out of the tomato field. It would be a year before we discovered the best solvent for the job: fresh tomato juice.

My father turned up one afternoon in his snazzy new convertible Camaro, having commuted all the way from New Hampshire. After parking the Camaro next to the empty swimming pool, he proceeded to do what only my father could have thought to do his first time back at Eckerton in half a decade. As we toiled away in the tomato field, he put on his in-line skates, in full view of us all, and practiced figure eights next to the wind-stripped weeping willow tree. My father bristled to see how the roots of the half-dead weeping willow could already be cracking the driveway he'd paid so much money to have resurfaced only six years earlier. It made for rougher-than-anticipated skating.

Dad started out running errands for me: picking up tomato boxes and supplies, scouting for a larger pickup truck. He stayed in a hotel nearby and brought me food when I had gone all day without eating. My father's presence even afforded me ad hoc representation when our neighbor, his former client and fellow Eckerton deed holder, bellowed at my infringements. The neighbor was bent on defending Eckerton from me the way Milt Miller once had, obsessively circling the grounds in a lawn mower, stopping here and there to move my crap out of the way. For sure, Milt Miller would never have put up with tomato boxes and garden implements and potted-up pepper plants strewn all about the property. How many times had I left Milt's Ford 8N sitting out in the rain? And who did I think I was, making the large gazebo into a sloppy packing shed?

Nothing blew the cork off the neighbor's fury more than the sight of my field. A pox on the landscape of northern Berks County, that otherwise flawless patchwork quilt of swirling contoured corn rows; dewy, lush alfalfa; willowy, tall, wind-tousled rye; corduroy rows of broad-leaved soybeans. There is something to be said for the general sense of harmony promoted by the tractor-riding, chemical-fortified farmer, the way his massive harvesting equipment cuts down the rows in uniform swaths. The eye for smooth-sailing symmetry ran aground at my renegade tomatoes, chiles, and eggplants. Planted by hand and never abetted by herbicide, my rows were woefully crooked and lost in a sea of run-amok weeds. And what to make of those laborers in their ragged green-stained clothes, toiling the way peasants used to, each with his or her own quirky methods, demonstrating above all the absence of anything remotely like an overall plan?

"I want to see rows of corn," our neighbor shrieked. "Nice, neat rows of corn. You have to pay me rent if you're going to make a mess of everything."

"Does that mean the other farmer has been paying you rent?" my father shot back accusingly, taking my corner the way he did when I used to trot out onto the mat as a high-school wrestler. "What's the other farmer been paying you?"

"Oh, him. He just grows a little hay. He doesn't make money." Ah! There was the rub! With slick niche marketing, I was attempting to supplant that noblest of creatures, the farmer who does everything a farmer is supposed to do and winds up owing money at the end of the day. For the artistic thrill alone, and never for profit, he goes out on his tractor and seeds his fields. Even as he is being taken to the cleaners by Cargill, he will smile and wave to you from his tractor in the middle of the field, this venerable old populist who loves nothing more than to dig himself deeper into debt. And there I was, his polar opposite, taking advantage of the volunteer labor of one girlfriend, one father, one mother, and one mother's boyfriend. Paying a pittance to an overworked Korean War veteran. Impresario of the tomato! Capitalist pig! I should be ashamed of myself.

"How much rent has he been paying you?" my father persisted. Year after year, back in the 1980s, my parents had turned down the annual set-aside subsidies the government offered them. "We're not farmers," they protested. The going annual rental rate for suboptimal land like ours was about thirty dollars per acre, although many landowners in the area, grateful to have anybody willing to keep the weeds mowed, turn their ground over to farmers gratis. Our farmer had probably been paying the neighbor a modest tribute of apples and other produce. What he really had offered was the satisfaction of having this twelve-acre swath of rolling fields fit seamlessly to the other swaths that covered the hills and valleys—all but the forested mountains and steepest hillsides—surrounding Eckerton.

"The place looks like a shithole. I want to see corn!" For a whole afternoon, the neighbor stormed around the premises with his lawyer, drawing up a line of division. Just what I needed on top of the eighteen-hours-a-day, seven-days-a-week grind: a brewing diplomatic crisis. To make matters worse, Cho skipped out on me for the first time, a pattern that was to repeat itself over the next couple of years. Throwing his hands up with indignation—*I am overqualified for this!*—he would storm out of the field, leaving me with the impression he had landed something administrative or technical, only to return a week or two later with his plug-in rice steamer, a change of clothing, and a grin of insubordination. *I'm retired, so what the shit?* The first time he left, I figured Cho was gone forever. Without him around, and with chile peppers and eggplants ripening on top of everything else, I needed my father to be more than just a counselor and a gofer. So he, too, came out into the field to pick cherry tomatoes. My tomato operation was as close as it ever would be to a family farm.

With more than seventy varieties of chiles and a dozen varieties of eggplant to pick in addition to the tomatoes we had already been picking, all organization went to the wind. We never had two hundred different containers just the right size to effectively separate out all of the varieties for the trip to New York City. Every week, a few varieties would get picked and then disappear mysteriously, like socks in a dryer. Late on the day before market, there was always some crisis point when the order went out to pick everything into the same basket. Turkish Orange eggplants, lime green Romanian peppers, Amish paste tomatoes, long crinkly red Aji Colorado chiles, tiny yellow currant tomatoes. Everything in the same basket. We would arrive at Union Square the next morning with these impromptu cornucopias that were appealing to the eye if a bit exasperating to chefs who actually expected some kind of uniformity in their purchases. *Uh . . . do you think you could go away for, say, twenty minutes, and I promise when you come back I'll have a full half bushel of nothing but orange eggplants?* The chefs put up with this because, well, where else were they going to find Turkish Orange eggplant?

With the tomato loads as big as they were, I had my hands full pushing brown and fuchsia globes of tender-fleshed perishability to a consumer raised on fridge-kept reds. How many times did I resort to that schmaltzy children's tale, the Ugly Duckling adaptation about the lonely magenta tomato that, having endured the ridicule of all the fire-engine reds, winds up prominently sliced atop the princess's sandwich?

By the time Cho returned, my tomato crop was in decline. The wet summer was finally catching up with me. Laden with unpicked, collapsed fruit, the cherry tomato plants died first. By mid-September, we were back to scavenging for whatever we could find. The seasonal restaurant menus moved on to beets, kale, spinach, and winter squash. My father went back to New Hampshire to gear up for ski season. Jill returned to my sweater, stitching it together and pulling it apart. After a sudden deep freeze finished off my chiles, Cho and I yanked all of the tomato stakes and cleaned up the field. I had stuck it out for a full season, which was more than I could say about most of the jobs I had held down in my adult life. But like Cho, I felt overqualified for this kind of work. It was time to move on.

Or so I thought. I moved back to Brooklyn, where I had every intention of burying my newfound aches and pains beneath a pile of office work. But nothing was the same. I was feverish and compulsive, sleepy by day and sleepless by night, more forgetful than I had ever been in my life. They didn't want me back at the old consulting job, either. "Boss isn't convinced you're smart," a friend at the firm informed me over a beer. *Who told the boss about my farming?* I wanted to ask. Rest and recuperation only made matters worse. When I did manage to sleep, my dreams were of Milt Miller coming to my dorm room at college clutching in his green, tomato-stained hands a kitten he'd run over with the Ford 8N. "I'm sorry," Milt would say in plain, understandable English.

With the ground frozen, Eckerton was in the hands of lawyers negotiating a line of division, an outcome that ranked right up there with Solomon's halving of the contested baby. The thought of Eckerton being divided only worsened my arthritic pain. Post-tomato stress syndrome is the only diagnosis I have come up with for this condition, which I experience every winter. And there was but one antidote. By early December, I was back in Pennsylvania, working the farm dispersal circuit, hobnobbing at auctions with button-lipped farmers in their snowmobile suits and John Deere caps and Bruce Fegley lime spreading jackets. Over steaming Styrofoam bowls of chicken corn noodle soup, they traded hunting stories and bid on shoeboxes overflowing with C-clamps and washers, nuts and bolts, and ancient, weighty lead shapes. An endless supply of oddball hardware for mounting that prize nine-point buck or fixing the tractor on the cheap. I was there mostly to acquire hoes, rakes, and shovels and to pick some brains over the bigger things I needed. *How powerful is the International 786? What years did they make the John Deere 60? How many horsepower does it take to pull an eleven-tooth chisel plow?* The farmers exchanged glances that were not so much scornful of my questions as baffled that there could be a world out there in ignorance as to the laws that bind the universe; that, for instance, you needed ten horsepower for every tooth of a chisel plow. My old consulting boss was not the only one who wasn't convinced that I was smart.

I had about six thousand dollars to spend on a shopping list that included a moldboard plow, a chisel plow, a transport disc and cultipacker, a plastic mulch layer, a manure spreader, a water-wheel transplanter, a greenhouse, a full-size pickup truck, and a tractor. More than anything, I needed a tractor. After the sacrilege of my first-year raid on Milt Miller's Ford 8N, which, the way the Eckerton negotiations were proceeding, would fall into other hands anyhow, I decided that owning my own tractor might convince people, myself included, that I was truly a farmer. Moreover, I needed something bigger than the Ford 8N, something with a front-end loader for moving compost around.

The Case 530 with front-end loader—thirty-two years old, packing forty-one horsepower, and extremely rusty—went up for auction at a farm dispersal sale five days before Christmas. The farmer who was parting with his land, his house, his cows, and every loose screw and fan belt on the property was what they call a black-car Mennonite. Having long ago split with the horse-and-buggy church, the black-car Mennonites nonetheless continued to observe strict laws in matters of dress and internal-combustion-powered transportation. Because I could not rustle up my friend Daryl to come out and render a verdict on the condition of the Case 530, I cornered the old farmer, who told me the tractor ran just fine.

And so, figuring a retiring Mennonite farmer had to be more trustworthy than your car salesman, I began to pace and hyper-ventilate and seriously contemplate the rusty old workhorse. All morning long, as the auctioneer in the barnyard plowed through tables and tables of toys furry with dust, gun stocks, loose wire, chicken feed, steer de-horners, and scraps of unidentifiable metal, I shuffled nervously back and forth between the tractor on display in the icy field and the huddled warmth of the barnyard crowd. I stood watch over the Case 530 as the more mechanically inclined farmers boarded it, pumped the clutch, started it up. The puff of smoke rising from the exhaust pipe was blue at first—not a good sign, that much I knew—but then turned black.

At noon, the property went up: a developer outbid the farmer who lived next door in a test of nerves that didn't need to be as dramatic as it ended up being. Your developer will always outbid your farmer. Then came another excruciating hour and a half of petty bidding on bits and scraps. Nobody else seemed to mind that the auctioneer took two minutes to squeeze seventy-five cents out of the winning bidder for the bent rim off an ancient Ford Ferguson. Your seasoned auctioneer will have a sixth sense about not only the value of a piece of farm machinery but also the amount the crowd is willing to bid and even, sometimes, who will be the winning bidder for each item. Ralph Zettlemoyer, founder of the Zettlemoyer Auction Company and descended from the very Zettlemoyers who owned Eckerton before it was Eckerton, is a case in point. Once, I saw Ralph pick a stodgy cross-armed farmer out of the crowd and say to him, "How about thirty-five hundred for that New Idea manure spreader?" The farmer stood there chewing on his tongue and looking at his feet, so Ralph threw out lower numbers on the manure spreader: fifteen hundred at first, then all the way down to seven fifty, where the bidders jumped in. Back up it went—"a thousand, seventeen fifty . . . twenty-five hundred, how about twenty-seven fifty?" Up, up, up, until Ralph got back to his original figure of thirty-five hundred and sure enough, the old farmer who couldn't be bothered to acknowledge him the first time around put up his hand and won the manure spreader for thirty-five hundred dollars. "Ay, ay, ay," Ralph said proudly to himself, like Babe Ruth trotting around the bases after having pointed out, before he even swung the bat, where in the stands his home run ball was going to land.

But my auctioneer was no Ralph Zettlemoyer. He spent too much time extracting pennies on broken field cultivators, disassembled grain-drill parts, moldboard plows with cracked shins and shares. When a combine shot up over fifteen thousand dollars, he worked the bidders up in twenty-five-dollar increments. Nervous anticipation tickled my bladder. When bidding started on the Case 530, the sun was a ruby disk half tucked behind the horizon and I was returning from my third trip into the woods. I forced my way up front, so the auctioneer could see me clearly. But nobody would bid as the price plummeted all the way to four hundred dollars. I didn't bid either, figuring all of those clutch pumpers must have known something I didn't know. But then two farmers jumped in, one pointing his finger in the air, the other making henlike nods. The one with the finger dropped out at about twenty-two hundred dollars, so I jumped in, waving my bidding number until the auctioneer saw me. Up, up, up the price went, me against the Mennonite with the surreptitious, henlike nod, until it hit twenty-eight hundred dollars and I had the winning bid. The Case 530 was mine!

But wait! I had won the tractor, but the front-end loader, which was removable, was still up for grabs. Nobody had told me this. I needed that old, rusty Dunham Lehr loader as much as I needed the old, rusty tractor, so I started bidding at four hundred dollars for the loader and kept nodding yes yes yes when the auctioneer turned back to me. It seemed to me I was up against one Mennonite farmer and then another. They were taking turns running up the price on me. But I held on tight until the loader reached a thousand and it was mine. For thirty-eight hundred dollars, I had my tractor and loader.

But wait! The tractor was still not mine. "What we do now," announced the remorseless auctioneer, "is we put the loader and tractor together and start bidding at thirty-eight hundred." The package deal shot over four thousand dollars, and all around me heads were sneakily nodding as the price went up, up, up. I felt outnumbered by clean-shaven Mennonite farmers in their black narrow-brimmed nylon hats. The feeling was a little bit like driving down Lexington Avenue during rush hour, with taxis cutting you off and blaring their horns and stopping abruptly in front of you to pick up a passenger. The yellow cars seem to be in league against you. So it seemed with the black-hatted cousins and brothers and nephews of the man whose tractor was on the auction block. *Let's run up the price on this young city slicker!* At forty-five hundred, I tried to throw them off with feints and hesitations, as though I had reached my limit on the Case 530 and they would be stuck with the old tractor forever if they kept bidding me up. But my slackening resolve only encouraged the other bidders. In smaller and smaller increments, the auctioneer kept coming back to me. Forty-five fifty? Forty-six? My bladder felt full to bursting. My stomach went topsy-turvy. I discarded the wavering ruse, firmed up my jaw, and took a blind leap of faith, nodding like a fighting rooster each time the auctioneer turned back to me. At forty-eight hundred dollars, the Case 530 and loader were truly mine.

In a daze, I wandered around the implement-strewn field as the auction wound down and the other farmers gathered up their used merchandise and started up their newly purchased tractors and combines. Up to this point, farming had been a relatively risk-free venture for me. My truck patch had gotten off the ground for the price of some spark plugs, fluorescent lights, and seeds, family and friends willing to work for little compensation. But the Case 530 tractor changed all that. In my life, I had never done anything so radical as pay forty-eight hundred dollars for a heap of rusty machinery that might not even work. There was no way I could fall back on consulting now.

I lived too far away to drive the tractor home in the dark, but I wanted to start her up all the same, so I mounted the Case 530 and turned the key in the ignition. But the tractor engine didn't make a sound. There was a button that said STOP, so I pulled the button all the way out and tried the key again. Nothing. I pushed the STOP button all the way in. Again, nothing. I got down off the tractor and walked around it, checking the battery connections and the engine block. Was that a crack in the engine? And what were all those jerry-rigged wires that seemed to be leading nowhere? I walked away from the tractor, the only one left in the field now, an old rusty heap that would probably cost me another two thousand dollars to get home. *All equipment is sold AS IS*, I could hear the auctioneer reminding me with law-abiding sincerity. Other voices were inside my head, too, an all-too-familiar giggling, like the hyena laughter of Indians watching from the woods. At the age of ten, my schoolmates had had more common sense than I did now. And now that I was thirty-three years old, theirs was still the measure by which I judged myself. *Only a fool would blow forty-eight hundred dollars on a tractor with a cracked engine.* I got on the tractor and tried to start it again, but she refused to make a sound.

There was a light on at the Mennonite farmer's home, so I went to the house and knocked. A girl in a bonnet, fourteen years old or so, opened the door, and inside, a ruckus of kids rolled around on the living-room floor. The roughhousing laughter of merry farm kids. They, too, seemed to be laughing at me. "I'm surprised the Case 530 won't start," said the girl at the door. She put on a jacket and came outside with me. She climbed up onto the tractor and firmly readjusted the gearshift lever. The Case 530 started right up when she turned the key. "You have to put it into the start gear first," she explained, pointing at the shift lever. "See, here, where it says *S*." Before I went home, I took a lap around the field in my new tractor, and after I drove over the corn stubble and pulled the STOP button to shut it off, I could hear the laughter coming on again, in uncontrollable snorts. *Oy, now the farmer needs a little girl to show him where the start gear is.* Those sneering, leering wiseasses. I will be wrestling with them for the rest of my life.

A few days later, Daryl, my friend and tractor consultant, drove the Case 530 fifteen miles home to Eckerton. "Runs pretty good," he told me. To prevent rainwater from getting into the engine, I fitted a wide upside-down coffee cup over the opening to the vertical exhaust pipe and parked the tractor in front of my mother's house, where it accumulated more rust all winter as negotiations proceeded over the ground on which it stood.

There was an awful lot to do before another season could get off the ground. Jill finally finished my sweater, and in February we moved into a rented farmhouse five miles away from Eckerton, although she spent her weekdays working in New York City. In the kitchen of the rented house, I set up the germination rack that I had cobbled together in Brooklyn and, as the next generation of chile and tomato seedlings grew overcrowded beneath fluorescent lights, I worked frantically putting up a greenhouse to accommodate them. A friend of mine who had recently quit practicing law in West Virginia came to stay in the farmhouse, and the two of us worked on the greenhouse day after day. "Seems like an awful lot of toil just so a bunch of food snobs in New York City can have their tomatoes," Zeke would crack as heavy, wet drops of snow fell on us. But we kept at it, pounding steel support pipes into the frozen ground, bolting together the curved hollow steel frame pieces, and nailing together two-by-fours at the ends. I had started more than twice as many seedlings as I had the year before, and by mid-March, as the aches and pains of my December hiatus receded, I could see how another season of frenetic, one-crisis-after-another activity was coming my way.

We finished the greenhouse just in time to transplant all of the seedlings into hundreds of trays. I would never have gotten the fifty-foot by twenty-five-foot clear plastic covering over my greenhouse without the help of James Weaver, a Mennonite farmer and fellow grower of heirloom vegetables. James came early one morning with his brother, father, and son. Accustomed as they were to building barns, they maneuvered like acrobats over the high greenhouse framework, tightening bolts and sanding down sharp edges and redoing our flawed carpentry. James had also been instrumental in landing the rented farmhouse for me. In fact, James had almost overnight become, by virtue of his knowledge, experience, and eloquence, my mentor, fellow seed exchanger, and most trusted friend. Jill's aunt Toby, who had come to stay at the farmhouse after quitting her job proofreading for a San Francisco law firm, cooked an unforgettable lunch for the six of us. In a kitchen whose windows were perpetually foggy with the transpiration of thousands and thousands of seedlings waiting for the true sun, we feasted on onion-smothered chicken, winter corn pudding, homemade biscuits, and strawberry-rhubarb crisp.

Eckerton's ownership was still up in the air, passions subdued in anticipation of a surveying crew, when the fields became fit for plowing. Since I had blown all of my money on a tractor, greenhouse, and a scrappy old transport disc that I had dragged over the Blue Mountains with the Toyota pickup, I still couldn't afford a plow. So I hooked up the cultivator I had used with the Ford 8N, clawing it back and forth until the ground was workable. My wintertime maneuvers seemed to reduce tension between the two Eckerton families. Like the other farmer, I could come and go as I needed now, using my own tractor, harvesting my tomatoes, and transporting them to the packing shed we'd improvised at the rented farmhouse. All the chile pepper plants and tomato boxes and assorted paraphernalia would clog up arteries there instead of at Eckerton.

My father was the first one to show up when I needed a field hand. From my friend James, I borrowed a plastic mulch layer, which puts down four-foot-wide weed-suppressing strips of black plastic in a field. James took me out on his tractor to show me how the mulch layer attached to the three-point hitch and how it worked best if you had children to follow behind the tractor and shovel soil onto the edges the mulch layer didn't cover properly. As I laid plastic mulch in *my* field, my father took up the shovel and did the grunt work. The man who had resisted every group effort to improve Eckerton when he lived there followed behind the tractor with a shovel and covered the edges I missed. Together, my father and Toby seeded rows of corn and beets, which, when they germinated, were almost impossible to find among the weeds that germinated with them.

My endless trips between Eckerton and the rented farmhouse, fifteen minutes each way, became onerous, primarily because I kept forgetting things. Arriving at Eckerton to sow arugula and weed the beet rows, I would leave behind the seeds *and* the hoe. So back I would go to the rented house, where, seeing how the seedlings were drooping in the greenhouse, I would spend half an hour watering and then take the seeds along to Eckerton but forget the hoe. At least two hours of every day were spent shuttling back and forth to retrieve forgotten, twice-forgotten, and thrice-forgotten items. If only everything could be in one place! To boost morale, my father reminded his former management-consultant son how the magnificent British navy, too, had operated for hundreds of years out of a ragtag assortment of office buildings. The scrappy organizational structure gave freer reign to the piratical savvy of a Drake, the patrician instincts of a Nelson. When they got around to putting an extension on the Admiralty Building at the start of the twentieth century, the magnificent British navy became a centralized, overbureaucratized institution that could no longer rule the waves. The modern British Admiralty was a bit like the Jersey tomato, I joked, crown of the sandwich in its glory days, now an overpampered, egregiously uniform product of too much water and advertising.

With Sir Francis Drake–like pluck, my father went back to New Hampshire and returned shortly after with his girlfriend, an avid hiker and sedulous berry picker. The second woman he had brought to do hard time at Eckerton, Jeannine proved to be as diligent as my mother had been in her first years there. My father left Jeannine in the field and applied himself to running errands, hunting down a full-sized pickup truck for me, lending me money, mowing grass at the rented house, doing crossword puzzles, and pondering other aspects of a management strategy that might keep me afloat in the formative years.

Because I could not afford to have one ship go down at sea—the tomato highway at four o'clock in the morning is a desolate place to have to wait for help—the pickup truck my father scored for me was a brand-new three-quarter-ton Ford. "I can't afford that," I protested. But he gave me some money to make a down payment on the truck, and the first thing I did when I got it home was have a friend of mine weld a frame on the truck to which my market tables could easily attach from the outside. This way, I could avoid the previous year's repeated late-night mistake of having to unload the truck and reload it because I'd forgotten the tables.

As the summer heated up much faster than the previous summer, I knew it would be tyrannical to expect a mostly voluntary work force to get me through. With persistence and a little luck, I scored Joseph from California at about the same time Cho turned up. A language savant, Joseph had served as a war interpreter in Vietnam, translating for an enemy-interrogation unit. Fluent in Spanish and Vietnamese, Joseph had more tomato-growing experience than all of us combined, having run picking crews in California and Mexico. Joseph chafed at our lack of mechanization, at the way we transplanted by hand and relied too much on hoes and shovels. Worst of all, not a single Mexican was represented on the labor force. He tried scouting the local mushroom houses for Oaxacitas or Guatemalans, but the mushroom farmers were hoarding them. Overworked and underpaid, Joseph conversed with Cho in a sort of Indochinese Esperanto to keep himself amused. And Cho would share with him the potluck field lunches he brewed up in his electric steamer, the porridges of rice and overripe tomatoes and whatever obscure weeds he had foraged from the fields that morning.

There were countless employees who came to work and disappeared before I could even remember their names. In those early years, if I could have identified the telltale characteristics of a tomato person, I would not have been so quick to hire anyone who turned up. In retrospect, the non–tomato people were easier to put a finger on, attracted to the field either by dire necessity or some chronic obsession with short-lived alternative job fantasies. Art students from the local college seeking haven from the uninspiring mainstream workplace, only to cite lack of inspiration as a good reason for quitting a few days later. There was Howard, for instance, who worked in a tweed coat, his pockets laden with the CDs of spontaneously arranged white noises he produced and tried to hawk to his fellow pickers. I once made the mistake of leaving Howard alone to pound tomato stakes; when I came back, his zigzag arrangement of sticks looked like some kind of art installation. It was Memorial Day weekend, and my earliest tomatoes, thriving in the unseasonably warm spring, were already lying on the ground. With no one to help me, I spent all of Sunday and Monday pulling out Howard's stakes, pounding them back in the right way, running strings between the stakes, and training my fallen tomatoes to stand up again.

There were new hires who asked up front how long they had to work before they could get fired and collect unemployment. Others took one look at the field upon arriving for the first day of work, hopped back in the car, and raced away at breakneck speed. Joseph would line up a dozen people to come pick the next day and we would be lucky to have four show up. He finally drew a line when Mary celebrated her $350 winning lottery ticket by buying a new television and blowing off a week of work to watch it. She hadn't even bothered making up an excuse, and she dragged her best friend out of the field to watch television with her, so Joseph told her to take the rest of the season off when circumstances finally brought her back to pick cherry tomatoes. When Joseph brushed off Junior for similar reasons, Junior came to my house with his whole family in the car, wife and four kids staring wide-eyed through the station wagon windows as he showed me the latest court order to get a job or go to jail. *I promise it will be different if you please hire me this once more . . .* They had a blue-lipped underwater look, those hungry, gaping faces. Convinced, I overruled Joseph and even forked over subsistence money before Junior's next work week was over. But Junior's was a purer strain of subsistence. Cash in hand, his sentence commuted by the little note I had written for him, he disappeared, abandoning me to the irate phone calls of his case worker.

And by no means was Junior the only Eckerton Hill Farm alumnus to flirt with the law. We've watched them move on to become bank robbers, accessories to murder, bail skippers. I began to have nightmares of workers sleeping off hangovers under the gnarled apple tree in the far corner of the field. Worse, in the mind-altering humidity I lost my sense of where reality left off and the nightmares began. That second year was dry and excruciatingly hot, the first of three memorably oppressive El Niño seasons. When I wasn't at Greenmarket, I devoted myself to tweaking water from a severely challenged irrigation system. Sufficient for a medium-sized garden at best, my well kept drying up on me. Each time this happened, I would wait half an hour for the well to replenish before hiking a quarter mile up to the top of the hill to start up the pump. Then I would cut back on the plastic drip-irrigation lines receiving water, until the tap was delivering at a trickle. When a thirsty mouse or groundhog would take a bite out of one of the running drip lines, the leak would overwhelm the well so that the pump would shut off and I would have to repair the leak and wait half an hour before trudging up to the well again. I was becoming familiar with something Milt Miller had learned years ago: Eckerton's soil was well drained. I became consumed with seeing to it that every one of my plants received at least a few drops of scarce water each week. Toward this end, I would set my alarm clock for midnight and then again for four o'clock in the morning so that I could hightail it up to the field and fix irrigation lines and restart the pump in the pitch black. Before going to market at three thirty in the morning, I would head up to the field to work on the irrigation. Although the plants drooped within a day of receiving their ration of water, they continued to squeeze out intensely flavorful fruit.

When lack of sleep started to catch up with me, Joseph took on more of the daytime irrigation responsibilities. Reduced at times to a de facto picking force of one, Cho couldn't help but go and go and go. In my exhaustion, I joked about posting elixir-wagon-variety help-wanted signs:

ECKERTON HILL FARM BLUES CAMP
Two months and you'll sound a little bit like B.B. King
MONEY-BACK GUARANTEE

At last, within a two-week span, Bonnie, Heidi, and Craig arrived. Three tomato people through and through. Bonnie in clogs and sweatpants, her gift for diplomacy and teamwork honed at a dentist's receptionist desk and the various country grills where she had waited tables. An energetic ball of get-up-and-go, Bonnie reminded me of my grandmother with her lickety-split decisiveness. She even kept two caged canaries, Cheech and Chong. Pensive and self-sufficient, Heidi spent the non–tomato months following the sun to places like New Zealand and Mali and Swaziland, an itinerant vegan with a working knowledge of obscure languages like Bambara and Sosotho. Craig was an old high-school classmate who stumbled upon us while combing the field for arrowheads and the shapeless rocks he was fond of carving into Rodinesque shards of human form. "I never thought in a million years I'd be working for you, Starkey," Craig confessed after two weeks had passed and he had stayed on board.

Joseph immediately put Bonnie in charge of smoking-policy enforcement. Another characteristic the non–tomato people had in common was that they all smoked. To prevent a devastating outbreak of tobacco mosaic virus, employees were sent a quarter mile from the field to take cigarette breaks. Afterward, they were required to wash their hands in a bleach solution and put on surgical gloves before handling the fruit. Even as she diligently picked cherry tomatoes and chatted to Jeannine or my mom, Bonnie enforced this policy like a hawk. To Heidi were assigned technical chores—things like fixing irrigation leaks and organizing the packing shed. Craig kept pace with Cho, whose nightmares of squirted seed-beady tomato rot began, at long last, to dissipate.

With the fresh arrival of solid help under Joseph's tenure, the golden age of our operation blossomed, the time when the Hugh's and the Brandywines, the Nicky Crains and the Mango tomatoes grew plump as sugar pumpkins. Pounding the longest stakes we could find into the ground, one for every two plants, we strung the vines up with a Florida weave. But those Florida hybrids were engineered to grow only four feet long. Aiming for the sun, our unruly indeterminate vines soared as high as the stakes would allow before spilling down over the sides and twining together into a bosky morass you had to struggle with to get at the fruit. We even found the time to label the hundred-some-odd varieties growing in the field. The labeling seemed so critical then. There were so many different shapes and sizes and shades of color, it seemed they would never get picked at the right ripeness without customized instructions.

Bonnie was the one who first referred to those nasty dark green stains on our hands as "tomato tar," and Heidi figured out that the juice of split tomatoes was best for cleaning it off. A tomato person could tell you from touch alone whether a fruit was perfect for picking. It was much more than mere competence, though, that placed one in this select company. Mind you, neither I nor my employees even knew to refer to ourselves as "tomato people" in those early years. In fact, we seemed as unlike one another as the varieties of tomatoes themselves. The similarities rested on indefinable hunches. I'm thinking of the way Bonnie and Craig and Heidi would park their cars so meticulously in the same place every morning that each dripping oil pan only darkened the uniquely circumscribed oil stain already formed on the macadam. "Tomato people" was an impression, a barely perceptible outline whose completeness needed a few years to rise to full consciousness.

Joseph had an expression for that moment the night before market when, amid the sounds of chirping crickets and gulping frogs, the last box of tomatoes was stacked precariously on the overloaded F-250. "That is one ay-ass of tomatoes," he would declare with a drawled South Carolina chuckle as I tested the driver's seat to determine whether the mountain of tomatoes I was sharing cab space with was going to bury me the first time I made a right turn. If there was room up front, Jill or Aunt Toby or my father would ride to market with me. "The tomato people are here," customers gushed when we made it to market. We still showed up as late as ever, the same old chaos of trying to unload and set up the stand as people inspected the boxes of tomatoes. The hundred varieties of tomatoes that had been painstakingly labeled in the field once again lost their identity on our Greenmarket tables.

A golden age is always a hindsight epoch, unhinged by some mortal flaw. The high point of the farm's second season was succeeded by the crash of the third season. Catching wind of Cho's relapse into peasantry, his family demanded his return to Seoul. After wintering over in California, Joseph was forbidden to leave his home state on account of family obligations about which he was vague. Almost weekly, I was finding Craig alongside the road, scratching his head over the 1969 GMC pickup with the hood that had to be unbolted every time he added oil. As the engine hissed, he would make threatening gestures with the rusty seized-up socket wrench he used to open the hood. The truck was like some high-school tart he still hadn't gotten over now that he was nearing forty. He had already drained so many resources that pure stubbornness was keeping him from trading it for another or accepting a ride to work from Bonnie. Instead, he ended up trading his tomato nature for a Pygmalion dream, settling down in his leaky trailer to the disconnected elbows and torsos and breasts he was so good at creating out of stones he found in the fields. Gwendolyn, the first of our two children, was born, which meant Jill had less time for pulling weeds and picking cherry tomatoes. While cutting grass at the rented farmhouse, my father tipped over the riding mower and cracked a couple of ribs. Toby moved to New York City, where her cooking expertise was more valuable at our market stand.

I was left with two good women. Bonnie took charge of execution, tenaciously running the cherry-tomato picking crew, the rag band of lukewarm adventurers who might or might not get out of bed on any particular morning. "I have fifteen flats of Sun Golds, ten flats wild Mex, and lots of Isis Candy ripe for picking," Bonnie would report, always using first person in the manner of a snappy waitress presenting the breakfast specials as though she planned to grill them up herself. When the crew was particularly slim, Bonnie would race home and drag her boyfriend or her cousin or her neighbor's kids back up to the field with her.

Heidi took charge of design, fixing the irrigation lines and stringing the plants. She could spend hours inspecting the tomatoes for blight or hornworms or a better way of doing things. On the subject of hornworms, which we handpicked and splatted on the ground, Heidi had to struggle with the hypocrisy of her organic-farming vegan soul. Whereas among humans, she found dinner companionship among like-minded consumers of grains and leafy greens, she was expected to turn coat in the realm of insects, allying herself with carnivorous spiders and praying mantises, squishing the mint-green guts out of the vegetarians. Good bugs, bad bugs. They all seemed to strike a balance without our taking sides one way or another, without our having to construct a whole damned religion for the universe of squirming organisms encountered in a stiflingly hot tomato field. Conflicted, Heidi opted for a middle ground, pulling the hornworms off the plants, gently setting them in between the tomato rows, hoping maybe the bluebirds or the braconid wasps might take care of them. Or maybe not.

Arguments broke out. Bonnie wanted to know why Heidi was dicking around with the weeds and the hornworms when there were more tomatoes than we had hands to pick. To which Heidi would reply by reaching into a picking basket and coming out with gouges and split tomatoes, green ones hard as billiard balls. *You call this picking?* Execution and design. Two warring principles in the farmer's tortured soul. Resorting halfheartedly to my consultant's bag of tricks, I lightly suggested to Heidi during a pretzel break that she ought to draft a flurry of procedural memorandums for distribution to new hires: *Quick snapping wrist action is critical to picking an unsplit wild Mexican tomato . . . The Green Zebra is ready to pick when a yellowish sheen appears . . . Cigarette butts must be discarded in the receptacle at the designated smoking area.*

In truth, I too was conflicted about the hornworms. But secretly, I wished to hell that one employee—*just one tomato person*—could come up with an unflinching strategy for controlling them, as well as the groundhogs who took single bites out of the low-hanging tomatoes. Or for the myriad rodents who bit into my irrigation drip lines. Another summer of tiptoeing through my fields in the middle of the night, a tick magnet brushing against musky tomato vines as I listened for the hiss of pinpricked irrigation lines. I could not spare a single drop of water. No wonder Milt Miller went crazy. We were falling behind again. The weeds were growing as high as the tomato plants and there was not enough manpower to get the staking done right. Some of the workers took to stamping out their cigarette butts right in the tomato rows. My memorandum-writing campaign incurred the ridicule of both Bonnie and Heidi. At last, they could agree on something. Behind a wall of staked tomato vines, I eavesdropped on Heidi's imitation of my voice, spooned out, amid giggles, in dollops of drollery: *"Do you think you could put together a little . . . memorandum?"*

I assigned Heidi sole responsibility for picking the technically challenging tomatoes, those whose woody stems had to be scissored with surgical precision. I helped her when I could, squiggling on my back like a mechanic under a car, snippers in hand, trying to get a good angle on the stem of a Marizol Purple. All this effort for just one ungouged tomato! Further and further behind we fell as the sun poured it on like never before. The water from the well was abysmally insufficient for even my plants' minimal survival needs, so I started bringing trash cans full of water up from the rented farmhouse so that we could water the most exhausted plants by hand. Those pea-green flotillas of clouds that delivered half a minute of spit and drizzle could nonetheless pack gusts strong enough to snap hundreds of tomato stakes. Too busy picking and watering, we had no choice but to leave the plants where they fell. From six in the morning until dark, Heidi and Bonnie worked without breaking for anything more than water and broken pretzels. Peak harvest was still a few weeks off, but you would hardly know it from the field hand defections.

At last, fearing imminent disaster, Bonnie pulled off something Joseph had never managed to do: she went into the city of Reading and came back with Mexicans. They all came from the same town in Michoacán, and their leader was Enrique, who drove them out every morning in his Chevy Lumina van. Enrique was a twenty-five-year veteran of North American agriculture, healthy and punctual, devoted to his children and his Alcoholics Anonymous meetings. His crew, which included two of his sons, was relatively young—Chicago Bulls caps, dark suck marks on their necks, swastika tattoos. There was a standoff at first, Enrique's crew flexing experience and self-worth born of many seasons in the San Joaquin Valley. We were something new and amusing to them, a farm run by two *gringas*. And what to make of these Stone Age irrigation methods, hauling water from trash cans in milk jugs? A few of the Mexicans, sensing mismanagement and doom, hightailed it back to the air-conditioned piece-rate predictability of the mushroom houses. But beneath the sniggering of those who stayed, I sensed a feeling of familiarity and comfort. This was how they irrigated back home.

Swaddled in fabric to keep every square inch of skin protected from the sun, they moved slowly and methodically, picking what was ripe and removing the most cumbersome weeds along the way. They chattered constantly, a little bit in Spanish but mostly in their native Purépecha, a modulated pitter-patter with guttural sounds akin to the clicking language of the Bushmen of the Kalahari. Thriving just to the west of the Aztec empire Hernán Cortés encountered, the Purépecha were one of the few pre-Columbian native peoples to survive the Western onslaught of assimilation and smallpox. Enrique and his crew taught us the virtues of working at a sustainable pace, taking regular breaks and making time for at least one half-hour siesta involving tortillas as well as tomatoes, tomatillos, and weeds scavenged from the field. I could see how the work suited them, how it beat the hell out of hacking off heads of broccoli and placing them on a field conveyor day in, day out. I got the feeling they had been in search of us more than the other way around.

Bonnie and Heidi were more than happy to concede to Enrique his fiefdom. And anyhow, as if to maintain balance, Wayne and Dennis arrived about the same time. Wayne, the professional student with his groaning, oil-guzzling tan Lincoln Continental, its trunk a cavernous library of dog-eared Kerouacs, Burroughses, and Bukowskis. Dennis was supporting a wife and four kids on his wages, seven bucks an hour with no bonuses for the ample supply of self-deprecating jokes he liked to crack, jokes that kept the English-speaking crew in hale spirits. Not the smallest object of Dennis's ridicule was his Ford Bronco which often got used to transport the tomatoes to the packing shed at the rented house. The drought was a blessing for the windowless Bronco. Like Wayne's Lincoln and Enrique's Chevy Lumina, it dripped oil. A whole new archipelago of unique stains graced the macadam edging the tomato field. I was beginning to see the whole picture.

To keep the packing shed in order, Lee and Ernie came on board, two retirees who'd been working jobs together since they were teenagers. As if we weren't already glutted with obscure languages, Lee and Ernie conversed in the local dialect, Pennsylvania Dutch, a language their children refused to learn. Lee and Ernie enjoyed listening to the mariachi music the Mexican crew cranked up when they came to help in the packing shed because its *BOOM-pah, BOOM-pah* sound was so similar to the polka heartbeat with which they were familiar.

At last, I could focus on selling tomatoes and getting water to my plants. Up and down the hill I went, to the well and back, my anxiety-prone stomach flipping and flopping like the inside of a lava lamp. In 1999, the year of the millennium-ending drought, we hung in there by virtue of the most unorthodox of methods. As the surrounding farmland deteriorated into a dusty federal disaster area, slapping us across the face with back-to-back-to-back hundred-degree afternoons, we spent whole days, every one of us, watering thousands of plants by hand. Still, that wasn't enough. I tracked down another old Little League teammate who hooked me up with a water pump and an ancient International truck with a thousand-gallon water tank attached to it. What with all the restaurant orders to be taken and the buckets of water to be hauled from the rented farmhouse and the feeble hilltop pump in constant need of maintenance, I was lucky if I could run the water tank three times a day down to the mountain stream at the foot of the hill, the stream that had supplied the swimming pool with water back when Milt Miller had the pipes and the old pump house in good order. I will never forget 1999. It was the kind of year—like 1957 or 1964—that pushed Milt Miller to the brink of insanity. And I understood only too well about his stomach trouble. I tried Milt's oatmeal diet, but it did nothing for me. In pulling every shoestring available to my undercapitalized farm, I opened myself up to fresh attacks from neighbors who saw me helping myself to scarce water. The organic farming snobs on top of the hill who contended that my quarter-gallon-a-minute well was pumping the whole aquifer dry. The lady in Milt Miller's old farmhouse who stuck her nose into my misery when I pulled next to the stream with the rattletrap water truck. "You're using up all the water. The reservoirs are drying up because of you." No matter that the total amount of water I succeeded in drawing on my best day was less than what a typical vegetable farm in South Jersey used in ten minutes.

Somehow, the plants managed to hang in there. My patched-together organizational structure produced a tomato that was to the New York culinary scene what the British navy had once been to the Atlantic Ocean. The fruit was smaller than I would have liked, and drought stress was causing an unsightly outbreak of blossom-end rot. But flavor was all that counted with my customers. Since we didn't have a full *ay-ass* of product to pick, I upped the price and sold homely specimens I never would have dragged to market before. The years of heartwarming tomato fables were paying off. Consumers had grown suspicious of the faux reds. The patches of black, the woody scars, the multiple signs of tomato suffering were now the draw among the cognoscenti. My methods grew bolder. When they came back asking for a Radiator Charlie's Mortgage Lifter, an Aunt Ruby's German Green, or an Extra Eros Zlatolaska, rather than ensure the hundred different varieties I had brought were piously categorized, I came up with new names and fairy tales: *And this would be a Monica Lewinsky's Emperor Tempter. Named, of course, not after the newsworthy White House intern but after a little-known balalaika strummer in the court of Peter the Great.*

Again and again, we were written up: *The holy grail of tomatoes. Best tomatoes on the planet.* Once the laughingstock of all nightshade-dom, our tomatoes graced the cover of *Gourmet*. People from as far away as Mexico, birthplace of the *pomi d'oro*, were FedExing gobs of cash, anything to get us to pop some real tomatoes in the mail. Even the man who had come to survey Eckerton so it could be

divided insisted I sell him some tomatoes. The orange demarcation
flags he left behind in the field got bleached by the sun and the rain
as the saber-rattling threats of litigation subsided.

"His middle name is chaos," Bonnie said of me to the NPR
interviewer who came out to the field and remarked upon the pro-
liferation of weeds. The seasoned farmers, those who'd dedicated
their careers to growing orbs of weed-free, spit-polished perfection,
came to steal secrets from our trendsetting operation. And there on
Eckerton Hill, they would see scrawny tomato plants swamped
by perennial weeds, a melee of grasshoppers and hornworms and
multilingual field hands competing for a meager supply of zip-
pered, wheezing fruit. The farmers would bristle and quake and,
fearing contagion, hurry away from the field muttering to themselves, "This is not farming. Not even organic farming. This is not
farming at all!" But that was precisely our secret. The less farming
we did, it seemed, the greater our success. Perfection is attained
when nothing more can be taken away. We cut out the pesticides,
the fungicides, the calcium spray for the blossom-end rot. We
wore stiff trousers to prevent Canadian thistle from scratching
our shins. Like weeds themselves, the tomatoes were volunteering
from previous crops, brand-new cross-pollinations springing up
and joining the native perennials, toughing it out with pigweed
and hydra-headed quack grass. Given half a chance, a tomato will
try to become something else. Thus, the appearance on Eckerton
Hill of the Bowling Pin tomato, the Baby Carrot tomato, the
Honkleberry Honk. To find these newly spawned varieties, you
had to bushwhack through untamed field. The food magazines
would send out photographers at first light and, hard as they tried
to enhance and edit the shots, they just could not bring themselves
to print pictures in which the tomatoes were either impossible to
make out or didn't even look like tomatoes. One food critic went
so far as to comment that the search for an Eckerton Hill tomato

bordered on a truffle hunt. Another accused me of subjecting my tomatoes to Calvinist suffering.

No matter. Similar varieties were now being grown by other farmers who were perfectly capable of pumping their tomatoes up with fertilizer and purging the weeds for the glossies. With the competition mounting, I rose to the challenge. If a wet-behind-the-ears chef queried me for a per-pound price, I sniffed at the mere thought of my forage-worthy delicacies enduring comparison to so many overwatered, obliging upstarts. "Really," I would reply. "If you need to ask." Before such an ego, even the chefs were doing a double take.

It is still so difficult to pin down what makes a tomato person. Facility with a dead-end language? Knowledge of edible, rarely eaten weeds? A swastika on a brown forearm?

One thing I've noticed is that during the most brutal part of summer, the tomato people go at it with an extraordinary singleness of purpose. Eckerton Hill has a daunting southern exposure, canted like a target for the sun's angled rays. When the sun is burning holes through the afternoon, the tomato plants soak up light until they are limp with molten exhaustion. At night, all that suffering transfers to the fruit, turning the tomatoes every shade of the sun—off-white, pale yellow, dusky purple, blazing orange red. Come morning all these colors are hanging from the plants like gifts from some summertime Santa. By midday, the brightness and the weight of all the humidity leave you standing there, shadowless, the bare fact of yourself. You can either leave the field, as most would, or you can join in the activity orbiting the two sources of magnetism: the tomatoes, softening as fast as you can pick them, and the jubilant sun. I am always astonished at how the crew will stay out there until the last of the fruit is picked.

The talk of defection doesn't start until autumn. A northern blast of wind will come sweeping in, the temperature barely making it past fifty, the fruit unwilling to ripen, a late and pathetic generation of lackluster hornworms jaundiced in sickly imitation of the listless yellow tomato leaves. Overnight, the whole field succumbs to a gloomy factory-town grayness. And the tomato people react as though this is the end of everything. "I can't take it another year," Bonnie would tell me when the frost finished everything off, refusing to set foot in the field of papery dry husks that a few weeks earlier had been thriving tomato vines. She would crawl under a rock and I wouldn't hear from her for months. Saying, "We'll see," Enrique and company would head back to Mexico or to Florida for the citrus crop. The rest of the tomato people would get all uppity on me, in much the same way I had become accustomed to Cho doing. There were just too many other openings out there, cozier situations without ticks or blossom-end rot, intellectually stimulating opportunities with twice the pay and benefits to boot. I've done my own fair share of murmuring. "Someday I'm just going to plow it all over," one writer quoted me as saying. But this resolve to quit has become as much a part of the annual cycle as the appearance each June, right around the summer solstice, of the tomato hornworm.

Bonnie stayed on for a few more years, and Heidi went off and started her own farm. Although Dennis moved on, he grows a huge garden each year for his family. But Wayne is still with me, thank God, and so is Ernie. And a crew of Purépecha-speaking, tomato-savvy people from the same town in Michoacán starts coming on board in April each year, with the last of them arriving right about the same time those hornworms appear.

From the golden age of the farm until today: ten years. Turn the telescope around and those plump tomatoes are as infinitesimal as the tenacious pea-sized mother of the whole race. Surely, our methods have devolved into something more art form than science, a reversal of so-called progress, an attempt to swim against the waters like salmon back to some original spawning ground. How else to further a hypothesis about a people supposedly versed in rocket propulsion who chose to blend in among a race still struggling with the rudiments of the wheel, a people whose intelligent and motivated descendants were to be found today driving outdated, oil-hemorrhaging cars, engaging in a style of farming that bore resemblances to hunter-gathering? Could it be the original tomato people were escapees from a brainy planet bent on high-tech hara-kiri, meek enough to know the new world would be better off if they ditched the rocket and latched onto the virtues of Montezuma's beloved fruit?

I am confident that, if enough monkeys playing on typewriters can eventually tap out the full text of *Hamlet*, then somewhere, at some time, in a language more ancient than Purépecha, there must have existed a story, a creation story of sorts, that went something like this:

A long, long time ago, the moon was brilliant with light, as bright as the sun. Day and night, brightness reigned continually on earth so that there was no cause for tiredness and no need for sleep. Life was everlasting and hunger was unheard of because tomatoes flourished in the ever-present light on vines so muscular there was no need for staking. The fruit was so plump and abundant and ever growing, there was no need for planting seed either.

But then, in a great war for control of the sky, the sun soundly defeated the moon, shattering it, reducing it to a mere foil for its own brilliance, coloring it red and then peach and then umber and then bone white as the first darkness engulfed it, surrounding it like a tomato seed embedded in black, loamy soil. As hunger, cold, tiredness, and death took hold upon the earth, fragments of the moon's once magnificent brightness rained down upon it, falling in all the colors that make up the spectrum of light, tomato colors. With the moon's light halved, the new tomato vines that took root were spindly and weak and with fruit so small it was barely larger than the seed itself. For as long as there was daylight, earthlings had to pick the tiny fruits just so there would be enough to survive on.

In time, however, these first farmers came to realize that a greater supply of tomatoes could be assured by scattering the seeds about and that careful seed selection could ensure larger fruit. And so, as the tomato began its slow, embryonic growth—now as big as four seeds combined, now half the size of a pea—the peasants who knew the story of the once-brilliant moon developed an insatiable optimism about the day far, far off in the future, when man could coax the tomato to grow huge again, on vines so tenacious and strong the moon could be reached upon them and its brilliant raiment of light restored.

What is the most sublime contemporary cuisine but a refinement of the peasant's querulous methods, an acrobatic balancing of fish heads and garden whatnots, all plated in such a way as to resemble nothing if not modern art? And what is modern art but a headstrong longing to go back to some smithereened epoch?

From the golden age of the farm until today. In a decade, we have reduced to an art form what it took eons of peasant optimism to make possible. And still, I don't deserve to say "we." I'm just a salesman now, too smoked by the first years to be of much use in the field. While I am at market juggling tomatoes, everything is really happening back home on the hill.

ONCE UPON A SUGAR SNAP

My wife—the farmer's wife, always sticking her nose where she got no bidness—wants to know how come I decided at midnight, with deliveries finished and two hours of driving ahead of me, to stop for a beer before leaving New York City.

The short answer to your question, my dear, is peas.

And the long answer?

Need I remind you of the warm spell we had back in early March? The ground dried enough for me to disc up some shaley hillside, and I got out my walk-behind Earthway garden seeder and sowed half an acre with Sugar Ann, Sugar Sprint, Sugar Snap, Premium, Eclipse, petit pois. It stayed warm the rest of the week and—bonus!—my peas germinated by St. Paddy's Day. Before the north winds blew in again, Wayne and I got out there and covered the peas with lightweight protective fabric. We pounded tomato stakes around the perimeter of the pea patch and attached seven-foot-high poly deer fence to the tomato stakes and fastened the deer fence to the ground with six-inch hand-push staples to seal it off from the groundhogs and rabbits. Since our uninvited dinner guests are not so easily deterred—indeed, they long ago deciphered the meaning of those white tent cities I construct in early spring for my peas and lettuce (sequestered from the muddy, ice-limp winter fare, such tendrils of satin sweetness!)—I sprang for a quarter mile of chicken wire, which I used as a border around my fence to impede burrowing. There is time in March for such preventive measures.

At some point in mid-April, the first of the Mexican crew straggled in, so I started them off in the pea patch, hoeing weeds for half a week, then building trellises. Somewhere in the middle of trellis construction, the door closed on my peas' ability to pay the rent. As you are sure to point out, my March would have been more profitably spent flipping burgers at McDonald's.

But that is not the point. Peas are like poems, priceless on their own terms. What an ego boost it is for a sentimental farmer to be first to roll into town with bucket loads of crisp, sweet peas! As you know (remember when it was just you and me picking?), the trick is to move them as quickly as you pick 'em, since peas start on their descent toward starch the moment they disengage from the vine. So I decided to pick everything in the morning and make my deliveries in the afternoon. Whoa! Did I ever misjudge the pea load. Especially the petit pois. Those teensy-weensy petit pois? What talented young kitchen extern, charged with shelling a brick load of petit pois, wouldn't find himself ruefully contemplating another blow-off summer at the beach? It takes me half an hour to fill a picking basket with petit pois. The Mexicans are faster, but we still didn't get out of the pea patch until noon. And then there were baby heads of lettuce to dunk into ice-cold water. Mesclun greens to snip, clean, and mix. Spinach, wild arugula, spring onions, radishes, yellow chard, lovage. The first ripe sun-fragrant strawberries, barely enough to fill one flat.

By the time we were done harvesting, cleaning, weighing, boxing, and loading the truck, the kids were coming home from school. On the way to the interstate, I got caught behind a school bus, starting and stopping, starting, stopping. I was in no mood to witness the rituals of preadolescent disembarkation—the high fives and catcalls and the bus driver waiting to make sure the kids didn't decide they wanted to jump back on the bus to take one last farewell bow. Into the loving widespread arms of one candy-dispensing mama after another they chugged, the roly-poly, pink-cheeked balls of amiability whose sole purpose in life seemed to be to impede my progress. If only I'd had the time and the tact, I would have gotten out and taught them how the sweet tooth can be satisfied with freshly picked peas.

Okay . . . so maybe a couple of the kids were lithe and nim-ble, capable of scaling a steep escarpment without the asthmatic breathing. Okay, okay . . . so maybe my fuming was more appro-priately aimed at my own inability to manage. Because for the fourth straight day now, there wasn't going to be enough time to plant those tomato seedlings that were getting leggy in their cell trays. Because, once again, I couldn't find my cell phone. Because I lost my order sheet. Because there was no way I could afford to pay somebody else to do this delivery, not after all the money I'd already sunk into those peas. After ten years, I had learned noth-ing about peas. I was better off letting the deer eat them. Or not planting them at all.

But I made good time on I-78, stopping to drop off micro-greens and peas in New Jersey, then cussing my way through a forty-five-minute delay at the George Washington Bridge. At Sixty-ninth and Columbus, I pulled in at the fire hydrant in front of Telepan, where service was kicking into high gear. Bill Telepan came out nonetheless and, as I showed off the goods, he whistled the tinselly ice-cream-truck song. "Mmm," said he, tasting a Sugar Snap. "You got my baby romaine?"

Yes, I did have Bill's baby romaine. But everything had gotten loaded pell-mell, as usual, so I had to dig deep for Bill's romaine, my feet sticking out the back of the pickup truck. He also took yellow chard, spring onions, French Breakfast radishes, red-stem spinach, and, of course, peas. More digging beneath boxes, the peas spilling out of the little handle holes, peas spilling onto the flatbed, peas spilling onto the sidewalk. "So early," Bill said. "So sweet. This makes me very happy." And off I went, with Bill whistling the ice-cream-truck song behind me, my spirits lifting measurably. No telling what I might have done had he told me my peas sucked.

Down Columbus Avenue, past Lincoln Center, onto Ninth Avenue, where traffic bottlenecked behind horse-and-carriage rides. *Ka-lip, ka-lop. Ka-lip, ka-lop.* A hundred and fifty years ago, that might have been the sound of some curmudgeonly, ruddy-cheeked, whiskey-snorting renegade Stuyvesant headed for the city with peas grown in Harlem. But all I could think was how the entire world was in collusion against my progress. I reined in my impatience, went nip and tuck with the cabbies, stopped to let an old, disoriented lady cross in front of me—the cab horns blaring protest—then turned right onto Forty-third Street.

Esca's kitchen was a beehive of activity. Not a good time to show up with two kinds of spinach, the neighbor's feta cheese, rhubarb, wild arugula, scrapple from the butcher, mesclun greens, asparagus, microgreens, spring onions, red-stem spinach, three kinds of radish. I even had a lamb aboard for Dave Pasternack—the neighbor's lamb, fed on goat's milk, dressed out at a mere twenty pounds. Dave sent out a crew to haul the ice-packed lamb cooler and other bags of goodies into the kitchen. He even turned his back on the kitchen to come outside and personally try a pea.

The tasting of the first pea is an annual ritual between farmer and chef, a sign the race is on, a race that's every bit as thrilling as the Indy 500, this long-anticipated race called the northeastern growing season. Oh sure, the asparagus and rhubarb and spinach and spring onions have been sizing up for weeks, but there's something about the first peas plumping up beneath the big sun: you better not blink now because right behind those peas—*VROOM!*—come sun-coddled berries and cherries and plums and peaches and tomatoes. Ears of morning-picked corn whose kernels burst clear and sweet in the mouth. If you do blink, you'd better have access to a farmer who has his eyes wide open. Because *VROOM!* and all those sweet squirty sun juices are gone. Gooseberries and nectarines and strawberries and apricots and blackberries. *VROOM!* and bright Phoebus Apollo, that heavy-hearted fiddler, will be chasing after the flower-drenched *dulcequitas* of Argentina.

"Outstanding," Dave declared to my sticking-out feet as I dug under boxes of lettuce and peas. "But there's gotta be a better way to execute, Tim," he continued, crunching on another pea. "You and Guy Jones, you're the last of the Mohicans." Dave always says that about me and Guy. Which is a stretch, the way I see it. Guy Jones is a forager extraordinaire, a maestro of ramps and fiddleheads and nettles. Guy Jones really *is* the last of the Mohicans. I'm just a farmer with too many peas to pick. Dave checked the cab of the truck for stowaways. A gardener himself, he was savvy to what should be coming in, knew what he was looking for, saw it. "The strawberries you got hidden under the rhubarb, they taken?"

"You want them?"

"Do I *want* them?" I gave him half of the strawberries and placed a pint of them on the dash for myself. For a lip-smacking follow-up to the two pounds or so of snap peas whose stems littered my dash, Dave sent out a crispy piece of striped bass on the fly. Like my peas, the freshly fired striped bass, perched atop grilled artichoke flesh, had its moment, which I couldn't afford to let pass. I scarfed it down hot, breaking off slithery, delicate pieces and pushing them into my mouth, then swigging down the sweet, warm cocktail of fish and vegetable juices en route to Becco, where

I contorted my half-bushel-box-laden body through a packed dining room, leaving a trail of peas behind me.

Then across town, another delay at Times Square—spilling out into the street, a surge of tourists surrounding a well-formed Adonis with long dirty-blond hair strumming his guitar in a pair of spanking white briefs with the words NAKED COWBOY stitched into them. In the snow, I've seen the Naked Cowboy serenading in his underwear, making a whole lot more money than I could ever dream of making on peas. No use breaking into a rage, so I went into survival mode, cranking up the radio because Sandy Denny was singing her hauntingly beautiful song "Who Knows Where the Time Goes?" Every face I saw on the street seemed to mirror my own panicky sense of entrapment: mothers pushing perambulators, businessmen exhausted by that after-dinner drink, pretty girls checking their cell phones for messages: *Why doesn't he call?* If I knew where my cell phone was, there would be plenty of messages that I couldn't do much about anyhow: *Just reminding you, Tim, we're expecting those mesclun greens for dinner service tonight.*

It was already past nine o'clock and I still had to head across town, then downtown, and then into Brooklyn. *Who knows where the time goes?* On account of the tall buildings, Sandy Denny's song broke up in front of a glowing store sign that said 99 CENT DREAMS. I considered my predicament. Forget about getting my mesclun greens on the table tonight. The big question was, would I make it to all of the drop-offs before the kitchens closed?

At Restaurant Daniel, the curb was taken up with black cars and limousines, so I double-parked and struggled in the dark of the back of the truck for peas and micro mâche. Behind me, a garbage truck let out an air horn blast: *BRRRROOOOOOP!* "C'mon, c'mon, I can't get through, you're holding up traffic," shouted the driver as I stumbled out with boxes of peas.

"I'll be in and out!" I answered. With the clock hanging over me, I didn't have time to drive around the block, but I sensed one very unhappy garbage truck driver, so I reached into one of the boxes for a handful of snap peas—an old and dependable tactic—and walked over and gave them to him. "Eat everything but the stem," I advised.

"Better make it fast," he said. Down the steps to the prep kitchen I went, then back up and outside for three more boxes. Back into Daniel and out again. "Hey, hey," the garbage truck driver shouted as I started to put my tailgate up. "Can I buy some of those off you?" With my fingers, I raked a handful of peas off the floor of the flatbed and handed them over as a chorus of horns flared behind him.

After Daniel, traffic ruled more in my favor. A stop at Payard on Seventy-fourth and Lexington—in a cloud of steam and worry, Philippe Bertineau nonetheless smiled after biting into a pea—then a string of green lights on the way down Lexington. It was well after ten o'clock when they buzzed me in at Gotham Bar and Grill. I chatted about baby radishes with Alfred Portale and his sous-chef, Adam—watermelon radishes, black radishes, spicy Japanese radishes—and endured the usual jokes about how a farmer should rightly be in bed by this time. "I still have to go into Brooklyn," I said, racing out the door.

But before Brooklyn, there was the Tasting Room, the second-largest delivery of the night. How it is Colin Alevras could need so much with a dining room a little bit larger than the flatbed of my pickup truck, I don't know, but a couple of end-of-shifters came out to gather up asparagus and baby lettuce heads and yellow chard and baby beets and red-stem spinach and feta cheese and English peas and snap peas and petit pois. I also talked him into taking some unclaimed bags of green spinach, red Russian kale, and micro celery.

"I've been running around the corner all night for asparagus,"

Colin said. "Each time a customer asked for it I got just enough for the order and hoped you'd get here before the next order came in. Can you hit me up with a little extra asparagus this week? Hey . . . now *that* is a pea."

A heavy wave of self-pity came over me on the way across the Brooklyn Bridge. As I parked on Smith Street, I braced myself for what seemed to be the logical outcome of this day from hell: the Grocery closed for the night so that I would have to sleep over in the city and make the last pea delivery in the morning. Which meant the tomatoes would have to wait another day to get planted. Or maybe two days, since another bonanza of plump peas would be ready for picking the day after tomorrow.

Across the street from the Grocery, a girl was playing the violin; I could see and hear her through an open fourth-story window. One of those tricky Stravinsky pieces—jerky screaks of sound forming their own miraculous order. She played it quite well. Which made me think of my own violin, sitting unused for two weeks now, neglected because of, well . . . peas. As you know, my dear wife, I'll never be any good at the violin because I took it up too late in life. I tend to squeeze the fingerboard so much it makes my hand hurt. I play baroque music with emotion. "For Pete's sake, you're playing Bach!" my violin teacher has to remind me continually, always with that look of mirth and bafflement, as if I had just fixed myself a peanut butter and sauerkraut sandwich. "You're playing Bach, not Brahms!"

I only took up the violin, you'll remember, because I wanted to be involved personally in the musical instruction of our talented young daughters. I didn't want to be half-assed the way my parents had been with my piano lessons. If only my parents had pushed me harder, I would be playing Stravinsky and some other bumble-clot could be pulling in at Smith Street wondering whether the Grocery was still open to accept his peas.

1076271152

But then, you will remind me, I haven't found the time to work on the girls' music lessons these last two weeks. The pea falls not far from the pod, eh?

As if to stanch the bleeding of my melodramatic heart, Charlie and Sharon were still bustling about the back of the house. The Grocery is the sine qua non of the mom-and-pop bistro. Tired as she had to be, Sharon nonetheless waxed rapturous over the arrival of same-day peas. "Mmm. And you remembered our red-stem spinach?"

"Aw, crap." I had, in fact, packed three bags of red-stem spinach, but in my blind frenzy to reduce inventory once I got into the city, I'd already sold every bag. This is what happens when you get so discombobulated with peas that you lose your order sheet.

Sharon asked if I was hungry, so I said, "Yeah, sure," and she set me up at the bar in the little back garden, where I sat and ate grilled artichokes and chicken cacciatore and listened to the helicopter hovering overhead. The chicken cacciatore was rich and comforting. It had a smoked bacon flavor and I washed it down with a glass of Château de Pibarnon Bandol Rosé. My mood heightened by wine and repast, I thought some more about those long-ago piano lessons my parents didn't hold me to. *No way you're laying that rap on me, buster*, I could hear my mother protest. *Maybe I oversteamed the broccoli once or twice. Or I used that fired ceramic spoon holder you made in art class for an ashtray. But you never practiced, remember? What you were good at was whistling at the birds and jumping on your pogo stick and pulling that unsightly fold of skin down off your elbow to everybody's horror. I couldn't even get you to take a bath. Want to know why you're a pea picker? Look in the mirror.*

Into such maudlin wine-soaked ruminations entered Charlie, beer in hand, worn out at day's end. "Didn't we both say years ago we would never keep doing things this way?" he asked.

"Jeez," I said. "Can't the two of you just go to a movie and let somebody else run the kitchen from time to time?"

"Can't you get somebody to deliver your peas for you?" He laughed. "You want coffee?"

The thought of coffee turned my stomach, but I needed a pick-me-up to get home by. I knew exactly what I wanted. "Could I trouble you for a sliver of that chocolate cake?"

Chocolate fig cake is what I meant. The pastry table is Sharon's corner of the kitchen. It would have been very easy for her, especially at that hour, to dispense with the bells and whistles, but the chocolate fig cake came out full size in a perfect puddle of chocolate syrup and with the requisite scoops of coconut ice cream and passion-fruit sorbet. Even the mandarin orange slices. Oh my. The recipe holds back on the sugar, too, just enough to let the chocolate do most of the talking: the essence of bittersweet chocolate, with fig seeds to crunch between my teeth, the passion-fruit sorbet a tart counterpoint to the coconut sweetness. Bach and Brahms all rolled into one. There *are* some perks to the pea picker's trade.

Revved up with chocolate, I was ready for the ride home. *VROOM!* I stood next to the truck and listened to the girl on the violin for a few minutes before starting on my way, racing across the Brooklyn Bridge into Manhattan. But traffic came to a halt as I approached the entry to the Holland Tunnel. Twelve fifteen by my clock and New York City had one last bottleneck for me. I tried to hang in there, but the only movements any of the cars were capable of seemed to be the incremental squeezing out of the air between them. I was so wide awake that when a car from Canal Street wedged into the intersection, I got out and explained to the driver as tactfully as I was capable of that, thanks to his bonehead move, we were all in a state of gridlock.

"You shut your mouth or I'll rip your throat the fuck out," was his spirited response. For a moment, I stood at the ready, still holding on to the rage at my parents over those piano lessons, my fingers prickling for a confrontation.

But what if he had a gun or a knife? Read it in tomorrow's *Post*: GENTLEMAN FARMER DRUBBED AFTER DROPPING OFF PEAS.

I got back in the truck and slowly, delicately backed my way out of the Canal Street intersection. There are more ways than one in which a pea can get between a man and a good night's sleep. I headed to an old stomping ground: Bleecker Street Bar. Remember how we used to go there to play darts? I didn't see any of the old gang, but I borrowed the house darts and sprang for a pint of Guinness. Just a little something to take the edge off, a little something to rein in the bittersweet chocolate racing through my veins on this warm late spring night . . . er, morning.

Harvesting the DMZ

Huzzahs for the tamers of the forests of eastern Pennsylvania: scythe-swinging enablers of order and uniformity, breakers of oxen, wielders of axe and adz, salt-curers of shredded cabbage. They earned their names the old-fashioned way, those Millers and Weavers and Fenstermachers. By turns grumpy and wise, methodical and pious, they wasted nothing. Made scrapple from pig guts, soused the cow's tongue. Not in their nature to scrape off the bark and let the mighty oaks die standing up. They felled every tree, dragged them out of the woods, and squared them into barn rafters or lintels. Or rendered them into charcoal for stoking their pig-iron furnaces. They tanned hides with the bark and stirred the ox's hair into a paste that could hold a log home together. When stumps were all that stood in the way of the plow, they drilled holes and dynamited and *yooksed*. And *yooksed* and *yooksed* and *yooksed* and *yooksed* until the roots gave way like unwilling molars.

When the air cleared over their industriousness, every piece of workable ground was available to wheat or barley or corn. Here and there, a stump had refused to go, so they plowed around it, calling out *Gee, now! Gee!* then *Haw!* to the docile team of horses. They had gone overboard in places, clearing marshland that sucked on a horse's hooves. Or steep hillside where the deforested topsoil washed into the valley during spring torrents. Marginal patches best kept in alfalfa or timothy. Or allowed to grow back to forest.

In December, they could look out and see how the land they'd bared was exquisite as a woman's body, heaving up and folding down, elegantly caressed by long winter shadow, here and there a pubic cluster of leafless brush to denote a plow-resistant shale head, a spongy armpit of nonnegotiable swamp. On the borders of the cleared land, the beaten-back forest put up a natural fence line, where shiny-leaved poison ivy could twine in springtime around the barbed-wire canes of wild berries—blackberries, wineberries, black raspberries—a rustic DMZ beyond which only the morel hunter or the seeker after the ovenbird's song could be expected to tread. Wild black cherries took root on the same borders, as did the ancient elderberry shrubs.

Come summer solstice, when most of the farmers around me are bringing in hay or gearing up to harvest wheat, I find myself uncomfortably cash strapped and with little to pick for quick money. With peas on the way out and tomatoes yet to ripen, I invariably make a madcap adventure out of harvesting the wild fruit glistening at woodland's edge. Last summer, I spent hours with Nacho and Silvio in the bosom of my favorite wild cherry tree. Branches scratched my neck and scalp as I picked from the raised bucket of one tractor, my feet as high up as a basketball net. Silvio worked from the raised bucket of another tractor, while Nacho volunteered to be the monkey of the crew, easing out on a branch to where it was barely strong enough to hold his weight, a plastic grocery bag hanging from the elbow of his nonpicking arm. Wobbly of knee, I reached for a fruit so tiny it was half pit. Minuscule and packed with flavor, the wild cherries grow in clusters of five or six. If you pull one off without its stem, your cherry will bleed and rot by nightfall. Pick two successfully, pop the bleeder into your mouth. Silvio and I filled half-pint containers, which we placed in cardboard flats at our feet. Each tractor loader was equipped with a long-handled shovel. When Nacho's plastic bag was about one-twenty-fifth full, the critical point beyond which the delicate cherries at the bottom of the bag would collapse beneath the weight of the cherries on top, he would call out for either Silvio or me—whoever was closest—to reach out with a shovel so he could place his plastic bag onto the spade. Conveyed to one of the tractor loaders, the bag was gently emptied into the two or three half-pint berry boxes it could fill before being returned to Nacho. This was our system for harvesting nature's commercially unviable bounty, fruit designed to be eaten on site, by the birds.

But the special attention does not end with the picking. I always set my wild berries and cherries out on the porch with a fan blowing over them until we load them on the truck to go to market at three thirty the next morning. Even then, the two hours of market-bound confinement can bring on the condition Seamus Heaney laments in his poem "Blackberry-Picking":

> *We hoarded the fresh berries in the byre.*
> *But when the bath was filled we found a fur,*
> *A rat-grey fungus, glutting on our cache.*
> *The juice was stinking too. Once off the bush*
> *The fruit fermented, the sweet flesh would turn sour.*
> *I always felt like crying. It wasn't fair*
> *That all the lovely canfuls smelt of rot.*
> *Each year I hoped they'd keep, knew they would not.*

Me Irish heart waxes arrhythmic at the mere mention of that rat-gray fungus.

This year, for a change of pace, I've decided to hunt down elderflowers for Alex Grunert, the pastry chef at Bouley and Danube. Alex has been after me for years to bring him elderberries, the tiny clustered black gems he used to pick with his grandmother on the outskirts of Vienna. Against his will, she would drag him out to her favorite hunting grounds, marshy areas where the railroad tracks cut through forest, since the elderberry thrives wherever nature has been disrupted by human design. When they brought the elderberries home, his grandfather would set to work with tweezers, removing the tiny stems from the berries. Hours and hours of picking and destemming and boiling down just so his grandmother could put up a few jars of jelly. It pained young Alex to have so many potentially fun-filled hours diverted to those tedious little *hollunder* berries. Now that he is an ocean away from his grandparents' Old World influences, he sings a different tune. "Tim," he often said to me when I failed to deliver his elderberries, "if you want I can come down there and help you pick them."

To be quite honest, I didn't know where the elderberries grew. My grandfather used to enlist me in his elderberry expeditions out in western Pennsylvania. Like Alex, and like my father before me, I was not fond of the exercise, which involved picking the berry clusters and shaking the berries into a bucket, incurring purple-stained fingers and nasty flare-ups of poison ivy. It didn't matter to me that, cooked down, the berries had a rich and musky old-fashioned berry flavor, without that corrupting oversweetness wrought by hybridization. All I knew was that the raw berries, unlike all other wild berries, had a gritty, slightly bitter nothing flavor that wasn't worth the stained fingers. I never bothered figuring out where the elderberries grew in eastern Pennsylvania.

Sambucus canadensis, the most ubiquitous of all the native American elderberries, grows far up into Canada and south to the tip of Florida. It is hardier than and not nearly as tall as its European cousin, *Sambucus nigra*, which reaches thirty feet in height and can be found in Asia and North Africa as well as beside the railroad tracks outside Vienna. There are more than twenty species and subspecies of *Sambucus*, with every continent but Antarctica featuring at least one native.

The name *Sambucus* derives from the Greek stringed instrument, which is puzzling because elder wood, with its meaty, easily removed pith, converts conveniently into a flute or panpipe, as American and European natives discovered about the same time they were breathing life into what came to be known as our myths. If I were called upon to fact-check Ovid, I would not question his claim that a sexy wood nymph named Syrinx was turned instantly into a reed in the sandy waters of the Ladon. No. I would be more likely to wonder whether heartbroken Pan hadn't crafted his instrument of sorrow from worthier material than marsh reeds, from, say, the branches of the scrappy *Sambucus nigra* that surely thrived in its own damp leaf mold along the shore of the same body of water. To this day, the mountain folk of Italy still construct a wind instrument called a *sampogna* from the elderberry shrub.

Two millennia after Ovid, I am driving around the countryside hunting elderflowers with my friend Joe Bowman, whose roots in eastern Pennsylvania go back to the Swiss Mennonite Bowmans, one of whom founded Bowmansville, where Joe's ancestors lived until his father moved out into the country. No longer an adherent of the old faith, Joe is nonetheless instinctively drawn as any Mennonite to flora, which explains why he is the only person I know, besides Alex Grunert and his grandparents, who has eaten elderflowers. "I dipped them in tempura batter and fried them in vegetable oil," he explains. "We had a huge elderberry shrub growing on the edge of our yard. The recipe came from Euell Gibbons. The sweetness of the nectar offset the clear bitter taste of the flower. Right there's an elderberry."

"Where? Where?" I look in the direction Joe is looking but all I see is lush green spring growth. "What do you see that I don't see?"

"It's the shade of green. And the bush shape. But the flowers haven't opened yet. You'll know the elderberry when you see its flowers." There is no use stopping, so we continue in the general direction of the biggest cluster of elderberry bushes Joe knows of, in a swamp along the Saucony Creek. A sudden downpour slows the pickup to a crawl. Just as quickly, we're flashing through sunlight again, cresting a hill from which I can see, off in the distance, a dark thunderhead dumping bucket loads upon the village of Krumsville and environs. I don't bother looking toward my field, north of Lenhartsville, where I know the unabated sun is pounding everything to dust. It's easy in springtime for a farmer to look into the sky and see what the Greeks saw, that prototype of the dysfunctional family—Hera, Zeus, Athena, et al., each gliding along on his or her own cloud, playing favorites with a small community of farmers, the sky a rancorous bumper-car ride for immortals, the bemused farmer a futile slasher of his best lamb's throat. When it does finally rain in my field, it will be a gully-washer, five or six inches with silver-dollar-sized hail in it. I just know it. Then I'll bellyache even more than I do now. I don't bother looking for the rainbow. Seen enough rainbows and hailstones this spring, thank you.

Joe's got woman problems, so we talk a little bit about how he's being too honest with this girl. "Plants I can understand," he says. "If a plant is thirsty, I give it a drink of water. Easy as that." We decide it's probably best in the long run if he stays honest with the girl even though that strategy has never worked for either of us.

"Plenty here," says Joe when we reach our Saucony Creek destination.

"I don't see anything," I protest.

"Once the flowers open up, you'll know. But we'll have to wait until the weather settles for that to happen." There is no place to pull to the side of a busy road, and they're calling for scattered frost tonight, which means the thousand or so tomatoes that are unprotected in my field will need to be covered with special fabric before dark, so I keep on driving, still clueless about a plant my grandfather had tried so hard to teach me about. "Terry's old girlfriend makes her jelly from those elderberries," Joe says as I drive him back to his car.

"Oh yeah? It's her land?"

"Oh no. It's not her land. I just know she picks there."

"So . . . like, it's her territory?"

"Well . . . no. No. Not really." I'm not sure what to think. Is Joe getting back at his fickle woman by leading me to the elderberry cache of the wood nymph who spurned his best friend? If I go bumbling around Saucony marsh snipping elderflowers before they can produce berries, will I get conked over the head with a cast-iron pan? I think of all the local foragers I know whose eyes narrow to slits in my presence whenever I try to steer the conversation toward favorite morel-hunting grounds. *Yeah, right. The moment your secret is out, I'll have busloads of city sous-chefs trampling your tender-fleshed earth treasures.*

I get my tomatoes covered in time for the frost, and after three unseasonably cold nights, elderflower petals tight as a fist, the weather turns gray and misty for a week and a half. My body slips into winter mode on account of the low light conditions. Lackadaisical and bumbling, I let things fall behind, spending too much time convincing myself that the constant moisture will breed disease on the leaves of my tomatoes. I still do not know what an elderflower looks like, but a farmer tells me he knows of a bush growing along his tree line. "You're welcome to pick all the flowers you want," he says.

Late on a Friday afternoon, I call Joe on his cell phone. He's at a bar, rehashing his honesty policy toward women. He'd be happy to come look for elderflowers in the rain, so I pick him up and we go to the farmer's house and the farmer points out the tree line where the elderberry grows. "Walk out there five or six football fields and it should be there. I know it was there ten years ago." Ten years ago? The rain comes down harder as we set out along the edge of a cornfield, mud clumping on our shoes. Joe assures me the elderberry of ten years ago will still be around. "Elderberries live forever," he says. The rain lets loose when we're almost there.

It would seem that either Zeus or Hera doesn't want us anywhere near the sacred panpipe shrub.

We're both soaked through and through by the time Joe spots our shrub, but the tiny white flowers have barely attained what he terms the "balloon" stage, waiting for a little sun to open them up fully. Since we've already gone this far, I decide to snip a bouquet of about-to-open elderflowers, and we slosh back to my pickup truck so that I can return a sopping-wet Joe to his beer and put my bouquet of tactfully obtained elderflowers into a vase of sugar water. The next day, I present the bouquet to Alex when he comes by the market.

"Well, let's hope they open up," Alex says optimistically. But when I call him later in the week, all but two of the flowers have died. "It's okay. I can do something with two flowers," he assures me. Alex tells me that his grandmother is also an encyclopedia for all of the elderberry's medicinal uses. For longer than history has been recorded, the mythical shrub has served man also as a natural emetic, cathartic, diaphoretic, diuretic, alerative, emollient, and discutient. To translate: the flowers and berries help the body manage fluids like phlegm and sweat and urine. They also clear up respiratory problems and help settle the stomach and offer a natural defense against the common cold and flu. John Evelyn, the seventeenth-century English diarist, declared *Sambucus nigra* a "catholicism against all infirmities whatever." As with so many ancient medicinal plants, though, a good part of the shrub is poisonous.

But Alex is mostly after flavor. He's not only thinking of crunchy batter-fried elderflowers powdered with cinnamon and confectioners' sugar and served on a plate with ice cream. There's elderflower gelée, elderflower sorbet, elderflower-laced chantilly cream, and Danube's signature elderflower-infused champagne cocktail. "You know," Alex says, "I could use at least ten times the number of elderflowers you brought me."

But the sun is out now. The summer heat is pouring it on. With so much to do in the field, I don't have time for hunting down elderflowers. Not that I have to hunt for them anymore. Once you've seen the flowers, Joe had warned me, you will know the plant. Umbels of tiny upright-growing white flowers that will eventually shed their petals and droop from the weight of the plumping-up berries. The elderberry looks like an unpruned hydrangea whose flower clusters resemble Queen Anne's lace. Elderflowers are turning up everywhere in my daily orbit. At the edge of my field, one bush splits the branches of the giant maple that fell in a summer storm ten years ago but still manages to leaf out each spring. Another clings to the hillside beside the interstate exit ramp, right next to the little pull-off where the abandoned cars of fed-up out-of-staters become fair game for BB-gun-toting adolescents. In the wetlands behind my greenhouse, I saw off a fat, dead elderberry branch, fully intending to make it into a flute when the growing season is over.

It gets so I can sense the presence of elderflowers whenever I am near a meadow or a stream that has been tampered with by mortals. At the base of a steel electrical tower, the distinctive white umbels wave in an afternoon breeze. I can even hear Alex's voice. *Look, Tim. Elderflowers.* Alex has been such a good sport when you consider that all I've ever managed to bring him is two barely opened umbels. I think of the desserts he has offered me when I was delivering lettuce or tomatoes in a surly mood. One stands out: a chilled multilayered delectation of passion-fruit curd, espresso granita, spiced banana toffee, and toasted lemon me-ringue. All served in a tall, narrow glass. The deftly managed spoon slices through all four layers and delivers them simultaneously to the tongue. An icy liqueur, both sweet and mouthwateringly tart, subtly infused with the aroma of lovingly roasted espresso beans, the dessert brings equilibrium to the soul and sends a worn-out farmer home feeling a tad more enthusiastic about having to pick tiny vegetables and fruit.

On a Saturday morning, I wake before dawn, thinking how nice it would be just to forget about the usual springtime stresses for a few hours. Thinking elderflowers and how to go about harvesting them. I load up on used quart-sized yogurt containers and fill two gallon jugs with water. Since my foraging will undoubtedly trespass on the age-old supplies of unknown jelly gurus, I decide to snip only a couple of dozen flower clusters from each shrub I've identified, enough to fill one yogurt container. As it turns out, an already trampled-down path leads to each of my elderberry shrubs. In all, I visit eight previously visited shrubs, filling eight yogurt containers with white bouquets and leaving plenty of flowers to develop into berries. When the berries are ready, I'll help myself to a fair portion of those, too.

My work crew has the day off, so before I haul my elderflowers into New York City, I have to water the greenhouse, transplant a few trays of basil seedlings, pick some zucchini, and tinker with the irrigation lines in the field. By the time I'm set to go, it is scorching hot and my elderflowers are drooping in their makeshift vases. I decide to drive them up in the car with the air conditioner going full blast. Even then, the flowers droop more with each mile traveled. Halfway through New Jersey, when I'm about to turn back on account of my sagging bouquets, elderflowers begin to pop up along Interstate 78. Some of them are set back ten feet or so, while others waver on the very edge of the forest. Practically tapping me on the shoulder, the lopsided, fortuitous shrubs whisper: *Droopy elderflowers? No problem.* I make four stops to replenish my supply, hoping each time a police officer will pull up and issue a citation. What a story that would make. On the outskirts of Newark, the elderberry population is bigger than any I've ever seen, but I've got my vases full, so I zip right past.

Although I could have harvested all of Alex's elderflowers in ten minutes just fifteen miles west of New York City, I make a grand show of presenting him with my foraged delicacies, bringing a few vases down to the pastry kitchen—a little bit like presenting a bottle of good wine—and inviting him out to the car to have a look at the rest. "Here is what I made with the elderflowers you brought earlier," Alex says after helping me unload the morning's haul. He shows me a small bowl full of elderflower syrup, the flowers boiled down with water, Riesling, sugar, honey, lemon peel and juice. The syrup is both a medicine and a base for the creams, cakes, sorbets, and even salad dressings he derives from the elderflower. He offers me a teaspoonful of the flu-fighting syrup, and its flavor is at once floral and bitter, a cross between rhubarb and sassafras tea. Knowing Alex's reputation for innovation—he whips up a right scrumptious white asparagus ice cream when asparagus is in season—I ask the obvious question: "So what spin do you put on your grandmother's elderflower recipes?"

Alex gets a spooked look. "I would never tinker with my grandmother's elderflower recipes," he assures me.

Two hours west, some fifteen thousand tomato plants are crying out. Irrigation lines need changing. Overgrown suckers need pruning. As I head home from my successful delivery, the elderberry colony lounging just to the west of Newark is downright urban, thousands upon thousands of white umbels merrily waving halloo and good-bye to the breezes of passing eighteen-wheelers. An underappreciated medicine chest and flute supply thriving on the edges of the sprawling quagmire known as the Meadowlands, where stilted birds tiptoe among the moldering, hastily dumped remains of troubled city folk, where human habitation bucks up big-time against marshy arcadia.

More ancient than Ovid and born to outlive us all. Hell, I would wave, too.

THE MISUNDERSTOOD
HABANERO

IT'S ONE OF THOSE days at the farmers market—a bright October sky, tables piled high with late summer bounty, the sun so tolerable you can't get enough of it—where people are buzzing around my stand, not buying much, asking too many questions. People always ask too many questions when they see a hundred varieties of chile peppers arrayed before them like this.

"Excuse me, which pepper is the hottest?"

"The one in my hand," I answer.

"What is that, a chocolate-covered walnut?"

"It's a hot pepper. A very hot pepper."

"What kind of hot pepper looks like a chocolate-covered walnut?"

"Chocolate habanero. Or chocolate Scotch bonnet. In Trinidad, they call it seven-pot pepper." I add the part about seven-pot pepper as a temptation for these two ladies from Port of Spain who were lured to my stand by the familiar wrinkled brown pepper in my hand. But they're not buying yet. Like most West Indians, they are skeptical about the pungency of my Pennsylvania-grown specimens. "Okay, so maybe this one only fires up five pots," I say, cracking open the chocolate hab so its distinctive perfume wafts toward the ladies, eliciting the expected smile of recognition.

"I just need something to spice up a tomato sauce," says a red-haired college girl.

"Throw half of this in your sauce," I advise, handing over a weightless, papery-skinned Thai chile. "If it's not hot enough, throw in the other half. Need a bag?"

"A bag? Please. Drop it in with my apples."

"That'll be fifteen cents."

She gives me a quarter and says, "Keep the change."

"Which one is the hottest?"

"This one. Chocolate habanero."

"Are those real peppers? They look plastic."

"That's because they're fresh. Picked yesterday."

"Picked yesterday? They lose their heat if you let them sit around, right?"

"Um . . . no."

"That's what I heard. They get milder with age . . . don't they?" The man who says this has a beard and he's wearing a shabby tweed coat. He's holding a branch of yellow Thai chiles in one hand, a branch of red Thai chiles in the other. A warning flag goes up in the back of my brain: *It's him.* By *him,* I mean the philosopher guy, the one who always ties me up in metaphysical knots over some hitherto unexamined property of chile peppers. While my chiles have developed a cult following, and I can only deem myself grateful for, say, the woman who puts chiles in her socks to keep her feet warm (if anyone, I suppose, *she* would know whether the heat diminishes over time) or the sorceress who uses them to ward off evil spirits, the last thing I want to do just now is engage in a lengthy debate with this modern-day Socrates over the staying power of my chiles.

All the same, I can't resist falling into his trap: "If anything," I reply firmly, "it should be the other way around. The capsaicin gets more concentrated when the chile dries out. Pound for pound, the chile gets *hotter*."

"Hmm. Not what I've been told. You know, I don't like my chiles too hot. Which of these is milder?" He holds up the yellow and red Thai chile branches.

"Both of those are scorchers."

"But which is milder?"

"I would not advise you to bite into a yellow or a red Thai if you're expecting something mild."

"You call that yellow?" he says. "It's more orange than yellow, isn't it?"

Every one of my answers begets another question. He's just like Socrates, all right. So I'm grateful for the man with a colorful Hawaiian shirt who approaches with a jalapeño in his hand. "Mind if I try this?" he asks in a foreign accent, German maybe.

"Sure, go ahead." All eyes turn to the man with the jalapeño, who does more than just try it. He bites off all but the stem, chewing and swallowing with expressionless aplomb. "Not hot," he announces to a rapt audience before wandering off, putting a damper on the case I've been trying to make with the Trinidadian ladies.

They show up regularly at my stand, these culinary thrill seekers with uncommonly tolerant taste buds. Chile heads. The jalapeños I grow are not the wimpy version piled up in gringo grocery stores, bred by seed companies to conceal a bell pepper meekness beneath that glossy, slender facade. It's a no-brainer, as any MBA could tell you: Make the peppers mild and your heat seekers will just have to buy more of them. Dilute the hot sauce with vinegar and your chile heads will dump a whole bottle of it into a vat of stew.

So I guess my degree in English literature helps explain why I am trying to make a living off a pepper so hot it is reputed to fire up seven pots of grub. Your average customer cannot be expected to turn around and come back for more after unconsciously nibbling on a whole bag of chocolate habaneros during a walk through Union Square Park.

The chocolate hab makes a zinger of a hot sauce, too. A drop is all it takes. In the early years of the farm, my wife's aunt Toby made sauce out of the peppers we couldn't sell at market. Now there was a labor of love. We even named our chocolate habanero sauce Burning Love, although Toby originally wanted to call it Burning Fingers because the pain the chopped-up chile inflicted on the webs between her fingers could become so excruciating that nothing short of thumbscrews could make it go away. The blender fumes could set off a fifteen-minute coughing attack. It's been six years since we threw in the towel on Burning Love, but people still show up to tell us they just finished their favorite hot sauce and they'd like to buy some more. A little bit goes a long, long way.

With Burning Love no longer an option, what can I do with all of those extra chiles? Luckily, there are some unconventional sales outlets in New York City, where sex appeal lands my chiles in all kinds of nonculinary supporting roles. I once sold every red chile I had brought to market—eight bushels in all—to a photographer who had Penélope Cruz recline in a bathtub full of them for a promo snap for her movie *Woman on Top*. Another time, my serrano chiles were strung together into a bikini worn by Molly Sims for the *Sports Illustrated* swimsuit issue. My chiles have definitely been places I could only dream about.

I'm lucky, too, for New York City's unique ethnic mix. People from the remotest villages of countries far and wide—Peru, Mexico, Saint Lucia, Burma, Nigeria, Bulgaria—who break out in the most unabashed smiles at having chanced upon the unmistakable chile they remember from the dinner table at home. Citrusy South American ceviche peppers like *aji limon* and *aji panca*; the smoky, hot *mirchas* of southern India; the mild, thick-skinned orange-yellow paprikas of Hungary and Kosovo. Bird peppers, so named because birds farm them in tropical climes, eating the seed and then sowing at random, along with a white smear of that most organic of fertilizers, in backyards and churchyards, alongside the road, next to the liquor store. My customers bring me seed and teach me most of what I know about chiles. They are my mentors *and* my bread and butter. If I can only get these Trinidadian ladies to try some of my chocolate habs, I know they'll be back. Unfortunately, Beverly and Robin and Frieda and all of my regulars came first thing in the morning, as usual. They could have attested to the "true island heat" of my chocolate habs.

"Excuse me. I want to know which is the absolute hottest pepper you got."

"This one in my hand. Chocolate habanero. Some say *fatalii* is hotter." I hold up a slender triangular-shaped yellow chile. "This is an African version of the Scotch bonnet."

"Those grew in Africa?"

"The seed is from Africa. I grew everything in Pennsylvania. *Fatalii* and Scotch bonnet and habanero belong to the same species of chiles. The *chinense* species."

"Chinese? I thought you said these chiles were from Africa?"

"I said 'chin-*ense*.' *Chinense* is one of five species of chiles." Once the word "*chinense*" is out of my mouth, I slip into my broken-record curator-of-the-chile-pepper-museum routine. "The *chinense* has its origins in the Amazon River basin." My hand instinctively reaches for a tiny canary-yellow chile, about the size of a mung bean. "This one grows wild in Brazil. See how small it is, like a wild berry? It's called *cumari*. It may actually be the mother of the species. The distinctive feature of the *chinense* is its smell and flavor."

I drop the *cumari* on the ground and smudge it with my foot so the fragrance envelops the stand. How to describe that fragrance? Fruity. Floral. Apricot with a brace of doctor's office antiseptic.

That unmistakable don't-mess-with-me-I'm-a-habanero smell. Because it grows wild, packing an untamed wallop of fire and flavor in so tiny a package, *cumari* is the most fragrant of all of the varieties of *chinense* that I grow.

From Brazil and Peru, the *chinense* peppers were spread into the West Indies by indigenous people. Since chile peppers are notoriously promiscuous, taking advantage of every opportunity for cross-pollination, the varieties spawned by this migration varied widely in color, size, and heat. Every island has its darling. The Scotch bonnets of Jamaica, the Congo pepper of Trinidad, the goat pepper of the Bahamas. The slave trade probably brought the incendiary *fatalii* to Africa. When an orange version of the island-hopping *chinenses* arrived in the Yucatán by way of Cuba, the locals named it "habanero," meaning "from Havana."

The first chile of the *chinense* species that I ever grew is one I named "ton 80," in honor of Keith, who played on my dart team ten years ago, when I lived in Brooklyn. Keith brought seed for ton 80 back from Trinidad, where he had once supplied his village with corn and spinach and passion fruit from the acre and a half of ground he turned with a shovel. In Trinidad, the pepper was simply called "hot pepper." Or, on Keith's tongue, "ought peppa." Keith was one of the best dart players in Brooklyn, more likely than most to hit three triple twenties, or a ton 80, in one round. "I come home from the bar at three o'clock in the morning," Keith would say, "and me wife is blocking me passage at the door. 'At this hour, you are not welcome,' she tells me. So I reach into me pocket and pull out the twenty-dollar bills I won at the dartboard and she wraps her arms around me and says, 'Ohhhh, I love you, I love you, I love you.'"

The first time Keith saw all of my chiles arrayed at Union Square, he smiled and spread his arms out wide and said, "The United Nations of peppas."

"Excuse me," asks a sweet old lady. "What is that in your hand?"

"A chile pepper."

"It's beautiful. Can I chop it up in a salad?"

"Not unless you want to have smoke coming out of your ears."

"It's not as hot as a jalapeño, is it?"

"It's a hundred times *hotter* than a jalapeño."

"A hundred times hotter than a jalapeño?" According to the Scoville unit scale, the habanero is, indeed, a hundred times hotter than a jalapeño. To contemplate such a statistic is, for most, a little bit like imagining those one hundred Hiroshima bombs we've got stockpiled for God knows what purpose. Half a Hiroshima is unacceptable.

Just how hot is a hundred times hotter than a jalapeño? "If you give a 'ot peppa to a monkey," according to my friend Keith, "the monkey will hate you for life."

The lady who wanted to put my lovely pepper on her salad scoots away in horror. "But it has great flavor," I say in her wake.

"How can a pepper a hundred times hotter than a jalapeño have *any* flavor?" It's Socrates again, with another question. He has replaced the yellow Thai branch in his right hand with a branch of clustered Japanese *santaka* chiles.

I reach for a shiny, thick-skinned, reddish-orange pepper, about the size of a jalapeño and with a pronounced fold at the tip. The pepper, called "pimiento" in Trinidad, gives off that daunting habanero reek when I take a bite out of it. But it's not hot at all. The flavor of habanero without the heat. The Trinidadian pimiento is also called "seasoning pepper" or "flavoring pepper." Most of the Caribbean islands, having been blessed with an ingenious gardener who long ago figured out a way to neuter the habanero by means of cross-pollination and careful seed selection, have their own versions of the seasoning pepper. Some countries share the same seasoning pepper. The best known of these is *aji dulce*, a red pepper about the width of a quarter and shaped like a dented spinning top. Numerous grocery stores in Latino neighborhoods carry *ajicito*, a green, unripe, and less aromatic *aji dulce*, which has deep roots in Puerto Rico and elsewhere. At my stand, *aji dulce* once stopped a young lady from Venezuela in her tracks. As I was talking to her—gleaning everything I could about the chile and its culinary uses—a man who had grown up in Cuba pulled up and explained that he knew the same variety by the name of *chile cachuca*. "We just call that 'seasonin' peppa,'" chimed in a Jamaican girl in a rich West Indian accent. Only in New York City could such an obscure pepper engage four different people in conversation.

I have grown nine different varieties of seasoning pepper, including the one from Saint Lucia and the one from Antigua. My favorite is the pebbly skinned yellow Grenada seasoning pepper, whose seed was originally given to me by a market customer. "I'll take all of the pimiento you have," says one of the Trinidadian ladies. Unfortunately, the one I took a bite out of is the only one I have left. Word has gotten out in the West Indian community. When the seasoning pepper harvest is at its peak, as it is now, there are usually a couple of women waiting for us at six in the morning when we arrive at market. Since most of our West Indian regulars want to buy every seasoning pepper we have—they freeze them, chop them into sauces and pastes, pass them on to neighbors, and mail them to relatives—we have taken to dividing all of the harvested seasoning peppers among seven or eight boxes the night before market so we can hide all but one box behind the stand. This way, each comer leaves the stand satisfied that she has cleaned us out. If we're lucky, this strategy enables us to hold on to a supply of seasoning peppers until about ten in the morning.

Habanero essence is to Trinidadian cuisine what ginger is to Chinese cuisine, what lemongrass is to Thai or Vietnamese. The seasoning pepper brings a whole new layer of flavor to everything it touches, according to Beverly Williams, my biggest customer for that pepper. She stir-fries them with vegetables and chops them up into salads. Seasoning peppers are the key ingredient, along with Caribbean cilantro, in a classic Trinidadian condiment known as seasonin'. As long as there's a bottle of seasonin' in the fridge, says Beverly, the essence of tame habanero can be smeared onto fish, chicken, meat, anything.

While Caribbean cuisine also features the eye-watering *chinense* varieties (and indeed, the hot varieties had better be hot or they're not buying), this does not mean the habanero is off limits for all but the masochists and the jerk barbecuers. For instance, an unripe Scotch bonnet or habanero is typically dropped whole into a bowl of boiling rice, then plucked from the fluffy finished product, thereby imparting a fraction of its heat along with that much-desired aroma. But woe unto the taste buds if the pepper is punctured while the rice boils!

Hot or mild, the versatile apricotty essence blends well with tropical fruit like mango and papaya and passion fruit, playing a unique supporting role in the jumble of sweets and sours that makes for a great chutney. In Toby's finger-burning days, one of her hottest sauces was called Peaches and Scream.

A growing number of non-Caribbean chefs have taken an interest in the mild seasoning peppers, using them both as a bold "new American" flavor and as a twist on a traditional theme. Madhur Jaffrey first used *chile cachuca* the way they do in Cuba, to infuse *sofrito* with the fragrance so elemental to bean dishes like aromatic white bean and pumpkin stew, a classic from her *World Vegetarian* cookbook. She was so taken with the fragrance that she now uses the chile with vegetables like green beans as well as with chicken and fish. Every September, she stops at the stand to pick up a bagful for the freezer. Peter Hoffman at Savoy makes a Grenada seasoning sauce to flavor striped bass and a seasoning pepper vinaigrette that enhances raw summer fluke.

Alex Raij at Tia Pol uses both hot and mild varieties of *chinense*. She infuses oil with the tiny, fragrant, and fiery wild Brazilian *cumari*, then sprinkles the oil over tuna tartare in much the same way Spanish cuisine traditionally makes use of paprika oil. For dessert, she uses the Grenada seasoning pepper to enhance a tomato sorbet. The pepper adds a deliquescent touch of head-scratching mystery to the diner's experience, says Alex. "What *is* that flavor?" they are always asking.

There are risks involved in putting seasoning peppers on the menu, though, as Peter learned from hard experience. When a pickled Trinidadian pimiento he once served whole turned out to be chock-full of Scoville units, he had a traumatized diner on his hands. In saving my own seeds for seasoning peppers—there is no reliable commercial seed source—I try my best to keep them separate from the scorchers in my field. When they do cross-pollinate, though, they revert to full-blown habaneroism. My West Indian customers laugh when I warn them of this tendency. "They do that on the island, too," they say. Peter still buys seasoning peppers from me, but with caution. I usually scrutinize each pepper in his bag for the less agonizing indicators of cross-pollination—the slight shading of color, the absence of pebbly skin on the yellow Grenada peppers. And he no longer serves them whole.

"So which is the milder of these two?" Socrates asks, holding up the red Thai chile branch along with the *santaka*. Two fiery cayennes.

"*Machs nix,*" I answer, a Pennsylvania Dutch expression that means "six of one, half dozen of the other." I should not expect him to understand Pennsylvania Dutch, but I'm getting more than a bit testy. For all my chatter, the last twenty minutes of a fine Indian summer afternoon has netted me all of twenty-five cents. And only fifteen of those cents were earned.

"What's that mean? I don't like my peppers too hot, you know?"

"Both of those are *extremely* hot."

"But peppers get milder over time, don't they?"

Out of exasperation, the shark in me finally rises to the surface. "So if they get milder, then by all means buy either pepper and wait a long time before you eat it."

"Hmm." Before Socrates can formulate another question, the guy who ate the jalapeño is back. "There is nothing hot in this whole market," he says, looking at the peppers arrayed on my table. So I hand him a Bulgarian carrot pepper, a few notches above the jalapeño on the Scoville scale. He inhales the pepper, then gives me the thumbs-down.

I give him a serrano: "Nah!"

A cayenne: "That does not do much for me." He is in search of that quasi-religious experience known to all chile heads. The endorphin rush: a heightening of awareness, a euphoric sense of indestructibility achievable through a sort of crucifixion of the tongue. Maybe I'm not spiritual enough, but the closest I've ever come to an endorphin rush is a three-hour attack of the hiccups brought on by touching my tongue to the seed cavity of one of my chocolate habaneros.

I don't like giving peppers away, but I'm in a bind here. The ladies from Trinidad are watching intently. "He says your peppers are not hot," says one. I look at the chocolate habanero in my hand and then at the chile head. But no. I couldn't. Or could I?

I'm beginning to feel a little bit high. It occurs to me the pimiento I just ate is doing that endorphin thing to my inner constitution. In a variation of Pavlov's salivating dog, my body, having been alerted by the invasion of habanero perfume, is experiencing a profound sense of relief over the absence of the anticipated pain. All these comforting mechanisms are racing between my nerve receptors like polite and dutiful stewardesses who think the plane is about to go down. I think of Fyodor Dostoyevsky being marched in front of the firing squad only to be told, "Nah, we're not gonna shoot you." Endorphin rush. Yessiree, I am alive and well!

So what the heck! I hand over the chocolate habanero, and Mr. Chile Head takes a big bite out of it, as if it's a sandwich or a deviled egg. For a moment, he doesn't seem the least bit affected. But then he starts making this huffing noise. Huffing and puffing as his eyes open wide. His mouth opens, too, and he tries fanning it with his hand. Then he begins to hop. Hop, hop, hop. "Try milk!" I call after him as he hops away from the stand. "Or thumbscrews."

Call me evil. Call me a salesman. I sold five pounds of chocolate habaneros to those ladies from Trinidad.

Among the Mennonites

IF THE AMISH MEN were dead set on winning the game, they would have removed their wide-brimmed straw hats before stepping onto the playing field. The hats, like their full beards, make them larger targets for members of the opposing team, whose object is to peg them with the ball. But not only do the hats stay on, the two Amish men in the middle, twins named Stoltzfus, are putting on a show, larking for the crowd, nimbly bouncing on their feet, bouncing and splaying their legs in the air, Pepé Le Pew–like, as all the while their eyes follow the ball being tossed between the Mennonite players manning the four corners of the playing field. The ball is a homespun, rawhide-wrapped, softer version of the hardball used in the major leagues. It stings when it hits you. The Mennonite players pump-fake to rattle one Stoltzfus, pump-fake to rattle the other, pretend to take dead aim before tossing the ball to a teammate. Angling for a better shot.

With derring-do, one of the twins reaches down and pulls off a shoe. Pulls off the other shoe. Although his left hand is missing three fingers from some farm accident, he manages with thumb and forefinger to pincer his left sock and slide it off his ankle. As the ball shuttles quickly from one corner to the next, he removes the right sock. Planted there in the soggy, just-thawed early March Lancaster County soil, his toes must be getting numb. The crowd chuckles and heckles, drinking up his antics along with the late winter sunlight. Clowning makes you a bigger target, too, and sure enough the anticipated zinger comes straight for the barefooted jester, who drops to his chest amid oohs and aahs of delight. He springs right back up, a feather-light leprechaun, pieces of straw in his beard, fallen hat left on the ground, a crooked tooth lighting up his smile. If the ball had hit him, he would be out. Instead, the thrower who missed is out, replaced by a teammate.

The game is called cornerball, and if there are a few hundred spectators circled around the action the way there are now, if an auctioneer's bickering voice can be heard nearby, working up bids on grain drills, gravity wagons, and rusty old combines, you can be sure the Mennonites are squared off against the Amish. Word gets out through spring auction advertisements—*Cornerball will be played at the Weaver sale*—and enthusiasts, Amish and Mennonite alike, will travel hundreds of miles to watch the games. Or to "help," as my friend James Weaver, a member of the Old Order "Wenger" Mennonite church, always puts it. In a vocabulary accustomed to the language of toil, terms like "play along" collect so much dust on the shelf that they easily get trumped by an everyday word like "help." As if this were a barn raising. Or a field of mown hay that needed to come in before rain. In Pennsylvania Dutch, the word is "*helfen*."

James has a cousin from the western part of the state who once traveled three hours to Lancaster County to "help" a team of cornerball players at a spring auction. When he got unexpectedly smashed in the face by the ball, he knew his nose was broken, but he had to travel all the way home and then spend a couple of hours doing barn chores before going to the hospital. Work is always numero uno. But in late winter and early spring, when the soil is mucky and some field implements need to change hands, there is this sliver of an opportunity for play. "If the ground was fit to plow," James assures me, "believe you me, there would be no cornerball game."

The Amish against the Mennonites. Up close, their differences are easy to spot. In Lancaster County, the Amish ride in gray buggies while the Mennonites ride in black ones. The Amish men are forbidden to shave their beards while the Mennonites tend to shave religiously even though there is no proscription in their book against whiskers. The Amish men wear black zipperless broadfall pants while the Mennonites wear blue jeans. Amish women wear plain-color dresses. Mennonite women wear calico prints. While the bicycle is a common mode of transportation for Mennonites, owning a bicycle is *verboten* in Amish communities because of the easy opportunity it gives the rider to pass on the horse and buggy.

The Amish against the Mennonites. No currycombs here for scraping the flesh off those whose theological convictions differ in minor ways from yours. Anabaptists have always demonstrated their faith in peaceful ways. But their congregations are beehives of reform and schism. Their common ancestry dates back to the early Reformation, back to sixteenth-century Switzerland, when the Täufers, or Baptists, as they were all labeled then, were equally despised by Catholics, Lutherans, and followers of the Swiss reformer Ulrich Zwingli. Their ideas resonated with a Dutch Catholic priest named Menno Simons, whose first name eventually became synonymous with the movement. The Täufers, or Mennists, believed, among other things, that a second baptism, or conscious "baptism of faith," was required of the individual. It made sense to the practical-minded farmers who made up the Täufer community, and who noticed how religious reform brought no financial relief to the powerless and heavily taxed peasant, that an infant could not comprehend the significance of that brief submersion in water. But that first baptism, Catholic or Protestant, was the one that mattered to the state. The second was an act of civil disobedience. One common method of teaching a Täufer a lesson was by drowning him.

Bound together by persecution in much the same way the Jews were bound together by slavery in Egypt, the Täufers were recognized for their farming abilities by Karl Ludwig, elector of the Palatinate, who, in the interest of rehabilitating farmsteads decimated by the Thirty Years' War, encouraged the migration of these proven tillers into the German Palatinate after the war ended in 1648. Täufers were denied rights to citizenship and landownership along the Rhine, however, and by the time Louis XIV was laying waste to the Palatinate in the late seventeenth century, they were migrating again, across the Atlantic Ocean, this time at the behest of William Penn.

The Amish and the Mennonites were on the same side until 1693, when a young minister from Berne named Jakob Ammann took to calling for frequent and urgent meetings to address the unwillingness of certain members to "shun" the undesirable actions of other members. A prominent minister named Hans Reist declared himself too busy with the season's harvest to attend Ammann's ad hoc meetings, moving Ammann to question the elder minister's faithfulness. When Reist failed to respond to various summonses, Ammann excommunicated him. In much the same way that Martin Luther's more diplomatic brethren could only look on in disbelief as the great Western church was sundered by the nailing of those ninety-five theses to the door, Ammann's less vehement supporters mourned the division that Anabaptists carried with them across the ocean to the fertile county in Pennsylvania where they took again to clearing trees and swamps and excelling with the plow.

Cornerball is usually played in the barnyard. But today, because the barnyard is laden with auction-block items, the participants are playing in an open field. When they play cornerball, the younger Amish and Mennonite boys rely on their agility and pure muscle more than the married men, whose feints, hesitations, and balking motions provide another layer of amusement for the crowd. Waiting their turn to play, the clean-shaven Amish boys in their black clothing and straw hats stand together as a team in the crowd, like midshipmen at an Army-Navy game. James is fond of a joke about young Amish men, a joke that pokes fun at the more liberal Amish interpretation of *rumspringa*, the period before manhood when the youths are encouraged to explore the temptations of the wider world before undertaking the baptism that commits them in adulthood to the community. "A man is dining in an expensive restaurant," says James, "when he begins to suspect that the young men in fancy clothing seated at the next table are Amish. So he devises a plan to determine whether he is right. When he gets up to leave with his wife, he announces to her as he is walking past the table of young men, '*Ich schmock mischt.*' ('I smell manure'). When every young man at the table instinctively looks down to check his shoes, the man knows that he was right." No doubt, the Amish have their share of Mennonite jokes. The rivalry is carried out in other places besides the cornerball field.

Without James Weaver, I would never have survived my first years as a farmer. How many times did I show up at James's Meadow View Farm with a flurry of questions just as he was mounting his tractor to go out and work? *Is the ground fit to plow? What are these spots on the leaves of my tomato plants? How come my Scotch bonnets aren't setting fruit?* Sometimes, I would even walk right out into the middle of his field with my latest emergency, and he would stop the tractor and turn off the engine, and, if necessary, pull out a piece of paper and a pencil so he could draw a little diagram for me. If it was an irrigation fitting I needed—an elbow or a goof plug—he would come out of the field with me and root around in the barn until he found it. No cryptic answers, no tut-tutting or shaking of his head over my glaring practical shortcomings. James had been growing chiles and heirloom tomatoes for a number of years before I started growing them, saving his own seeds the way his ancestors used to save seed for their favorite pole beans and peas. In a typical year, he plants twenty-five acres of labor-intensive vegetables. And here I was, killing his time so that I could get my wobbly kneed two-acre patch up and running.

But the man loves to talk. In addition to being a good friend and mentor, James Weaver is my guide to all things Anabaptist. Whenever I am traveling with him in Lancaster County, he likes to point out historically significant landmarks. Just across the field from the farm where the auction and cornerball game are being held, for instance, stands Lichty's Church, where the great pulpit controversy of 1889 occurred. After members of the Lancaster Conference Mennonite church had constructed a small pulpit inside Lichty's Church, other members snuck in one night and removed the pulpit, which they could not tolerate because of its concession to popery and to the showboat mentality of the revivalist ministries that were storming the nation in the late nineteenth century. A bishop should never be placed in a pulpit. At the time, other issues were causing friction in the church. The new concept of Sunday school for children was frowned upon by conservative church members, who believed Bible instruction was the responsibility of parents. And church members were marrying non–church members, violating a precept from the Bible that gets a lot of airtime among Anabaptists: "Be ye not unequally yoked together with unbelievers" (2 Corinthians 6:14). While the identity of the pulpit thieves continues to be a subject of debate in the Mennonite community more than a hundred years later, the controversy boiled over into one of the more bitter church splits in 1893, when Jonas Martin and a few hundred members were locked out of the main-branch churches. Jonas Martin went on to found the Old Order Weaverland Conference Mennonite church. At the time of the Old Order division, my friend James's ancestors had been members of the Stauffer Mennonites, who had split from the Lancaster Conference way back in 1845. After the Stauffer Mennonites themselves split up late in the nineteenth century, James's great-grandfather's brother, Jacob B. Weaver, a Stauffer Mennonite bishop, elected to steer his family over to the Old Order church newly founded by Jonas Martin.

Even before the twentieth century, technological advances had caused friction within various Anabaptist communities. Early in the nineteenth century, recently introduced wooden springs on buggies were viewed by some as a godless luxury. The same happened when steel buggy springs were introduced a few decades later. One of Jonas Martin's great accomplishments was his diplomatic averting of a church division over whether or not the telephone should be allowed in the homes of members. But the car controversy outlived him. Jonas Martin vehemently opposed the car until his death in 1925, claiming the automobile gave its owner an undesirably "high and haughty" spirit. In 1910, one church member caused trouble when he mounted a one-cylinder engine on a wagon that was meant to be pulled by a horse. When the same member bought a new car, he was excommunicated. By 1920, a hundred members had been cast out for owning cars, and Jonas Martin, his health deteriorating, was forced to take a softer stand toward the automobile in order to avoid another division. Car owners were allowed to stay in the church, but the bishop would not offer them communion. Like the compromises that preceded the South's decision to secede from the Union in 1861, this was one compromise that could not last.

After Jonas Martin's death, Moses Horning became the bishop. In spite of his sympathy toward car-driving church members,

Bishop Horning was reluctant to take an official stand on the automobile, reluctant to upset a tenuous balance in a congregation where roughly half of the members were in favor of the car while half were opposed to it. Bishop Horning fainted and complained of ill health whenever it came time to weigh in on the car. He declared himself too sick to attend an emergency conference called to address the growing church discontent caused by the car controversy, but when conference members insisted on paying a visit to the sick bishop for advice they found him in the barn loading manure. Work was numero uno, even for a bishop. In 1927, two years after publication of the novel in which F. Scott Fitzgerald's fictional Daisy Buchanan—driving Jay Gatsby's roadster—ran over her husband's lover, Moses Horning took the critical step of offering communion for the first time to automobile-driving members of the church. Half of the congregation responded by refusing to take communion from him. The bishop wept. There was no turning back. The division was less rancorous than the 1893 division, with the congregation splitting roughly down the middle. To this day, the automobile-driving Horning Mennonites, referred to as "black car" or "black bumper" Mennonites, share numerous churches with the Wenger or "horse-and-buggy" Mennonites. And when a Wenger Mennonite abandons the church, it is usually to the car-accessible Horning church that he or she flees.

If you took the bat away from a group of farm kids who were playing baseball, cornerball is the game they might well devise in its place. The players throwing the ball from the four corners are allowed to run between corners but can only throw the ball from one of the corners. Beanballs are frowned upon. There are six players to a side and they play three innings in which the two sides trade off being in the middle. When all of the players from one side are out, either from getting hit by the ball or from throwing errantly, the half inning is concluded and the total number of players hit is tallied in the throwing team's ledger. Two players go in the middle at a time unless there is only one player left throwing, in which case the remaining players jump in the middle to dodge the last thrower's attempts to hit them. Sometimes a player intending to throw the ball to another player mistakenly hits an opponent and, after a cheer goes up from the crowd and the hit player begins to leave the field, acknowledges the true intentions of his throw. Because the throw was not meant to hit the player, both the thrower and the hit player stay in. If a hat gets hit while it is still on the head of one of the players, the player is out. But if the hat gets hit as it is falling through the air, the thrower is out. Like the Pennsylvania Dutch language the players speak, these rules are not written down, but everybody knows them.

In an earlier game, after a skinny Amish boy put on a dazzling display, twisting, leaping, and dodging so deftly you could hear the ball whistle past his elbow, James conceded that the Amish have some natural advantages on the cornerball field. "From working with horses," he surmised. "They are more loose jointed and flexible, especially those Amish men who walk with their horses instead of riding on a sulky plow. If you ever watch an Amish man walk, he takes bigger steps than the rest of us do because he's used to keeping up with his horses when he walks. And he rolls his hips. He's naturally agile on his feet. He's not so stiff and straight up when he walks, the way someone who spends a lot of time boxed up in a car or on a tractor is."

While a few members of James's Old Order Mennonite church farm with horses, the majority of them, James included, use tractors with steel wheels. Soon after the split with the Horning Mennonites occurred, the newly formed Old Order Wenger Mennonites were confronted with the introduction of pneumatic tires on tractors, which they decided unanimously to reject. A tractor on pneumatic tires, they reasoned, was no different from the automobile they had only recently spurned. What was to prevent a mechanically minded church maverick from changing the governor stop, from fiddling with the carburetor so that he could go racing into town at sixty miles per hour on a John Deere? The discomfort of riding on steel wheels would prohibit the driver from going fast on a paved road. As modern farmers went ahead and eagerly embraced pneumatic tires on tractors, the Wenger Mennonites were consigned to manufacturing their own steel wheels at an increasingly exorbitant expense. If you bought a used tractor with pneumatic tires in the late twentieth century, for instance, you then had to spend a couple of thousand dollars to have a Mennonite welder custom build steel wheels for you. All that extra expense for a bumpy, bone-rattling tractor ride. The use of pneumatic tires on a tractor or even a garden mower, however, would be grounds for automatic expulsion from the church and community.

As the years wore on, welders began to incorporate rubber pads and belts into the design of tractor wheels in order to allow for more driving comfort. The wheels became increasingly elaborate and expensive, so that by the 1990s a growing number of church members were grumbling that if so much rubber was permissible in the design of tractor wheels, pneumatic tires were hardly any different from the so-called steel ones. Opinion in the community began to polarize between those who favored the use of pneumatic tires on tractors and those who believed all of the unnecessary rubber on steel wheels should be disallowed. When I first started pestering James for farming advice a little over a decade ago, this growing conflict over steel tractor wheels was preoccupying him. Tempers were flaring on both sides of the issue, and sooner or later some decisions about tractor wheels would either bring peace to the church or split it the same way Moses Horning's decision to offer communion to car owners once had.

One way to really get the cornerball player in the middle going is to fake like you're going to throw low, then fake you're going to throw high, and then throw right in the middle and watch the guy try to jump and duck at the same time as the ball hits him smack in the pelvis or the knee or, if his legs are high in the air from jumping, in the foot, which is what happens to the barefooted Amish man. With a flesh-reddening smack, he gets it on the right foot. His Achilles heel, you might say. The irony of it brings a roar from the crowd. The players squared off against the Amish men this time belong to the Reidenbach Mennonite sect. The first time I saw a team of young Reidenbach Mennonites play cornerball, I thought they might be a squad of local high-school kids come out to try their hand at the Anabaptists' game. Their clothing was hardly any different from mine. "Don't let those jeans and T-shirts fool you," James assured me. "The Reidenbachs are more old-fashioned than we are." The Reidenbachs split off from James's church back in 1946, after a debate over whether or not young men in the community should participate in Civilian Public Service. Besides being opposed to mandatory involvement in government projects, the newly formed Reidenbachs placed stricter limits on formal interaction with outsiders and weeded out many aspects of technology that had crept into the twentieth-century households and farming practices of Old Order Wenger Mennonites. They disallowed telephones and electricity in most of its forms. And they jettisoned the steel-wheeled tractor in favor of the horse. In their zeal for purity, the Reidenbachs have continued to break up into new congregations since the 1946 split, but today all of those groups farm with horses and harvest their wheat the way it was harvested in 1900, cutting it down and bundling it in sheaves by hand, and bringing it into the barn to thresh out the grains of wheat in a great storm of sinus-stifling dust.

Reidenbach Mennonites, yellow buggy Amish, black bumper Mennonites, white buggy Amish. The question the curious bystander wants to ask over and over again is: *Why?* Why go to the extra trouble of harvesting wheat by hand? Why forgo the automobile when it could save you so much time? Why spend thousands of extra dollars to have some clunky steel wheels installed on your tractor when you could have kept the original, more comfortable pneumatic tires *at no extra cost?* On one level, all of these church-splitting differences in belief, all the scripture-backed rejections of technology, seem worthy of the same ridicule by which Jonathan Swift once mocked the original Catholic/Protestant division: one side believes the egg should be cracked on its broad end, Swift wrote, while the other side believes the egg should be cracked on its narrow end. Incurable schismatics. If you've gone to all the trouble of cornering the best soil for planting your corn (and in my part of Pennsylvania, the Amish and Mennonites plow up some of the richest and most productive limestone soils to be found anywhere), why not take advantage of every technological innovation available, especially when farming is such a struggle even *with* those technological innovations?

"One of these days," James keeps telling me, "I'm going to take you down to Kentucky to visit the Scottsville community." James has a brother-in-law who five years ago joined the Scottsville community, which was forged nearly four decades earlier by a combination of Old Order Wenger Mennonites, Reidenbach Mennonites, and even Old Order Amish. The Scottsville community showcases the most considerable rapprochement between Amish and Mennonites since the 1693 split. On all of the Scottsville community farms, there is no electricity, no engines of any kind. No lawn mowers. No chain saws or string trimmers. They use windmills or rams to pump water for irrigation. To wash their clothing, they use wringer washers that are powered either by horses or by hand. Horse-drawn grinders are used to make animal feed from corn or wheat. You'd think that the absence of technology would make paupers of the community. Quite to the contrary, the absence of technology makes well-to-do team players of everyone. They share threshing equipment and team up to hoe the field of a community member who is lost in the weeds. Every farmer's tomatoes and peppers and lettuces are transported by horse and buggy to a common packing facility, where they are packed and palletized for the trucks that come and pick them up. "And I'll tell you something," James says with admiration and even a touch of envy, "you will not see more beautiful produce anywhere." There is probably no more technology-averse community, Amish or Mennonite, than Scottsville. The community is a model of peace and organization. When a young man reaches the age where he is ready to buy a farm, he knocks on the doors of the other members of the community. By the time he is halfway through the community households, he will have accumulated his down payment in the form of no-interest loans. Imagine the same young man trying to cadge a few dollars from the midwestern farmer who is up to his ears in debt trying to pay off a farm, a quarter-million-dollar combine, a hundred-thousand-dollar tractor.

Nobody in James's Old Order Mennonite community believes that the automobile consigns its driver to an eternity of fire and brimstone or that the Bible spells out the amount of rubber that is acceptable on a tractor wheel. What is critical for the community is the need to maintain brotherly peace of the kind that has made Scottsville such a remarkable success story. How much technology one community member may use to his or her own personal advantage is a matter for public discussion. After becoming friends with James, I kept tabs on the brewing controversy over steel tractor wheels. In the seventy years since they had gained their identity through the rejection of the automobile, the Old Order Wenger Mennonites had blossomed to more than eighteen thousand members, with settlements in eight states besides Pennsylvania. Guiding principles for the community are set by the twice-yearly meetings of the Groffdale Conference, which is made up of bishops, deacons, and ministers from all of the Wenger Mennonite congregations, some of them as far away as Missouri and Iowa. The community had grown too large and varied to peacefully maintain common shared values throughout, I assumed. Although James warned that division had always been a painful experience for the community, I figured it was a necessary evil, a very practical necessity when the congregation became too unwieldy, like the pain of giving birth.

One clear outcome of the Wenger split with the Hornings over the automobile is that the horse-and-buggy Wengers have stayed in farming much more than the Hornings have. And the Lancaster Conference Mennonites who locked out Jonas Martin and his followers more than a century ago hardly farm at all. If you go back to Switzerland or the Palatinate to track down Anabaptists, you will find very few Mennonites or Amish who still farm, let alone drive around the countryside behind a horse. I assumed the Wengers would divide over the tractor wheel, with the pneumatic-tire Wengers perhaps helping themselves in the early twenty-first century to an increasing portion of technology as they worked their way up from farming, their children racing away from home on rubber wheels at the first opportunity, while the steel-wheel Wengers would carry on the traditions of the people who were wooed into the Palatinate 350 years ago because of their known abilities in the field. And do they ever know how to farm, the Amish and Mennonites who play cornerball in the barnyards every spring before the ground is fit to plow. Nearly every community has set up a central produce auction where everyone can bring their cucumbers and zucchini and spinach and eggs by horse and wagon three or four days a week. At the peak of tomato season, these auctions are so glutted with tomatoes that the buyers with the big produce trucks have a field day standing there and waving all of those fresh, pennies-for-the-pound tomatoes onto their trucks. The produce buyers and the folks who love to bring those beautiful tomatoes to farmers markets and sell them like they grew them all themselves. *Yessir, picked these babies myself.*

No sir, there are not many people left who are willing to do the work required to pick all of those babies themselves. I assumed that, since James had never applied much rubber belting to the steel wheels of his tractor, he would be one of the steel-wheel Wengers and that everyone would eventually be contented after the smoke cleared in the aftermath of the division. The community had gotten too large and schism was the only healthy alternative.

But I was wrong. The Groffdale Conference of ministers came up with a compromise that brought all parties into agreement at last. Two inches of rubber belting was permitted on the steel wheels, but any rubber beyond that was deemed excessive. Because of the exorbitant expense of correcting rubber-aided steel tractor wheels that did not comply with this requirement, farmers were given five years to come into compliance. Compromise spared the community the pains of division, holding together nearly twenty thousand men, women, and children.

Although James Weaver's religion limits his ability to travel, he has succeeded in making his farm so interesting that a wide variety of people travel great distances to visit him every year. Chefs and food lovers from all over come every August to taste his heirloom tomatoes. His hot pepper field day the first weekend after Labor Day is the premier event of its kind. His Scotch bonnets have become the rage for a growing number of Caribbean and Liberian immigrants, including a woman who recently returned to Liberia to join the administration of the first elected female president, Ellen Johnson-Sirleaf. James still ships a couple of bushels of Scotch bonnets to the woman's mother, though. It was chocolate Scotch bonnets and *aji dulce* peppers that attracted me to his farm more than ten years ago. I remember talking to him for more than an hour the first time I discovered his farm. The man just loves to talk. About the history of the Amish and Mennonites, about Scotch bonnets, about steel wheels on tractors, about the scrumptious pink paste tomato that appeared in his field a few years back, an apparent cross between a pink oxheart called Anna Russian and the long sausagelike red paste tomato named Paulina after the woman who had saved seed for it for decades, Paulina, the mother of a musician who first brought her seeds to James over a decade ago. And now, thanks to James and Paulina, there is Pink Paulina, a paste tomato that it has taken him three or four years of seed selection to stabilize. He has also stabilized a chocolate peach tomato, a mustard habanero, and a peach habanero from cross-pollinations in his field, where he grows hundreds of varieties of chiles and tomatoes every year. I don't know quite how he does it, but James finds time to talk about all of his new varieties and still get his field work done.

This past summer, a little over a decade after I met James, I took the opportunity to pull my head out of the mud long enough to see that I was not the only non-Mennonite tyro who has been regularly knocking at his door for advice. There was a young man who was interested in growing heirloom tomatoes. There was Nick, who came from Greece and couldn't understand why he wasn't getting more watermelons on his plants. And there was Kam, an immigrant from Malaysia who had thrown himself headlong into a farming adventure, planting acres and acres of mustardy Malaysian greens, acres of yard-long beans. In the middle of the night, Kam was running greens, beans, and bitter melons into New York City. By day, he was out in the fields, picking. His wearying routine reminded me of my farm in the early years. James let Kam store his vegetables in his walk-in refrigerator and rented him some of his land for cheap. But this year there was something wrong with

Kam's beans. "Mr. James," Kam said, showing up one evening, exhausted and malnourished, "the leaves of my beans are turning yellow. I am losing everything." So James called the extension agent and went out to the farm where Kam was growing his yard-long beans, the very same farm where James had started out growing tobacco twenty-two years ago, which was what everyone in his community was growing back then. Kam was using too much fertilizer, it was decided, so he laid off the fertilizer and within a week the yard-long beans came around again and Kam had more than enough of them to pick. More than he could possibly get picked, in fact.

I am sure that Kam would never have gotten his farm off the ground without the intervention of James Weaver. I'll never forget the spring I tried to build a greenhouse at the same time I was planting lettuce and seeding tomatoes and plowing my fields. Just when it started to look as though the greenhouse would not get finished, leaving me without a home for some six thousand tomato, chile, melon, and eggplant seedlings, James Weaver showed up at my house with his son, his brother, and his father. By the end of the day, we had pulled the huge clear plastic sheet over the top of the greenhouse structure and fastened it down. In the middle of a very busy spring, these four farmers spent the whole day on my greenhouse.

Knowing I was broke from buying a tractor and from buying all of the material that went into constructing the greenhouse, they refused to accept payment for their services. And I wasn't even a member of their church. So I tried to be a sport. I offered to help James's brother with the greenhouse he was putting up. I spent a couple of hours helping him, which was all it took since there were so many people there to help get the greenhouse up. But a couple of hours was not a fair trade for what I had received. After the greenhouse, I threw myself into the next job that had been lined up for the crew: putting the roof on a barn. I found myself fifty feet up, clinging to a roof beam, cowering and dropping nails to the ground as all around me Mennonites young and old tromped along without the slightest fear in the world. I hung in there for about forty-five minutes, nervously pounding a nail or two, clinging to dear life and dropping three nails for every one that I pounded in. When I finally said enough was enough, maneuvering over to the ladder and climbing down to safety, everybody up on the roof thanked me with such sincerity that, in view of my tiny, cowering contribution, I decided they could only have been thanking me for not falling and breaking my neck and leaving them with a real predicament on their hands.

Still feeling indebted, I decided, in the end, to repay James and his brother by taking them to New York City for a day. We drove into the city squeezed together in the cab of my beat-up Toyota pickup truck. It was early November and we had loaded a variety of James's heirloom squashes and gourds in the back of the pickup for delivery to a downtown florist who had visited his farm. We went up to the top of the World Trade Center and we ate Mexican food and we went to see the Union Square Greenmarket. James impressed me when he spoke to a deaf girl in what appeared to be fluent sign language, impressed me again when he naively allowed himself to get drawn into inane conversation with some crazy homeless lady, a conversation that turned out in the end to be not so inane when James zeroed in on what the homeless lady was trying to say. The man just loves to talk.

But nothing impressed me more than what happened that night as we were leaving the Museum of Natural History, where James and his brother had been enthralled by the representations of old-fashioned irrigation methods used by the Egyptians and the Sumerians. Probably not much different from the methods used by the Scottsville community. When the museum closed and we were walking down the steps outside, a horse-drawn carriage approached and James looked up and smiled at the horse, this comforting image from home in a city so crowded and foreign. Seated at the front of the carriage, a man in a thick, just-off-the-boat Irish brogue asked, "Wid ye like a ride?"

We all laughed a little bit at the thought of James and his brother coming into New York City and *paying* for a horse and carriage ride. "No thank you," James answered politely.

"I can't even *give* a ride away!" the driver spat back in exasperation. He was offering us a free ride downtown, which was where we were headed anyhow. Sensing one of those magical opportunities that come along every so often, even in a bustling city like New York, we piled into the carriage. Turns out the driver had recognized the clothing James and his brother were wearing from all of the trips he had taken to New Holland in Lancaster County to purchase horses. He'd had a terribly slow day—hadn't even raked in enough to supply himself with a pint of Guinness—and all he wanted now was some spirited conversation as he drove his horse down to the livery stable for the night.

And spirited conversation was just what he got from James Weaver. They talked about Aaron Zeiset, the Lancaster County carriage maker with whom both of them were familiar. They talked about carriages and horse equipment. When you're riding in a carriage, it never feels as if you're going too slow. Only when you're in a car does it seem that way. The whole city was just lit up inside that carriage as the livery driver talked. And James talked, too. Man oh man, the man loves to talk.

TRUCK·PATCH

I GOT MY BALLS BUSTED the first couple of times I loaded my tomatoes onto the rusted Toyota pickup truck and drove them into New York City. One look at the dark green stains on my hands and shirt told those produce guys everything they needed to know. Too many hours picking teensy-weensy wild cherry tomatoes. No time to develop a sales strategy. "Eighty bucks for the load" was a typical offer from Carmine or John, who would be assiduously unloading a truck full of produce from California as I looked on, throwing bushel boxes of sweet bell peppers, arugula, tomatoes, and romaine onto stacks. Something you could never do with my produce. Every wild cherry tomato would split. Even my lettuce would bruise if you tossed a box of it. Mario was one guy who knew this. And he knew I knew he knew. Much as he tried to cover this up, his eyes popped to see my dead-ripe Romas, my beefsteaks. Fifteen lugs of them.

"Eighty?" I protested.

"Tomatoes are in the doghouse. Want to know what I'm paying for a five by six out of Jersey? Forget it. You don't want to know." Everything I brought was in the doghouse. To be fair to Mario, I was a fly-by-nighter whose deep red tomatoes, delivered at ninety-five degrees, did not have much shelf life. Those reefer trucks with the durable produce pulled in anytime they were needed. I was determined to break into the game, getting my balls busted until I could figure out a way to bust some balls right back. I would work him up to a hundred—a pair of crisp fifties handed over on the spot—and on the way home I'd tell myself that, just for kicks, I ought to paint the name Fido on the cap of my Toyota pickup.

The Toyota pickup truck is an eyesore in the middle of my field now, full of hoes, rakes, trowels, fish-emulsion and seaweed-extract fertilizers. Deluges and droughts are notched into my belt. Take 1999, the year all the corn dried up without producing a single kernel. The bears came down out of the mountains that summer, looking for water and food. The family of foxes who had chased playfully after my tractor in spring developed heartbreaking cases of mange, their orange-red carcasses desiccating where they fell. Although the government seemed willing to write checks to anybody who claimed to be a farmer in '99, I declined disaster relief because it had turned out to be my best year to date.

What made it happen for me was that clunky old juddering International truck with the thousand-gallon water tank strapped onto it. Littered with chunks of upholstery foam and sprouted rye seeds, its cab smelled of grease and pond scum. The farmer I rented the truck from laughed to see me shelling out money for it. I drove that truck every chance I could down to the mountain stream at the foot of the hill. It took about twenty minutes to fill the tank, after which I would lug the heavy pump into the woods and cover it with leaves so nobody would steal it. I was not the only one in my field to experience the headaches, nausea, and constant chills of heat exhaustion. Fever or not, I kept on running that truck back up to the field, where my crew cleared the way for the bouncing, belching, clattering beast with its sloshing four-ton cargo. There was this sweaty, exhausted feeling of noble purpose, of busting the balls of the hundred-degree days before they could bust mine, a heroism that was the closest I'll ever come to what the Allied forces must have felt pulling into Paris.

When the last of the bills was paid for 1999, I had enough money left over to go out and purchase a produce truck, the real thing, complete with a fourteen-foot insulated box and antiquated refrigeration unit. The lush red tomato emblazoned on the side of the truck, the logo of the produce supply company that had traded it for a new one, grabbed my attention when I saw it in a used-car lot. Beneath the tomato, in fat green letters, the logo said PRIMO. "You bought a truck with two hundred thousand miles on it?" scolded my father. Just what I needed to hear on top of my buyer's remorse. My daughter Gwendolyn, who had just turned two, christened it "the funny tomato truck." Our second daughter, Charlotte, newly born, was monopolizing my wife's attention. "Daddy, let's go sit in the funny tomato truck," Gwendolyn would say at least once a day. And so we would go out and she would sit in the driver's seat, pushing buttons in and out, moving levers up and down, going *VROOM!* and laying on the horn, which made this barely audible *eep* sound.

Eep. What a contrast to the burly, orcalike air-horn blast of the produce truck pulling up beside me on the interstate one evening as I drive home from New York City in the funny tomato truck. *BAAARROOOOOOP!* I nearly hit the roof of the cab. Plated with chrome and decked out as if a ninety-mile-an-hour trip to Lake Tahoe and back would be a warm-up, this truck is emblazoned with a logo identical to mine. PRIMO. Another funny tomato truck! Even though he is fully loaded and I am empty, he could pass me with ease. But he stays beside me. *BAAARRROOOOP!* This is more than just a howdy do. The driver is pointing at me with his cell phone and motioning to the side of the highway. I have an idea, as I pull off, what this is about.

"Boss wants to speak to you," says the driver, walking up to my door and handing me his cell phone. As the boss's voice scratches my ear, I'm imagining what he looks like: a tree-trunk neck and a snug-fitting suit. Although he may not have a grandfather who used to harvest San Marzano tomatoes from the once-alluvial soils of the Bronx, some venerable old salt who got tired of getting his balls busted by the banks and opted for the less treacherous art of distributing other farmers' produce, he'd like to think he does. Because of me, he has interrupted dinner with a potential account. "Twenty-five trucks on the road," he has just assured some big-time deep fryer of Maui onions. "In two years, we'll hit thirty-five." He lives for putting additional trucks on the road. But not trucks that look like mine. "Can't you paint over our logo?" he asks with exceptional politeness. Which pricks my ego. Because of me, I point out, his logo regularly graces the entrance to some elite restaurants in New York.

"You couldn't get that kind of advertising if you paid for a billboard in Times Square," I boast.

"We'll pay to have it painted over," he offers amicably. What a contrast the two trucks make on the shoulder of I-78, the old rickety one on its way home from delivering four-star Pennsylvania-grown produce to the chefs who write the cookbooks and the chrome-plated, turbocharged fortress on wheels transporting its cargo on the last leg of a long, long journey that terminates in the walk-ins of Pennsylvania chefs who, in less than fifteen minutes, could be standing in a farmer's field. The California-grown tomatoes he is bringing back from Hunts Point Market in the Bronx probably sell for half what I get for my tomatoes. The perversely circuitous conveyor belt of our cross-country economy. There is no doubt who is making more money here. And yet, how much can I get away with charging for friggin' tomatoes?

Wax beans turned the tables for me back when I was trying

to break in. Mario called to ask if I could score him some wax beans from another farmer since I was coming up to deliver my tomatoes. One of his restaurant accounts needed nice beans and he couldn't find them anywhere. This was in the midst of the bone-dry summer of '95, not as bad as '99, but dry enough that no farmer in his right mind would waste time irrigating beans. "These babies are going sky high at the produce auction," said the farmer who sold me Mario's wax beans. On the basis of this tip, I decided to charge a whopping twenty-five dollars for the half bushel.

"You crazy?" Mario reacted. "This is wholesale."

"Twenty-five dollars," I repeated.

"Twenty-five bucks for a half bushel? It's not even full." They were perfect waxers, slender and succulent. I caught a glimpse of his rejected box: fat, dry as straw. Some incensed chef had busted his balls over the crappy beans, and now I was angling to do the same over some good ones. I started to put the box of wax beans back on the truck, even though I had no other place to go with it.

"Okay," Mario said. "Okay, okay. I'll take the beans." I swear I could have charged him forty for the beans, almost half what he was paying for fifteen boxes of perfect tomatoes. But I'm not a gouger.

A ball buster? Yes. Mario himself had taught me this lesson, a transfer of knowledge that had a father-to-son tenderness about it. Any self-respecting father has to pull his boy aside at some point and say, "Listen, lad, you've got to bust some balls from time to time. Just don't get greedy."

"You want your own logo?" says the boss on the cell phone. "We'll pay for that, too." Twenty-five trucks on the road, two hundred juiced-up chefs ready to bust his balls anytime his delivery-man shows up late for lunch service. At night, he starts awake from the same kind of nightmares I'm prone to: rat-gray fungus growing on the raspberries, romaine dissolving into mush, the rancid juices of one collapsed cantaloupe rotting the whole box. Something about the perishable nature of our product makes you want to go out and bust somebody's balls half the time.

But I wouldn't trade trucks with him, even if the reefer unit on mine blows warm air. "Don't worry about the logo," I say into the cell phone. Call it farmer's pride, mixed with guilt for not having expunged the old logo in two years of owning the truck. I shell out more than any two-bit farmer should on my redesign: five multicolored heirloom tomatoes to cover the red one. A tomato hornworm dancing the cha-cha atop a Cherokee Purple. My truck now says Home of the Tomato People where it once said PRIMO. On the way home to Pennsylvania, when the chromium funny-tomato truck shimmers past me, the driver no longer knows who I am.

Groundhog Days

I've heard it said by people with firsthand knowledge on the subject that groundhog is good eating. "Tastes like a cross between a chicken and a squirrel," confided Joe, who choreographs my herb and flower garden each year. "A gamy, dark chicken. Best eaten young. Unless you want a mouthful of skunk, though, you better remove the scent glands on his back and legs. But he's a clean little beast. A vegetarian, for the most part. And a smart feeder. Just look at what they eat in your field." He's referring to my organic lettuces, award-winning tomatoes, and sweet multicolored beets.

The day is not far off when truffle-stuffed groundhog (aka woodchuck, aka whistle pig) will be the next peasant fare, in the tradition of garlic, bouillabaisse, pig's feet, and scrapple, to achieve white-tablecloth status. When that happens, there will be a ready supply of local farmers only too glad to let the chuckling buck-toothed balls of flab have their fill of carrots and peas before skinning them and charging some versatile kitchen trendsetter for the damage.

Since I belong to that new generation of bleeding-heart farmers who are apt to sit out the hunting season, my groundhogs get right of first refusal on peas, carrots, strawberries, lettuce, and broccoli. What they leave behind gets divvied up between New York City restaurants like Daniel, Esca, Bouley, and the Tasting Room. Many are the opportunities I have squandered for running down a groundhog in my driveway, slamming on the brakes in time to watch the blubbery thief, bloated on the fruit of my labor, struggle across my path like some obscenely obese mermaid with nothing but two overburdened flippers to paddle him home. I have been merciful, in part, because the groundhog is lukewarm to the musky leaves of the tomato, my principal crop, although his appetite can get so far out ahead of him that he will occasionally wolf down three or four small tomato plants before turning his back on them in favor of my lettuce patch, where he is partial to frisée as well as a speckled Austrian heirloom romaine called Forellenschluss.

But tolerance has its limits. For me, the line was crossed when a groundhog entered my greenhouse and made a shambles of one perfectly manicured red and green bed of mesclun greens. "What do you mean you don't have salad greens for me?" I heard from every chef except Jean François Bruel at Daniel. "So Daniel gets all the lettuce this week," they joked. "Is that what you're telling me?" Chefs can be competitive that way.

"Actually . . . uh . . . ," I said to the chef at Esca, Dave Pasternack, who rarely fails to answer the kitchen phone, always poised to make room on the menu for the latest seasonal sensation, "do you have a recipe for groundhog?"

"So that's what happened to my lettuce," Dave said, quick on his feet. This time of year, his celebrated crudo is served with pickled rhubarb, the soft-shell crabs are slathered with sautéed ramps, and the ricotta-rhubarb tart takes center stage on the dessert menu. "I've never cooked groundhog but . . . you got him? You got an Eckerton Hill Farm lettuce-fattened groundhog for me?"

"Not yet, but how would you prepare him?"

"I'd break down all the meat into its parts and brown it," he fired back. "Add garlic, onions, carrots, and half a bottle of red wine. Cook down the wine and add crushed tomatoes, water, bay leaf, sage. Cover it and let it simmer. Tough meat like that needs to be cooked a long time. Madison Avenue groundhog stew, we'll call it. So are you bringing me a groundhog? Or does Daniel get it?"

"I would gently roast the groundhog at low heat," suggested Colin Alevras of the Tasting Room. "Or poach him in a vacuum bag. Then toss him in the oven until he's brown and crispy." Colin is a seasonal purist whose ever-changing spring menu currently features cattail shoots, morels, mustard garlic, branch lettuce, and wild onions. He's a forager's dream come true. And what is groundhog but the consummate forager? "He would need to cook for a long time," said Colin.

"Because of the tough meat?" I asked astutely.

"Exactly. You know, guinea pig is the national dish of Ecuador. They roast the guinea pig and serve him standing up on a bed of potatoes. The dish is called *cuy*. We could make a gringo version of *cuy*, cold roasted groundhog served standing up on a bed of your mesclun greens. That would serve him right, wouldn't it? But you have to kill a groundhog the right way, you know, sneak up on him in a moment of bliss, finish him off with one fell swoop. If he gets too stressed out right before he dies, the rush of adrenaline will make his muscles too tough and inedible."

Not quite as potent as Proust's madeleine, the word "groundhog" nonetheless triggered for David Bouley this memory from his teenage years: on a chilly November evening with a ten-gauge shotgun over his shoulder, he and his hunting buddies brought some sportsmen's appetites to a potluck dinner at a hunting lodge in Waterville Valley, New Hampshire. Groundhog was served along with pheasant, partridge, quail, guinea hen, and hare. The groundhog had been marinated in hard cider, then stewed with hearty cider-saturated winter vegetables: turnips, potatoes, carrots. A sort of Tom Sawyeresque bourguignon, the stewed meat gamier than a white-tailed rabbit's, but not as gamy as a hare's.

Determined to bag me a groundhog, I go out and buy a Havahart trap that's big enough for a raccoon or an armadillo. Even as I bring the trap home, I'm steeling myself for the impending confrontation with a live groundhog. I think of an Elizabeth Bishop poem, the one that starts "I caught a tremendous fish" and ends with "I let the fish go." Who knows? Maybe I'll let my groundhog go. Or maybe I'll write a poem. I'll just have to wait and see what happens.

I use cantaloupe rind for the bait, with some sweet orange flesh still attached to it, and set the trap right next to my patch of mesclun greens, which have already started to grow back in the summery warmth of the greenhouse. In a week, I should have presentable greens again, so long as I can get rid of my groundhog.

I check the trap after an hour. Nothing. Another hour. Still nothing. I go out into the field to plow the section where I'm going to plant my chile peppers. The usual headaches. My tractor wheezes when I try to turn, a power-steering-cylinder leak. The tractor is more than four decades old. I walk down to the shed for some power-steering fluid, and when I finally get plowing it's hard going because of my bricklike clay, clouds of dust rising around me, my lungs ticklish. So dry and it's only May! My fava beans won't produce. The lettuce heads will bolt early. I'm so stressed out that if some cannibal were to sneak up at this moment and club me over the head, my flesh would be too tough to be enjoyed.

Buried beneath all the other anxieties of spring, my groundhog is forgotten until the plowing is done and I return to close the greenhouse for the night. Sure enough, I've caught him. Unharmed, but with no place to go. He wrinkles his nose at me. Up close, I can see what an efficient feeding machine he is, a ball of stomach muscle tapering off to the point where two sleek, thin incisors stick out sharp enough to puncture a can, his head a little wedge of destruction for the grower of leafy edibles. He growls at me, too. The poor guy is frightened, miserable. This is my Elizabeth Bishop moment, but I'm too tired to write a poem. I'm all set to drive him someplace far off, someplace where he'll have to settle for clover or alfalfa, when I notice the mesclun greens. Ripped to shreds again. The much-maligned rodent supped in civilized fashion, finishing off his salad before turning to a most sensible dessert. Most of my lettuce will have to be reseeded.

If he was crossing the driveway in front of me at this moment, I would run him over. If I had a gun, I would shoot him. The cloud of vengeance clears long enough for me to see exactly what I must do. I tie a length of tomato twine to the handle of the Havahart trap, and as I pick up the trap, I can almost hear his protestations, his clever plucking at my heartstrings: *You're doing this because I ate a little lettuce?* I throw the Havahart trap in the pond, and his death struggle is not unlike what a lobster tossed into boiling water appears to endure.

No, I am not Elizabeth Bishop. Nor am I the same ten-year-old who once cried for hours after shooting a rabbit with his BB gun. I wait five minutes before reeling in the trap by my tomato twine. Next to the entrance of my greenhouse, I showcase his dead body. The kind of thing watermelon farmers do with crows who peck holes in the watermelons. Kill one and display him in the watermelon field as an example to others. *This is what happens to crows who peck holes in watermelons.*

Next day, feeling depressed about what I've done, I have to hear it from one of my workers. "I couldn't do that, just drown the poor bugger," says Wayne.

"Meaning what?" I snap. "I'm a sadist or something?"

"You couldn't put him out of his misery quicker? Shoot him or club him over the head?"

"What if he gets away after I club him? Then I've got a groundhog with a migraine who's still eating my mesclun greens. It's so easy to be morally superior when you're not the one whose paycheck depends on how much the groundhog eats."

"You don't have to be so defensive." Within a day, the groundhog is gone, carried off by some dog who does not find the adrenaline-toughened flesh objectionable. A few days later, another one moves in, nibbling on radish leaves and decimating the few mesclun greens that survived the first groundhog.

Unfortunately, I don't have the time to hide in the greenhouse and sneak up on my merrily gorging nemesis, thereby minimizing his suffering and ensuring the palatability of his flesh. But my Havahart trap is set again. I'm thinking this time I'll let him live, maybe drop him off in the field of my nearest competitor, some other gun-shy twenty-first-century lettuce farmer.

Or how do I know the same grower of lettuce isn't secretly delivering his groundhogs to me? We farmers can be competitive that way.

Abu Groundhog Revisited

(A THIN-SKINNED RESPONSE TO THE OUTRAGED
READERS OF "GROUNDHOG DAYS," ORIGINALLY
PUBLISHED IN *GOURMET* MAGAZINE)

To all of you who would come down hard on my "manhandling" of one errant groundhog: Can you maybe find just a little something in your heart for a writer/farmer whose joints ache like hell and whose final planting of six thousand tomatoes is succumbing fast to late blight? Okay, so I drowned a groundhog and got paid some money for recounting the experience in prose. A terrible thing to do, I know. That's why I wrote about it.

I say writer/farmer, but farmer/writer would be more on the money. Whatever the rain and the wind and the droughts and the hornworms and the aphids and the blights and the weeds and the deer and, of course, the groundhogs leave untouched, I gather up two or three times a week to sell to the general public and to some chefs. I don't use any chemicals, you see, but I'm not allowed to call myself an organic farmer because you must first pay the USDA a pile of money to do that. But my point is this: take the "farmer" part off my label and all you would have is "starving writer."

Late blight on the tomatoes. I should have known it was coming. There was an outbreak in Lancaster back in June, which is not late at all for tomatoes. *Phytophthora infestans* is the proper name for it. The very same disease that decimated the Irish lumper potato in the mid-nineteenth century and sent my great-great-great-grandfather to this country. Brian Sheehe of Templetuohy, County Tipperary. He signed his name with an X and in the only picture I ever saw of him he had that determined chin you see on all of the Sheehes until my mother's generation, when easier living and an infusion of English and eastern European genes softened the camera-ready pose.

Brian Sheehe was less than a groundhog to those laissez-faire Brits: *Sorry, pal. All this food gets exported.* (I can't get him out of my system. He's bringing the thin-skinned writer down with him, my groundhog. So farmer, then. Just call me farmer.)

But late blight is the absolute worst thing a tomato farmer can endure. Greasy stains appear on the leaves. A week later, nine out of ten of your plumping-up tomatoes have horrible brown shellaclike stains. Kaput. Though supposedly rare, late blight has broken out within a one-hundred-mile radius of me in each of the last three years. This is due, I'm willing to bet, to the great tomato revival of the late twentieth century, the overwhelming consumer response to the cancer-fighting lycopene with which tomatoes are loaded. And, of course, to those irresistible heirloom varieties. There are more farmers growing fresh market tomatoes than ever before, and so the airborne *Phytophthora infestans* spores need only to waltz from one field to the next. The outbreak in June sent a ripple through the burgeoning tomato-growing community. The overwhelming response was to run down to Daniel's Farm Store just outside Lancaster and stock up on all the prescribed fungicides: Acrobat, Bravo, Tanos, ProPhyt. Acrobat is aptly named because it works wonders, taking up residence within the plant tissue, functioning like an antibiotic or a vaccine, rendering the tomato impervious to the *Phytophthora infestans* spores. Unfortunately for me, this wonder drug is off-limits if I am to label my tomatoes "chemical free." I sprayed my tomatoes with one application of an organic fungicide, copper sulfate, although the prevailing wisdom is that copper sulfate won't do squat if late blight finds my field. One application. I got too busy to apply copper sulfate a second time, let alone once a week as recommended on the label. I decided instead to hunker down and scout for the greasy leaf stains and the snowy white crystalline stuff that turns up under the leaves.

In other words, I was going to wait until it was all but too late to do something about late blight. Which is just about the stupidest thing in the world to do when you consider that I had just taken a beating on spring crops like lettuce and peas. A chemical-free environment is one your groundhog will jump all over. One even snuck into my greenhouse and helped himself regularly to my high-value mesclun greens. So I finally broke down and caught him in a trap and drowned him in the pond and threw his body next to the greenhouse in hopes of scaring off any other mesclun-loving groundhogs. It was the first groundhog I had killed in ten years of farming, and I was hoping I would never have to do it again. You have to understand how nice I had been to the groundhog community up to this point. I as much as said to them, "Listen, guys, eat all you want. You're welcome here in paradise. All you need to know is, the tree of knowledge is inside that greenhouse." *He compares himself to God! Arrogant murderer!* If groundhogs could speak and I were to give up growing lettuce because of their voracity, they would come a-knockin' at my door, those garrulous rodents. "What's the deal?" they would ask. "Not growing any frisée this year? No romaine?"

At any rate, another mesclun-loving groundhog quickly took the place of the first one, whose carcass got carried off by a dog. The whole experience had about it an existential pointlessness that encouraged me to write about it and give what I'd written to a friend, a sympathetic chef who smuggled what I wrote into the editorial offices of *Gourmet* magazine. I tried as best as I could to forget about my unforgettable groundhog and basically conceded the greens in my greenhouse to his brothers and sisters. Once again, lettuce was a bust for me. Once again, like every year since I started farming, I had all my eggs in the tomato basket. Only this year, *Phytophthora infestans* was alive and well less than fifty miles to the west of me. And I had not sprayed for it. I was dancing with the same devil who drove my ancestors out of County Tipperary 160 years ago. Organic farming is a tempestuous endeavor. My joints throbbed with pain. My stomach was doing endless flip-flops, and my ears rang for hours at a time. At midnight, starting awake from nightmares of winter snow falling peaceably on my unprotected crop of tomatoes—*Oh my God, it's snowing out!*—I would be unable to fall back asleep, tossing and turning beneath the sheets, my heart racing ahead of me, repeating "LATE-blight, LATE-blight, LATE-blight" until the sun was up and it was time to get out into the field.

But my early and midseason tomatoes came through miracu-lously unscathed. The combination of warmer, dryer, un-late-blight-like conditions, combined with all the spraying going on in other tomato fields, retarded the progress of those dreaded spores. And then *Gourmet* called to say they were going to run the piece about the groundhog. Whew! I was recouping some of my groundhog losses. ("There must be someone . . . who doesn't value a dollar more than a life," one critic screamed.) If I hadn't been so wrapped up with converting my crops into cold, hard cash, I might have contrib-uted some of the green stuff I got from *Gourmet* toward the erection of a memorial plaque for my groundhog who, I will admit, did not receive a proper burial. *Did not receive a proper burial? Understate-ment of the year!*

Things were looking rosy again, as I say. For a couple of weeks, the only thing going wrong was the pain in my joints, which has been ongoing since 9/11. In my most confused and reflective moments, I tend to put my finger on 9/11 as the cause of this pain. My tomatoes were at their peak when the terrorist attack occurred. For more than a month, the only folks New York City chefs had to cook for were firemen, so one night I took a truckload of my unsold heirloom tomatoes down to ground zero and donated them along with my time. I even got a police escort through the maze of confusing ad hoc one-way emergency alleyways. Next to a volunteer from Mexico City, a saintly, smart, and attractive young girl who said she flew straight to the city when she'd heard what happened, I stood at a cafeteria line ready to serve up magnificent helpings of char-grilled lobster; pearly, rich potato-leek soup; and sautéed al dente multicolored fall vegetables. Weary firemen from Iowa and Oklahoma surveyed the elaborate city fare and confessed rather sheepishly, "I'll take that hot dog over there." Familiarity is a lifesaver in an atmosphere of holocaust and devastation.

When I point to 9/11 as the cause of my pain, I do not mean the contaminated air I breathed at ground zero. "The author needs some psychological counseling," one of my incensed-by-the-groundhog readers suggests. My family doctor agrees, although I've come to the fairly solid conclusion that I have Lyme disease. When I argued with my doctor that traditional Lyme disease testing, by which I have received three negative determinations, is notoriously flawed, he pulled out a two weeks' supply of mood stabilizers and said, "Tim, I think you need to try these." So I took the mood stabilizers home and left them, unopened, in the medicine cabinet next to the unopened painkillers and the unopened sleeping pills prescribed by my rheumatologist, who had told me I suffered from myofascial pain on account of a lack of quality sleep. (Those eye-opening dreams of snow falling on my tomatoes!) I also have an unfinished container of antibiotic capsules big enough for a horse, the third container I'd been directed to take by my urologist for blood in my urine, which is surely not a symptom treatable by mood stabilizers. Nor was the excess calcium flooding my bloodstream, which my endocrinologist suggested was the likely cause of my pain. So I opted for his recommended parathyroidectomy—a tiny marble removed from my neck—and, in spite of the subsequent reduction in calcium being siphoned from my bones, the pain remained the same. On to a holistic doctor, who suggested the urologist's antibiotics had killed off the good bacteria in my stomach, resulting in an overgrowth of candida albicans yeast, a bone-pain condition sometimes referred to as candida. I sprang for a cabinet full of half-gallon-sized brown glass jars that said things like "Springreen's Intestinal Cleanser." Honest to God, these bombastically labeled, old-fashioned bottles brought to mind the elixir remedies fast-talking river folk sold to gullible bumpkins in rustic nineteenth-century novels. The intestinal cures I conscientiously made from them were so putrid I gave up on alternative medicine after a month. For now, the only thing the doctors seem willing to confirm is what my CAT scans show: a kidney stone, a gallstone, four lung nodules (probably from field dust), and no cancer. Hooray! No cancer! Still and all, what of the aches in my shoulders, knees, elbows, fingers, shins, and teeth? The ringing in my ears? The commotion in my stomach? The persistent brain fog? The dreamed-up symptoms of one fraught and overimaginative farmer, according to my family doctor. Your farmer needs a cast-iron constitution, an ability to knock off fifty groundhogs at a pop without flinching.

Until I met up with similarly ailing farmers, I shrugged and called it 9/11 disease. "I'm telling you, it's Lyme," these farmers told me. "Don't wait as long as I did because I developed Bell's palsy."

"Bell's palsy! You mean . . . ?"

"I mean don't wait until the skin droops on your cheek before doing something about it."

Still, my doctor insisted mood stabilizers were the way to go, hinting there were lots of quacks out there making money off Lyme disease. But the thought of Bell's palsy forced me to act on my own. I ordered a vial of one-hundred-milligram "pharmacy grade" doxycycline from a veterinarian supply company, popping four of them a day. (More fodder for the cruelty-to-animals camp: helping myself to an antibiotic labeled for birds.) I've been on bird doxy-cycline for a week and a half now and I actually think—although I'm not absolutely sure—that I'm starting to feel better than I have felt since 9/11. The high dosage is taking a toll on my stomach, so I'll have to reconsider those horrid intestinal cleansers. I'm also experiencing severe light sensitivity. Even when I wear shades, the glances of sun are surreal and painful.

More painful still is the sight of my late-blight-stricken toma-toes. Luckily for me, it came late, like it's supposed to. "Salvage what you can," I've instructed my employees. *"Lo que puede,"* I bark to Nacho and Silvio, who look at me like, *Who are you, Mr. Movie Star Shades, coming out of your dark house to bark orders in the overbright day?* Nonetheless, they sort through the brown-stained tomatoes—*Manchado, manchado, manchado, ah! Aquí es un bueno.* This morning they started pulling up stakes on their own initia-tive. It's too much to witness, this collapse of the vines that give us all sustenance. I'm not popular with anyone these days. *If you knew this was going to happen, why didn't you spray? If you caught the groundhog in a Havahart trap, why didn't you let him go?*

Torturer! For once, I've managed to reach a wide audience with something I've written. "This article made me lose sleep," says one reader. "What he did to that groundhog is called torture," says another. "And civilized people frown on that, whatever the current Administration says."

Civilized people. Perhaps the greatest poem of Western civilization takes as its hero a man named Achilles, who slew his adversary Hector and then, in his anger, dragged Hector's mutilated corpse around the walls of Troy before leaving him for the birds to pick over. While anger may have had something to do with my decision to kill my groundhog, I had humane reasons for not burying him and not eating him, either.

He dares to compare his treatment of a helpless groundhog to the valor of Achilles! The nerve! I can go one better. Here's a question: What did Agamemnon, Odysseus, Menelaus, and Achilles have in common besides the fact that they sailed off together to slaughter the men of Troy and enslave the women?

Answer: They were all organic farmers. Remember how Odysseus sowed salt before the enlistment committee? Back then, an organic farmer like Odysseus was much wealthier vis-à-vis his contemporaries. Most of us twenty-first-century shlumps lack the resources to construct Trojan ramparts between our tasty produce and the animals who like to eat it. The deer can jump over a seven-foot fence and, if hungry enough, are liable to knock down a temporary nine-foot fence. The groundhogs can burrow beneath the fence. Forget about those thirsty crows who will fly in and, one by one, peck a hole in every single watermelon if you don't intervene. You can't build a fence high enough for a crow. There is only one reason why I quit growing watermelons. It sets my recovering joints to throbbing all over again, the thought of those crows.

For all his reportorial tenacity, Michael Pollan was unable to get clearance in order to view an industrially farmed steer being slaughtered, noting: "The meat industry understands that the more people know about what happens on the kill floor, the less meat they're likely to eat. That's not because slaughter is necessarily inhumane, but because most of us would simply rather not be reminded of exactly what meat is or what it takes to bring it to our plates." There's more death on a farm than most people can stomach, even on a farm where only vegetables are produced. You could round up all the vegetable farmers in the country and you will not find many who have killed fewer lettuce-loving creatures than I have: to date, one groundhog.

Shall we call this the herbivore's dilemma?

If you want to eat a vegetable whose survival did not depend on a fur-bearing creature having to be killed, your safest bet is in the mustard family: arugula or mizuna. But if it's between the months of June and August and your arugula is not shot full of tiny pinholes, that means your farmer probably sprayed chemicals on the gazillions of flea beetles who descend upon arugula in summer.

But you could have done something other than drown the poor guy. So I am imperfect. I did not waterboard the groundhog. *That* would have been torture. And I assure you, much worse has been done to groundhogs on other farms and in backyards. *But you seemed to take pleasure in killing that groundhog.* It may be the case that, deep inside of me, some nitwit utilitarian impulse sensed that confessing to the savagery of my actions with the earnestness of a Saint Augustine would not have been a very good read. But I assure you, I was too emotionally wrapped up in the moment to think of writing about the groundhog as the events transpired. *Still, you could have thought of a better way.* If my exhausted, angst-ridden brain waves could have spat out an ideal, so-called humane method for killing a groundhog, my body would have eagerly obliged. A rat poisoned in the basement of an apartment building suffers a much more gruesome death than a drowning groundhog. Let's face it: the majority of rodent exterminations are carried out with poison. And really, there is no such thing as a humane way to take the life of a healthy animal, rodent or otherwise. The pastured hen who squawks and wiggles her legs as the blood drains from her neck, the lobster who clacks at the sides of a boiling pot of water, the dock-tailed hog squeezed into pen 65D, the mother rat beneath the sink with her little pink babies. They all want to live. Period.

On cloudy days, when my eyes can tolerate the sun, I sometimes squat down beneath the chestnut trees in the orchard and gather up chestnuts. *Horning in on the squirrel's means of winter sustenance so that what? A bunch of Manhattan wine snobs can sip an* amuse-bouche *of chestnut/bolete soup.* The chestnuts are Chinese, not the American variety, which, like my late crop of tomatoes and like the Irish lumper potato, was wiped out by blight. The American chestnut blight was, in fact, introduced by the late-nineteenth-century importation of the Chinese chestnut tree. If we could all have just stayed put for once, like the blameless, earthbound groundhog, whose claim to this soil goes back eons before the Native American's, the world would never have had to witness the dire consequences of Chinese chestnuts and smallpox arriving in the New World. Or potatoes crossing the ocean to Ireland.

And Brian Sheehe would never have left County Tipperary for Granville Center, Pennsylvania, where he raised hogs and six sons, most of whom started out digging canals when they were of working age. No sooner were the canals completed than the river barge was largely vanquished by the locomotive, so half of Brian's boys migrated to Clearfield County in western Pennsylvania, coal-mining country, where Brian's son John, my great-great-grandfather, worked his way up to the point where he ran a seventy-mule team down in the mines. That mule team was a great source of pride to John's grandson (and my grandfather) Joseph. Pappap Sheehe was also quite fond of his grandmother on his mother's side, an Englishwoman, a Hatherill, a staunch member of the Anglican Church. Pappap's grandmother adored him so much she would take him and his brothers and sisters wherever she was going, even to KKK cross burnings.

My great-great-grandfather kept an impressive gold watch in his pocket, too. But the team of mules was what most impressed his grandson. "Isn't that something, Pap," we would say. "A seventy-mule team."

They all went blind from being in the dark for so long, those poor mules. And there were not enough blacks for the KKK to point a finger at in western Pennsylvania. No. The purpose of those cross burnings was to intimidate Catholics. Pappap and his Catholic brothers and sisters did not love their Anglican grandma any less for being dragged to those cross burnings. But what was she thinking? I can only guess.

"Shot a man in Reno," sings Johnny Cash, to great fanfare, "just to watch him die." People love that kind of stuff. But kill one groundhog, a groundhog who has proven himself to be an intolerable nuisance! *What man sits there and watches a [groundhog] die painfully, panicked, slowly? One without a soul . . . there are layers of hell reserved for people who are cruel to animals, he has no excuses at all.*

And yet . . . I once met a priest who called me a saint. It happened in the Catholic churchyard in Troy (Troy!), Pennsylvania. The churchyard where Brian Sheehe is buried. This was in my wanderlust years. I was like my father, the former Eagle Scout/burned-out lawyer, teaching himself Swahili so he could converse with Chaga tribesmen as he led a tour up Mount Kilimanjaro. Only I was always too poor to afford airfare to someplace like Tanzania. I rode a bicycle everywhere and stayed with people I met along the way. Anyhow, it was on a Sunday, and I was in the Catholic churchyard in Troy, Pennsylvania, having arrived there by bicycle. It was just after mass had let out. The priest, who was the only one there to assist me, provided me with some paper and a blue crayon so I could make a rubbing of Brian Sheehe's tombstone. I was halfway through my rubbing when I noticed some keys on the ground next to me. I picked up the keys and took them into the church, and when the priest saw the keys he said, "I've been looking all over for those. You're a saint."

If you meander around on your bicycle for too long, pretty

soon the world of smart résumés and matching bedroom furniture leaves you in the dust. Unless you want to go down in history as one of the great ne'er-do-wells in the family, you might find yourself taking up the plow, struggling with the elements, trying your hand at a profession your great-great-great-grandfather was the last generation of the family to toil away at.

As my diseased tomatoes cower beneath the threat of an impending frost, I naturally think a lot about death this time of year. I have no idea what will happen to me when my time comes. I know that some of my most venomous critics, enemies for life, believe that when I enter the door labeled Judgment, I will find that on the other side there are four groundhogs seated around a table playing poker and smoking cigars and shoveling handfuls of peas into their mouths. One of the groundhogs (my groundhog!) will look up and say, "Oh, it's you." If that happens, well, maybe I will be in trouble. But I personally like to hope that if there were such a thing as a heavenly realm, it would be one in which pure understanding supplants all petty condemnation and finger-pointing. Maybe one farmer's openly confessed brutality toward a member of the animal community would be weighed in light of the fact that he labors hard at a job that does not pay huge dividends, that he has children he would like one day to put through college, and that, as for himself, neither saint nor demon, he would like only to fend off the onset of Bell's palsy and maybe make something respectable of himself, something of which his great-great-great-grandfather would be proud.

The rubbing I took in the cemetery says this:

Brian Sheehe
Died October 8, 1878
Aged 68 years
Town of Templetuohy
County Tipperary

In the only picture that survives of him, he locks his chin for the photographer, in part because he has no teeth. I imagine he holds a hat in his hands, too, although you can't tell from the photograph, but I imagine he holds the hat tightly, thinking to himself, *I'm going to make a go of it here.*

Would it soften your opinion of me if I were to tell you that I have a reputation for wrestling thirty-five-pound snapping turtles off to the side of a busy highway, holding up traffic in both directions, horns wailing in front and behind as I carry the plated creature, incensed, neck stretching to bite me, into the woods where he can amble away to safety? Or that I will always pluck an unlucky spider from the downward swirling maelstrom of a flushed toilet?

If the doxycycline proves not to be the wonder drug I'd hoped, I may give those mood stabilizers a shot. And who knows? In the right mood, maybe I'll open the doors of my greenhouse to all the beasts of the field.

But probably not, although another drowning is out of the question. If you're disinclined to give a groundhog murderer a break, at least say a prayer for a pig farmer who got late blight much worse than I will ever have it, Brian Sheehe of Templetuohy, County Tipperary, known to all posterity as X.

Dead of Winter

THE BUCKET ON MY tractor snapped when I tried to clear the snow that finally stopped falling at noon on Valentine's Day. Carrots and beets had been locked in place since the ground froze in mid-January. Two weeks earlier, I had opened up my greenhouse so the single-digit night temperatures could lay to rest the aphids, spinach, thrips, mâche, whiteflies, mustard greens, and radishes. *Au revoir* to greens fresh enough to stand up to olive oil and balsamic vinegar. I had three cans of soup in my pantry: lentil, lentil, and lentil.

Two days after Valentine's Day, down to my last can of lentil soup and with snow drifted halfway up the side of my greenhouse, I called up Colin Alevras, chef/owner of the Tasting Room. I had stopped bringing my vegetables to market in November, so he was surprised to hear from me. "The conveyor belt from California must be going full speed for you," I cracked.

"Not at all," said Colin. "I'm headed to market now."

"For what? Snow cones?"

"Conuco Farm for baby greens, Tremblay Apiaries for clematis flower and bamboo honey, Samascott Orchards for Newtown Pippins and Winesaps."

Out of the slush of my housebound self-pity rose this vision of Colin as ambitious contestant on the latest Bravo channel spin-off: Market Chef. Pacing before the contestants, Tom Colicchio presents the latest challenge: *You are going to create a menu from the ingredients you score from a handful of farmers set up in a blizzard. Ha-ha-ha and good luck.*

For fifteen minutes, I thought, I, too, could be Tom Colicchio. I didn't tell Colin I was coming for dinner until noon of the following day, by which time he had already done his shopping and I was on a bus to New York. From Port Authority Bus Terminal, I headed first to Union Square Greenmarket, where Colin shops three days a week. Morse Pitts from Windfall Farms was surrounded by baby mustard greens, mesclun salad, arugula, and sweet-pea shoots, all picked in his greenhouse a day earlier. His multicolored winter carrots tasted as sweet as a carrot could be. Morse showed me a picture of his stand on Valentine's Day, when he and seven other farmers had braved the blizzard. If I had not known better, I might have guessed the photo was of the Peary expedition.

"How did you manage to sink your stand into that snowbank?" I asked.

"We had to pile that snow on the sides," Morse answered, "so the stand wouldn't blow away." Talk about loyalty to your customers. Loyalty is a two-way street. Morse had brought less than what he normally would to market, but he sold out in the blizzard of '07.

To my surprise, there were lots of things at the market, besides Morse's sweet yellow and purple carrots, that you would have a hard time finding anywhere else on the Eastern Seaboard. Dandelion greens and fresh edamame, both husked and unhusked, from PNS's Long Island farm. Oak Grove Plantation's ears of popcorn and inimitable bacon. David Graves's honey collected from New York City hives; Jim Grillo's duck eggs; Vince D'Attolico's sorrel, garlic shoots, and Jerusalem artichokes; John Adams's pristine microgreens; Alex Paffenroth's burdock, salsify, and porcelain garlic. Nothing out of the ordinary about the wide array of tangy, flavorful upstate apples. But who in the world, besides Samascott, whom Colin had visited Friday, was carrying Thomas Jefferson's favorite, the matchless Newtown Pippin?

Alex Paffenroth's stand was a mind-blowing smorgasbord of winter roots and vegetables. Eight varieties of potato, including German Butterball and French Fingerling. Stripetti and Sweet Dumpling squash. Red and yellow cipollini onions. Black radishes, purple-top turnips, parsnips, leeks, beets, daikon radishes, celeriac, yellow and orange carrots. To harvest his salsify, parsnips, burdock, and Jerusalem artichokes, Alex had been using a pick to break off frozen chunks of his root-embedded muck soil before bringing the soil indoors to thaw. Talk about farmer/chef loyalty. In the dead of winter, Alex was still supplying a dozen New York City restaurants.

At Colin's restaurant, the Tasting Room, I started with a walk-in audit, noting one lamb (from Paul at Violet Hill, a Greenmarket farmer), a goat (from Vermont), and a pig ("Missouri raised," Colin confessed. "If only I had a nearer source for the glorious eighteenth-century Red Wattle breed."). Half of one walk-in was taken up with Alex Paffenroth's unmistakable produce. There were Bosc pears and apples from Samascott and Locust Grove. Green chard, collards, and dandelion from PNS.

Seeing what a bulldog I insisted on being, Colin made his first disclosure: "The porcini came from Tanzania. But you know how crazy I am about wild mushrooms. Not farmed oysters or shiitakes. Truly wild mushrooms. And I prefer them fresh. When Honey Hollow Farm shows up at market with shaggy ink caps or apricot jelly mushrooms, those babies go right on the menu." Colin picked up the evening's menu and it took him three minutes to write down sources for every ingredient. Of sixty-five listed ingredients, fifty-six were local. While the locals included things like Wild Hive's stone-ground grits, Ted Blew's popcorn, and Stone Church's Normandy duck, the nonlocals included wild ivory king salmon from Alaska and South Carolina black grouper. The homemade XO sauce, I was pleased to note, featured my own hot peppers. I left Colin to his busy kitchen and sat down to dinner.

What I ate went far beyond what I expected of winter fare. More like reaching deep into the slumbering sun-deprived soul of a region's leafy population and finding the flavors, both pungent and sweet, of milder days. The garlic shoots, for example, served with raw Alaska salmon, imparted a flavor that only comes from fresh-out-of-the-ground garlic. Parsnips, puréed beneath collards and savory slices of Normandy duck, were a revelation in the art of winter sweetness. Roasted beets with buckwheat, a dish owing many ingredients to Alex Paffenroth, was a buttery, beety delectation with a just-right sinus-clearing snort of horseradish. Green cabbage, shredded beneath Long Island striped bass, tasted like freshly made sauerkraut due to a few squirts of oloroso sherry vinegar. Dandelions packed a springtime pungency that cut into the ricotta made by Tonjes Farm in the Catskills.

I kept on eating. I was still eating when Colin retired from the kitchen for the night. Okay. So he was not some television elimination game enthusiast. Nor was he a martyr to seasonality, buying local because it helps some ragtag band of Nordic growers. The reason Colin is addicted to his sources is because, even in the dead of winter, local tastes better. "I've learned some lessons," he told me. "One is that winter farmers take a week or two off right after New Year's. Did I ever get burned the first time I went to market and found they had stayed home. We had to buy in from California. I'm not one to pour salt and butter on inferior ingredients. This year I doubled my orders at the end of the year."

"So long as you're willing to slosh through snow two or three days a week, finding sources in the dead of winter is not all that hard," Colin went on. "March is the bigger challenge, when thawing conditions make root and potato preservation more difficult. When farmers like Alex Paffenroth turn their attention to spring crops." Those endless thirty-one days, when the first lamb-warm breaths of the year bring intimations of what is to come. Before the ramps bulb up and the fiddlehead ferns form those tight curls. Before supersweet overwintered greens like spinach, kale, and mâche have sprung back from the dead. "I pound the streets a little more in March, but hey, it's a challenge I look forward to when the time comes."

Colin is smitten with the idea of a truly deep-rooted American cuisine, one that showcases native ingredients like burdock, cattail shoots, ramps, Newtown Pippin apples, and fiddleheads; native fish like brook trout and yellow perch; and introduced game like ring-neck pheasant and Scottish red deer raised upstate: "The deer cheeks are the best part." To help close the March gap, Colin's developing a list of all-but-forgotten native forest delicacies for some willing and able farmer to hunt down. "I guess it's best if I don't broadcast your list," I said to Colin, hinting at the proprietary feelings chefs can have toward their sources. "You might have to kill me if I did that."

"Kill you?" said Colin, perplexed. "If I killed you, who would I buy my tomatoes from?"

So You Think You Want to
Be a Farmer?

EARLY AUGUST AT Union Square Greenmarket in New York City: Our display tables are linked together like a single multifaceted sea of tomatoes upon which baskets of fingerling potatoes, Gold Bar zucchini, and gnarly little Padrón peppers are barely noticeable. We manage to sell some basil—purple, Genovese, and the green confetti-leaved Greek variety—but that's only because of the tomatoes. Wednesdays and Saturdays, I handle restaurant accounts off the back of the truck while Walter, Wayne, and Toby sell to customers at the front table. Every so often, when I get hit hard—seven or eight chefs arriving simultaneously to pick up—Wayne jumps on the truck to give me a hand. Forced to wait their turn, the chefs will wander off to another farm stand or light up cigarettes and fall into conversation with one another, looking on with amusement. This rare opportunity to observe somebody else in a familiar predicament. In the weeds, as they say in the kitchen.

Toby is my wife's aunt, a New York City resident and scholar of good food who once ruled our farm kitchen, where she filled thousands of five-ounce "woozie" bottles with her imaginative, much-in-demand hot sauces, legendary flavor enhancers with names like

Burning Love, Paradiso, and Smoke. Walter was my landlord and housemate when I lived in Brooklyn, the man who once blocked my efforts to cover the roof of his brownstone with freestanding glass cold frames, forcing me to move back home to Pennsylvania and become a proper farmer. Wayne is my indispensable right-hand man: young, energetic, and passionate about the thin-skinned, highly perishable darlings that keep both of us on our feet round the clock in summer. At three thirty in the morning, Wayne shows up at my house in Pennsylvania and we get in the truck and head for New York City, arriving at Union Square around six. By seven, the stand is set up, tomatoes are organized, and we have some sales under our belts. A little breathing room before we get slammed—and if it's not raining hard, we are going to get slammed—during which Wayne will go to the deli across the street to buy each of us a toasted bagel with a schmear of cream cheese. When he comes back, I'll sink a plastic deli-issue knife into a tomato that didn't survive the journey: a gouged Brandywine, a cracked, dripping Striped German. Meaty, sun-ripened slice of bursting sweet yellow or musky acidic pink slathered upon cream cheese and bagel. Pride of Pennsylvania oozing over pride of New York City. The mere thought of it makes me want to lick my thumbs.

As tomato juice trickles down my chin, I'll sit on the back of the truck and observe the work-bound masses. People watching is one of the best things about coming into New York City to sell tomatoes in a park: every nationality, every philosophy, every point of view. Old ladies whose jaws drop at the outrageous prices—*Greedy farmers!*—and young professionals who roll their eyes at our reasonableness and insist, "Keep the change." Obsessive-compulsives who insist on a separate bag for each item and obsessive-compulsives who organize their tomatoes, cucumbers, garlic, raspberries, and cut flowers together in the recycled

swizzle stick sack they tote every time to market. Hopeless urbanites who think every farmer must be organic (otherwise we would
have purple skin or strange appendages sticking out of our foreheads) and hopeless idealists who question the authenticity of any
organic farmer who doesn't brush his teeth with Tom's of Maine
toothpaste. Early birds who sweep through first thing for the perk-
iest sun-sweetened day-neutral strawberries and wheeler-dealers
who wait until the shadows of the west side buildings are stretched
across the park to cut a deal with a homeward-leaning farmer.

Natalie pulls up. "Tim," she says, "want to buy a picture?" Anyone who has worked Union Square Greenmarket in the past decade
has had opportunities to buy a picture from Natalie. Hunched and
fragile, well into her seventies now, she fell and badly bruised her
face a few years back. Ever since then, she shows up with a young
aide by her side. If you tell Natalie your birth date, she will tell
you, after ten seconds of contemplation, what day of the week
you were born on. She says I was born on a Wednesday; I've never
checked up on her. I assume she's a savant of some sort. The pictures Natalie paints are of fairyland settings. Cats with lipstick-red
kissers. Hovering, UFO-like eyeballs with mascara-thick lashes. Or
electrical nightscapes: Grandma Moses–esque riffs on van Gogh's
Starry Night. Today's picture is a self-portrait: Natalie presiding
like a witch over a bubbling kettle of what look to be Greenmarket
apricots. I've got more than a dozen of Natalie's pictures floating
around my packing shed.

"I bought a picture last week, Natalie."

"What's your wife's name?"

"You know her name."

"Is it Jill?"

"It's Jill."

"How about five dollars for a picture." While my prices have
gone up regularly since Jill and I first came to market ten years

ago (today I get more than twice what I originally charged for my tomatoes), Natalie's price has remained unchanged: five dollars.

"I'll pass today."

"What's your wife's name?"

"Aw, Natalie."

She winks and heads for another stand, self-portrait flapping in hand. "Have a nice day, Tim. And have a nice Thursday and Friday and Saturday and Sunday."

A muscular biodynamic girl with hairy armpits noshes on a big, sweet onion as if it were an apple. A svelte, high-heeled culinary architect in a navy blue dress inspects my variously colored tomatoes with an eye toward constructing a multilayered chèvre-and-Greek-basil-crowned ziggurat for Friday night's dinner party. Walter answers her questions about flavor and shelf life.

Across from the stand, a woman in her twenties with French doll looks—corkscrew curls; blue-bordering-on-amethyst eyes; porcelain, rose-tinged cheeks—raises a violin to her shoulder. Sunlight twinkles in the treetops as more people flood the market, most of them bustling through, a few stopping off. Savvy gourmands who buy from the same farmers who sell to the chefs and plain folk who get so angry at farmers for selling out to restaurants that they'll go where the chefs don't shop. Snobs who refuse to eat a tomato not grown in New Jersey and demurrers who think the Jersey tomato is the biggest marketing hoax since Tang breakfast drink. People who come only for the tomatoes. People who come only for the heirloom tomatoes. A tall, gawky young man locks eyes with me—an invitation I hadn't meant to extend—and walks up to brag: "I'm getting married to Minnie Mouse. And Mickey doesn't like it at all." He's serious, too, gloating over Mickey's misfortune. But he moves on quickly.

People smoking cigarettes, talking on their cell phones, looking at their cell phones, stopping to watch a squirrel bury an acorn in the soil of a potted herb on display at Katrina's plant stand, across from me. College girls who only come to the market for sweets: peas, apricots, raspberries, cherry tomatoes. Housebound widowers in need of somebody—anybody—to talk to.

Greenmarket is in its thirtieth year, a milestone that was not lost on the Office of the Mayor of New York City. Back in May, Mayor Bloomberg held a gala event at Gracie Mansion, to which every Greenmarket vendor was invited. The event took place on a market day, a fact Wayne and I neglected to consider when we set off at 3:30 a.m., so that neither of us had anything more than jeans and torn T-shirts in which to present ourselves alongside our fellow farmers, most of whom had managed to show up more formally attired. It was a splendid after-work outdoor catered affair, with Greenmarket produce, cheese, and breads piled high on tables around the grounds and the sun taking its good old time setting on a shimmery, summery lawn. Years ago, almost twenty years ago, I had worked for the mayor's budget office—the end of the Koch years and the beginning of Dinkins's term—so when I saw David Dinkins in the crowd, I smiled. And he smiled back, not because he remembered a former staffer who was so junior he would not have been recognized in the first place, but because he appreciated a farmer, grubby clothes and all.

Greenmarket continues to be that rare thing: a win-win success, saving farmland in the region; providing nutritious, flavorful food to urbanites; creating open-air, cornucopia-lined forums for urbanites to meet one another and browse in; cleaning up neighborhoods; fueling a culinary renaissance; restoring vigor and dignity to scores of farm families. After cocktails and locally produced hors d'oeuvres, Mayor Bloomberg emceed the main event: the presentation to Greenmarket's founders, Barry Benepe and Bob Lewis, of the twenty-third annual Doris C. Freedman Award for "a contribution to the people of the City of New York that greatly enriches the public environment." The mayor was more comfortable and pleased with himself than any executive politician I've ever observed. His high approval ratings, good humor, and disinclination to engage in dirty politics seem to prove that the worthier politician is the one who can bankroll his way into office. He cracked jokes about the fact that Barry's son Adrian was the commissioner of New York City's Parks Department. He drew even more laughter when he recited the oft-quoted observation of one Greenmarket farmer, on the day in 1976 when the first market opened on Fifty-ninth Street and frenzied New Yorkers had set upon mountains of fresh corn, peaches, and tomatoes, not letting up till noon, by which time every farm table had been stripped clean of vegetables. "Is there a famine going on in the city?" a bemused Ron Binaghi had asked a reporter.

Thirty years ago, Barry Benepe and Bob Lewis were Manhattan-based urban planners who understood all too presciently how both the quality of food in the city and the surrounding landscape pointed to the same disturbing trends. In our post–World War II exuberance, we believed the same technology that had whupped the Nazis and the Depression could enhance our everyday lives. Plentiful petroleum, five-lane boulevards, a television in every household, a car in every garage. C-rats for civilians: Campbell's Soup, Chef Boyardee, the burger franchise, TV dinners. Did anyone notice, amid the glitter of all that aluminum-foil-wrapped optimism, that the loamiest farmland was getting paved over by subdivisions, office parks, industrial warehouses, monstrously large neon cowboys lassoing consumers by the carload for a taste of that char-grilled burger? Barry and Bob did. Barry's skills as a city planner were grafted onto a boyhood spent partly on a Maryland farm. He remembered how good a tomato could taste. And he remembered how bidders at the local produce auction would collude to ensure that the farmers got next to nothing for the surplus they hauled there. Inconsistent wholesale prices were crushing the small farmer. The laws of comparative advantage dictated that potatoes were best grown in Idaho; apples in Washington; lettuce, carrots, tomatoes, and broccoli in California; field corn in the Midwest. Left to its own devices, the invisible hand of the marketplace would start planting our seeds in Mexico and China. Our beef would be raised in the cleared forests of Argentina. And the place to make a killing on real estate would be in the expanding metropolitan regions, those amorphous blobs oozing mindlessly into the hinterlands. A hundred homes where a farm once stood. Gone forever.

The bureaucracy I was a tiny part of nearly two decades ago was then the fourth largest in the United States, after Uncle Sam, the state of California, and New York State. New York City's sanitation budget alone was as big as New Hampshire's state budget. The team of Lewis and Benepe faced two daunting tasks: luring farmers into Gotham and acquiring a pile of city agency approvals. I can imagine how they worked together, Barry as the seasoned, senior-level ideologue, gentle but slightly aloof, with a bumblebee's patience and persistence, constantly on the move, his heart always with the farmer, trying one city office after another, shaking hands and toeing the line, seeking an organizational structure on which to graft a seemingly ungraftable idea. Bob Lewis as the young, ambitious implementer of an evolving strategy, down in the trenches, researching market locations, interviewing local agricultural agents, recruiting farmers. Greenmarket ultimately found a home with New York City's Council on the Environment, a privately funded organization within the Office of the Mayor.

"Life's nonsense pierces us with strange relation," wrote Wallace Stevens, the poet who was born in my county seat, Reading, Pennsylvania. If, on the same day I went to Gracie Mansion, I had pulled aside Keith Stewart, the farmer set up to my immediate left at Greenmarket, and told him the good news I had received a day earlier, that a publishing house had offered to buy this memoir I was writing about how I had chucked a consulting career to take up organic farming, he would have said, in his thoughtful New Zealand accent: "Well, isn't that funny. I've just published a book along the very same lines. Mine's called *It's a Long Road to a Tomato*." Of all the titles! Keith was a forty-two-year-old consultant in a midcareer slump when he and his then-girlfriend moved to the sticks of Orange County, New York, in 1987. They knew the farm they wanted the moment they saw it and they purchased it. Although there is plenty of sweat and toil common to Keith's story and mine, the dissimilarities are more striking. To begin with, I still don't own a farm after twelve years of farming.

Before I was a consultant, I was a bureaucrat. In the Community Board Relations Unit of New York City's Office of Management and Budget, I fell under the influence of one Stephen Lyon. Bearded, six feet five with shoes off, Stephen looked like a ruddy Abraham Lincoln, the man whose speeches he could recite by heart. Stephen had been a champion debater in high school, and he was fluent in seven languages. In those precubicle days, he had audaciously turned his desk so it faced the middle of the office room instead of the wall. Between budgets, there were these interminable lulls during which some of us took to hiding our subway reading behind office documents. Squared off at a sociable angle to the rest of us, Stephen refused to make any such pretenses. Right there in plain view, he translated my unpublished stories into Spanish, Portuguese, German, and Russian. He read the *Economist* cover to cover and snored unabashedly when he napped. Stephen taught me to memorize the presidents' names in chronological order: "Don't forget to say Knox between James and Polk." With less success, he tried to get me to memorize the British monarchs from William the Conqueror to Elizabeth II. After eight years in the office, the most intelligent civil service employee I have ever encountered was still an entry-level assistant analyst. The only reason he was staying on, Stephen would insist, was so he could collect his Lucite cube for ten years' service. I fell eight years shy of that elusive Lucite cube. After two years in city government, I became a freelance consultant. But my future as a paper pusher was doomed. I could never shake the Ignatius J. Reilly–like futility I had learned from Stephen. At least, if anyone asked me how my writing was coming along, I could honestly answer that my stories had been translated into four languages.

But those farmers at City Hall! Tuesdays and Fridays, there was a small Greenmarket across the street from the Municipal Building where I worked with Stephen. I would watch the farmers and think about the cider I made back home in Pennsylvania. Every other year, when our unsprayed apple trees produced a bumper crop, I would make as much as five hundred gallons of cider. Seven Apple Cider, we called it. The trees, which had been planted in the thirties, were so enormous you couldn't reach most of the apples with a ten-foot picking pole. Northern Spy, Rhode Island Greening, Grimes Golden, Stayman Winesap, Baldwin, Banana Apple, and a seventh whose name we didn't know. I had to climb out onto the limbs to where they were strong enough to hold me yet thin enough to be shaken. My forearm muscles would burn from the effort of shaking those limbs. A bushel of those gnarly, spotted, wormy fallen apples would yield about three gallons of cider that tasted the way cider tasted before World War II. Sweet but with a lingering tang that made you thirst for more. I always sold out when I took it to the local market. The old-timers would taste Seven Apple Cider and you could see how it nearly brought tears to their eyes. I drooled over those Greenmarket farm stands the way I drooled, as an aspiring writer, over the pages of *The New Yorker* or *Harper's*. Give me a chance and I could blow city folk away with Seven Apple Cider.

Grimes Golden was my favorite apple for eating out of hand. Sweet yet tangy, like the best of the old-fashioneds, it was shot through with spice. Grimes Golden was too small and perishable for the supermarket trade, which is why it got bumped decades ago in favor of the larger, artlessly sweet Golden Delicious. Rhode Island Greening held up best when baked. I learned this when I was living in Walter's brownstone in Brooklyn. Before he started working for me, Walter ran his own advertising business a few blocks from Union Square. The business did well for more than a decade, until a number of factors, including skyrocketing real-estate prices, forced him to run everything out of his brownstone home. He eventually threw in the towel. When I lived on Underhill Avenue, our landlord-tenant disputes were anything but typical. Mostly, Walter would get angry at me for not showing up in time for dinner. He liked to cook Szechuan, Italian, and French peasant fare. Walter's spacious, cookbook-lined, gadget-equipped kitchen eventually compelled me to start chopping up vegetables, sautéing garlic, and baking pies. Paradise Pie was my specialty: slices of Rhode Island Greening, Baldwin, and quince mixed with cranberries. My golden, unsprayed quinces had these pithy brown spots you had to cut around, but their tree-ripened fragrance and palate-zinging tang was . . . well, paradise.

I was but one of thousands of ambitious writers and artists who'd moved to New York City and found himself being swirled into the culinary vortex. In October, after a trip home to Pennsylvania to make cider and clean up my garden before the killer frost, I would come back to Brooklyn with my Toyota pickup truck loaded with bushels and bushels of harvested goodies. Apples, quinces, tomatoes, chestnuts, basil, hot peppers, hickory nuts, garlic, cider, and red, yellow, and chocolate bell peppers. If it was a damp October, there would be a sizable bag of larch boletes, which were the only wild mushroom, besides morels, I trusted myself to pick. I would make a rich, fragrant chestnut and wild mushroom soup with them. On the fourth floor of the brownstone, I would fill two or three five-gallon office water tanks with cider and put air locks on them so that all winter long the cider would slowly ferment from the wild airborne yeast. Baskets of tomatoes would be piled up in Walter's kitchen, while most of the tree fruit went into the backyard, where the busybody squirrels would cart away the chestnuts one by one until they were gone. To bring the chestnuts inside, where it was warmer, invited mass incubations of these maggotlike worms that would bore out of the chestnuts and squirm on the floor. It would have been better to refrigerate the chestnuts, but the fridge would be packed solid with bell peppers and radishes and carrots and arugula.

For weeks, Walter and I put up food. A couple of dozen batches of pesto for the freezer. Tomato sauce. Vats of sweet red pepper sauce. The first heirloom tomato I ever purchased seed for was a pale paste variety called Yellow Bell, which I grew so that I could combine it with yellow bell peppers to make a sweet yellow pepper sauce. We would run out of freezer space and still there would be bushels and bushels of apples, quinces, and tomatoes going soft on us. The kitchen and backyard would be permeated with quince fragrance. We started canning: hot pepper sauce, quince chutney, jelly. Walter emerged as the jelly expert. From the way the simmering liquid spilled off his spoon, he could gauge the gelling point of the naturally occurring pectins in apples and quinces. Paradise Jelly was his specialty, made with the same combination of fruit I used to make Paradise Pie. When Walter was just out of college, he had been extended an invitation to join the Trappist monastery in Spencer, Massachusetts, where they make Trappist preserves. And he came close to joining. So this was a karmic activity for him, to be making Paradise Jelly in his own kitchen. My job was to cut the usable meat from the gnarly, misshapen quinces. On occasion, we ran out of quinces because the unusable spots were so dominant. But we were in luck because there happened to be a quince tree on our block, at the intersection of Underhill and Prospect Place, next to the corner bodega. The first time I went to score some Brooklyn quinces, I asked the three teenagers who came out of the house if they knew what kind of tree they had in their yard, and the first one said, "It's an apple," the second said, "It's a pear," and the third, "It's an apple-pear."

Among the many things Walter and I have in common is our Slovenian heritage. Hardworking peasants who'd arrived in their teens around the turn of the century, his ancestors settled around Cleveland while mine landed in western Pennsylvania. They worked their way out of the coal mines or the menial factory jobs they started out in and they planted spruce trees in their yards. Eager to put the Old World behind her, my Slovenian-born great-grandmother, Geggy, adored all things American, boning up on phrases like "hit the road" and "you big palooka." She baked an angel food strudel and adored white bread. Unlike most grand-mothers, she harbored no reservations when dresses started to show more leg in the late fifties, avidly taking the hem up on the skirts she sewed for my mother. But when my parents moved to the country, Geggy just as avidly partook of Old World pleasures when she visited, putting on those sneakers with the bunion holes in them so she could take long walks through the orchard and fields with a basket on her arm, foraging for blewit mushrooms under the apple trees, hunting dandelion greens, bread and but-ter plant, the obscure Slovenia-named weeds that she steamed like spinach. "She could make soup from a dirty skillet," my grandfa-ther used to say of Geggy.

Walter and I drew the line when it came to Geggy's specialty, *potica* (pronounced "puh-teet-sa"), the painstakingly rolled Slo-venian pastry made with a finely-chopped-walnut custard rolled up in a superthin dough. We could have cracked all of those tiny hard-to-crack hickory nuts I'd brought back from Pennsylvania and chopped them up just as fine. In terms of flavor, a hickory nut is to a walnut what white truffle is to black. But no. There was no way two bachelors in a Brooklyn kitchen were going to bicker over the intricacies of *potica* construction. We had the finished pastry mailed to us from Cleveland, where Walter's grandfather ground up the walnuts and his grandmother meticulously rolled the dough out to a paper thinness and his mother and grandmother worked together to spread the chopped-walnut custard over the pastry and roll the whole thing up tight as a six-foot-long snake they had to coil so it would fit into the oven.

To Walter, now standing behind a sea of tomatoes, I say, "The Cherokee Purple guy doesn't come anymore."

"What Cherokee Purple guy?"

"The lawyer guy. The guy who talks to me about the Pittsburgh Pirates." I'm terrible at remembering names. I've talked to this lawyer from Pittsburgh so many times, he probably stopped coming because he didn't like being called the Cherokee Purple guy. "Guess he's buying his Cherokee Purples from someone else."

"He was here this morning."

"He was?"

"He bought two Cherokee Purples and a Brandywine. You didn't see him?"

"What about Beatrice? I never see her." Beatrice (pronounced the Italian way, "Bay-ah-tree-chay") is an exuberant woman with a tattoo of some Maori amulet on her lower back. Beatrice runs a small, popular, jam-packed restaurant called Il Bagatto in the East Village and she has always got a Chihuahua cradled in one arm. She buys her tomatoes off the front table like the other customers and then comes back to the truck to chat with me. Nearly every week, she comments on the quality of the last batch of basil. Her enthusiasm gives me a much-appreciated boost in the morning.

"I think Beatrice is in Italy," says Walter. "Relax." Until business starts to pick up, I torment everyone with my worries. Nobody likes my tomatoes anymore. My first-thing-in-the-morning customers are a kind of canary in the coal mine. If they abandon me, the rest will follow. It's an easy way to get yourself worked up when you've brought more than a ton of tomatoes to market. Unlike author/farmer Keith Stewart next to me, who at all times displays a balanced variety of greens and herbs, potatoes, garlic, tomatoes, onions, you name it, I have devolved, for various reasons, into a kind of tomato monoculturist. For sure, I always plant three or four acres of assorted other crops: chile peppers, lettuce, arugula, fava beans, sweet corn, potatoes, shell peas, carrots, snap peas, sweet onions, beets, sweet potatoes. But I lose money on most of those other crops, in part because the deer, groundhogs, and rabbits are so fond of them. My fate is bound up with my tomatoes. And sometimes it's so scary it makes me sick to my stomach.

"Timmy, you got corn for me?" Joe in his van, pulling up on the street next to the stand. Every Wednesday morning, he delivers to a few restaurant accounts. Joe is retired from his job as a Broadway stage set construction worker. To keep himself busy, he restocks soft drink vending machines around the city. He always asks this same question when he arrives. If I have sacks of corn for him to deliver, that means he will have to reorganize the cases of soda in his van. Corn is the biggest loser for me because of the labor-intensive methods I've devised to avoid spraying it with herbicides and pesticides. I start the seeds in a greenhouse, in plug trays. When the corn sprouts are three inches high, I transplant them into the field by hand, the way you would a tomato seedling or a geranium, usually around mid-April. Then I cover the corn seedlings with protective sun-admitting fabric. This way the frost can't kill the corn sprouts, which get a head start on the weeds as well as on the various and sundry worms that make a living off the ears and stalks of the plant—European corn borer, corn earworm, cutworm, wireworm. To keep the deer and raccoons from devouring the stalks, I also build a temporary seven-foot-high fence around my corn patch. I lose money big-time on corn, but I sell every ear. Some of the farmers who live near me are amused almost to the point of intoxication by my techniques. And I can't rule out the possibility that my corn-transplanting trick demonstrates a pigheadedness on my part, a determination to discredit a seasoned farmer who once listened to my philosophies before delivering up his unwavering verdict: "Corn must be sprayed."

"No corn today, Joe. Tomatoes, tomatoes, tomatoes." Joe's helper—a young Italian kid pulling a hand truck—is new. His helpers regularly quit on him. They can't take his cursing and swearing in traffic, his over-the-top rage every time a parking ticket appears on his windshield. One hundred thirty-five dollars a pop. I once got three parking tickets in a one-hour time span. So I'm grateful to have someone else handle deliveries. This is hardly a cozy retirement job for Joe, who had bypass surgery last winter. But he keeps pressing me for work. And I'm charmed by his old-school integrity. You take care of me, I'll take care of you.

"I have a number for you to call," Joe tells me. "A chef who would like to buy your tomatoes. Please! Do me a favor and don't forget to call this gentleman." I take the chef's phone number and cram it into my pocket as Wayne comes back to help stack tomatoes onto Joe's hand truck.

A glint in her eye, Natalie swings by on her way back through the market. "Sold another picture," says she, raising her right hand to high-five me before moving on to high-five some more farmers.

Towing a six-foot-long four-wheeled hauling cart, Hollywood arrives to pick up for Jean-Georges Vongerichten's restaurants.

Raised on a farm in Jamaica, Hollywood gets his nickname from the flashy shades perched upon his nose—you can see your own reflection in them. While Wayne loads up Joe, I hand over flats of tomatoes to Hollywood. Ten flats of mixed cherries for Jean-Georges alone. White cherry tomatoes, green cherries, yellow with red marbling, pink, purple, brown, red, and orange cherries. Tiny red and yellow currant tomatoes. The evening before coming to market, we spend hours mixing and matching in the packing shed. Besides the cherries, we mix flats of egg-sized salad tomatoes like Green Zebra, fuzzy white Peach tomatoes, dusky ruffle-edged Purple Calabash, and flats of the beefsteak-sized heirlooms—pink Brandywine sharing space with White Wonder, tie-dyed Striped German, Cherokee Purple, and Aunt Ruby's German Green. Although I always make sure we have tomatoes to put on the front table for our regular customers, three-quarters of what we bring to market gets sold off the back of the truck to restaurants in one of these three mixtures. At the peak of the season, our day-before packing sessions will often continue into the dark, especially if we were unable to finish picking until late afternoon. Last night was one of those nights. But we've come a long way since the days when Jill and I would finish loading the truck after midnight and then arrive at market with a crowd waiting for us. The chefs made up their own mixed flats in those days. And as sales slowed toward the end of the day, Jill and I would slump into exhaustion, waiting as dark came on for Lawrence or Nate or Shorty to come along with a broom and a burst of energy to get us swept up, loaded, and on the road home.

Not all of us Greenmarket stand holders are former New York City management consultants who write books on the side. We are as varied as our customers. First-generation puritans who cringe at the thought of a single fungicide-treated squash seed besmirching their compost-enriched soil and seventh-generation stalwarts who grunt to themselves when asked if the corn is organic. Big-thinking, hundred-acre-and-growing mechanized operations whose twenty-four-foot trucks never fail to deliver mile-high piles of lettuce, radishes, beets, carrots, broccoli, tomatoes, onions, and kohlrabi. And glorified gardeners whose limited supplies of zucchini blossoms, fava beans, and shell peas get snapped up first thing by chefs who don't mind paying retail for something so exquisite. Organic growers who continue to maintain the certified label even though the federal government has taken over all the hippie certifying processes and "beyond organic" alternativistas who trust their customers to trust them and thumb their noses at the USDA. Keith Stewart next to me is still USDA organic, while John Gorzynski, who is as pure as anyone when it comes to organic principles, elected to substitute the word "ornery" for "organic" rather than register his farm with the federal program. Morse Pitts labels his previously certified organic vegetables as "unconventionally grown." I never tried to certify my farm even before the USDA took over the label, mostly because I could never organize myself enough to fill out the paperwork. Too much time down on my knees, pulling up weeds. Of the 157 farmers set up at forty-four Greenmarket locations around New York City, 21 are certified organic.

The nearest Greenmarket farm to New York City is Stokes in Bergen County, New Jersey. Bergen County starts on the other side of the George Washington Bridge from Manhattan. Ron Binaghi, the fifth-generation farmer who today runs Stokes, is quick on his feet, a good speaker, personable, and as alert as any of the upscale suburbanites who surround his placid, tightly organized seventeen-acre swath of silt loam. While many of Ron's neighbors are grateful for the fresh produce his proximity makes available to them, one dragged him into court over the most recent addition to his fleet of greenhouses. Another neighbor regularly chips golf balls into his fields. The number of golf courses in Bergen

County long ago surpassed the number of working farms. When you stumble upon Stokes's seventeen acres, an oasis of lush plant life and tractor implements amid office parks, million-dollar mansions, and fifties-era Cape Cods awaiting demolition (the postwar developments that first sent farmers packing are themselves being uprooted), it's easy to forget that this farm was not painstakingly shoehorned into its present location. When Greenmarket started, Bergen County was down to forty-eight farms. Today, there are seven. One of the other six remaining farms recently sold development rights to eleven of its acres. The cost to local taxpayers of acquiring a permanent agricultural easement for those eleven acres, thereby reimbursing the farmer for the development potential of this open-space asset, was $332,000 per acre, or $3,652,000. Even if this farmer were to sell those devalued eleven acres, it is virtually guaranteed that no other active farmer could afford them.

In spite of the easy one-hour commute, Ron Binaghi still rises early to make it to his market space by 6:00 a.m. Thirty years ago, at the age of sixteen, Ron witnessed the frenzy of fresh-starved Manhattanites on Greenmarket's memorable first day. "All you saw was hands," he recalls. "Hands and money. People going crazy over a head of cabbage, which I didn't think was such a big deal. They'd never seen such green cabbage before." Ron's father delivered up the pungent, oft-quoted observation about the crowd's faminelike behavior. But the green stuff waved in their faces by those first-day customers had a similar effect on the Binaghis. The farm was on the brink of starvation, socked by the mid-1970s spike in fuel prices, hobbling along on the proceeds of a roadside stand and a wholesale operation focused on four crops: tomatoes, peppers, eggplant, and strawberries.

Early on a Saturday morning, a few months after the blockbuster Fifty-ninth Street kickoff, Ron pulled into Union Square with a truck full of cabbages, tomatoes, and eggplant. The pissy-smelling, drug-saturated park had been recommended as a Green-market site by the New York City Planning Department. Farmers and their customers, it was hoped, might provide the city, itself reeling from a budget crisis, with a no-cost solution to Union Square's deterioration. The bustle of potato and cucumber transactions would muscle aside the illicit trades. As farmers market locations go, Union Square didn't seem early on like it had much shelf life. Not like Fifty-ninth Street, at any rate. "Back then, we used beach umbrellas to protect our tables from the sun and rain," Ron recalls. "One morning as we were setting up, this guy comes along and grabs an umbrella pole off the ground. 'Put that back,' I said. 'It's okay,' he says, 'I just need to hit a mothafucker over the head. I'll bring it back after I hit this mothafucker over the head.' What was I gonna do? He was big. He was scary. He never came back with our umbrella pole."

Umbrella poles for hitting motherfuckers over the head. Add that to the list of easily overlooked goods and services provided by your local farmer. "Dad was more concerned about my safety than I was," says Ron, whose youthful fearlessness encouraged him to stick with the iffy Union Square location. And it paid off. While the old city-owned parking lot at Fifty-ninth Street has since sprouted luxury condos, the presence of farmers at Union Square is credited with anchoring a culinary district in the heart of downtown Manhattan. In 1985, largely because of the farmers market, Danny Meyer established his flagship restaurant, Union Square Cafe, just off the park. The next four restaurants he opened—Gramercy Tavern, Eleven Madison Park, Tabla, and Blue Smoke—are all within hand-truck distance of Union Square Greenmarket. Today, Gotham Bar and Grill, Babbo, Fleur de Sel, and Craft are among hundreds of restaurants close enough to send kitchen staff out on the fly for fiddlehead ferns, yellow carrots, purple tomatoes, a head of green, green cabbage. Peter Hoffman, chef/owner of Savoy, ped-

als to Union Square on a bicycle whose snazzy front-end cargo hold
has a payload capacity of 250 pounds. Jean-Georges's refrigerated
van sits on the edge of the park while Hollywood collects goodies
from more than a dozen different farmers. Spurred on by the pref-
erences of chefs and city palates, Stokes Farm slimmed down from
a struggling forty-acre operation focused on four vegetables to a
shipshape seventeen-acre producer of more than seventy varieties
of fruits, vegetables, and herbs.

"The tide that raises all ships" is how farmer Guy Jones sums up
the effect restaurants had on the quality and variety of vegetables
coming into New York City in the 1980s, when the Idaho potato
and iceberg lettuce ceded market turf to mesclun greens, radicchio,
haricots verts, zucchini flowers, and heirloom tomatoes. Guy took a
roundabout route to his profession. The storefront law practice he
had founded in the 1970s catered to the dispossessed—prisoners,
illegal aliens, farmworkers. To support a largely pro bono workload,
he bartended and pounded nails on the side. Guy caught the agriculture bug in San Jose, California, where he had gone to provide
legal muscle to César Chávez and the United Farm Workers. As
a democratizing gesture, Chávez encouraged everyone associated
with his organization, including legal counsel, to toil in the fields.
During harvest season, Attorney Jones would board a bus full of
hardworking Mexicans and "hungover Bowery-types with rotted
teeth." Disembarking at his destination, he would wade into a sea
of broccoli with his harvesting knife. Or a sea of celery. In the early
1980s, burned out by the Sisyphean nature of his goodwill legal efforts, Guy headed to Cornell University for agricultural instruction.
He bought a small farm near Ithaca, New York, although it became
clear that, once again, he would have to supplement his income.
One neighbor was milking seven hundred cows but had to drive a
school bus to stay afloat. Another worked the salt mines to augment
the income he got from a thousand acres of cash crops. To position

himself closer to a viable direct market, Guy rented a ten-acre patch within commuting distance of Greenmarket. He refers fondly to the work crew that helped get Blooming Hill Farm off the ground as "hippies from around the world." They ate venison, canned their own fruits and vegetables, milked cows, and made cheese, butter, and wine. After Guy took on more land, he was harvesting ten thousand bales of hay a year. In a blue '54 Chevy pickup with wooden slats built up the sides to hold all the produce they loaded on it, he started bringing the standard fare to Union Square—sweet corn, beefsteak tomatoes, zucchini. "The Joads coming to town," chuckles Guy, whose willingness to experiment quickly earned him special requests from top chefs.

"Can't you cut your lettuce leaves about this big?" David Bouley asked the lawyer turned farmer, showing a little more than an inch of space between his thumb and forefinger. The restaurant bearing Bouley's name was poised to dominate New York City for nearly a decade, setting the sourcing standard for city restaurants to come. Like fish fresh off the boat or *fraises des bois* damp with morning dew, tender young mesclun greens, largely unavailable in New York City at the time, were a mainstay in the French kitchens where Bouley had worked in the late 1970s, when the nouvelle cuisine of Fernand Point, Paul Bocuse, and Roger Vergé was taking the tradition of Carême and Escoffier to a new level. Bouley had originally set off for France to study Renaissance painting at the Sorbonne, but soon felt the tug of culinary forces coming from sunny, olive-oil-drenched Provence, arriving at Roger Vergé's garden-surrounded Le Moulin de Mougins just as a young, talented French chef named Daniel Boulud was departing for Denmark. In its emphasis on simple, healthy, pure ingredients, nouvelle cuisine eschewed heavy sauces and unnecessary flavorings in favor of primary ingredients so fresh they didn't need seasoning, so fresh that only farmers, hunters, and fishermen could be counted on to provide them reliably.

So the lawyer turned farmer started growing mesclun greens for the art scholar turned chef. Pungent, nutty, fragrant arugula; mustardy, ticklish-to-the-throat mizuna; satiny sweet inch-high baby romaine; bitter, frilly-leafed frisée; spicy nasturtium flowers. Guy even got talked into planting *haricots verts*, which were a nightmare to pick because it took forever to fill a basket with the ultra-thin, delicate French beans. But restaurants were willing to pay five dollars per pound for the tiny *haricots*, where the larger beans, though only slightly less tedious to pick, could only bring in a dollar per pound. Thanks to chefs like Mario Batali, who started smuggling seeds back from their European tours, farmers like Guy Jones were growing previously unavailable greens like mâche and radicchio. Farmer-chef relationships of the kind that had put Alice Waters's Chez Panisse in Berkeley over the top in the 1970s were now stirring up New York City's kitchens. Before long, Guy had so many different varieties of esoteric vegetables that he had to hang baskets from the wooden slats of the Joad-wagon because his tables could not display everything.

Rick Bishop and Franca Tantillo were an innovative farming pair who also caught the attention of chefs, Rick with his rugged, gentleman lumberjack's look (in fact, he logged for years to supplement his farming income) and Franca with her Staten Island accent and her gutsy, tenacious farming genes inherited from a father who had grown up picking olives, tomatoes, grapes, and fava beans in Sicily. While Rick was at Cornell, the ag department was conducting greenhouse experiments on a tiny, flavorful strawberry whose sun-drenched fragrance and intense sweetness could be enjoyed all summer long. For well over a decade, strawberry breeders at the USDA had been hybridizing a wild variety from the Wasatch Mountains of Utah that, unlike virtually every other strawberry on the planet, continued to produce fruit regardless of the amount of daylight. The sun and heat and dryness of late summer imparted a matchless flavor to the resulting day-neutral Tristar strawberry. When one of the USDA strawberry breeders presented the day-neutral berry to some big California growers, one grower held a little specimen up to the side of his head and chuckled, "Come back when you've got one the size of your ear."

The summer after Rick's graduation, Rick, Franca, and another Cornell ag student showed up at Union Square Greenmarket with Tristars grown on a one-acre patch near Ithaca. They took a small table at the end of Phil Hoeffner's stand on a Saturday. Not one customer objected to the Tristar's diminutive size. The flavor was more reminiscent of its wild ancestor than it was of those California-bred titans. And that fragrance! From blocks away from Philly Hoeffner's stand, customers claimed to have picked up the scent that led them to the flavorful mountain-grown berry. A year later, Rick and Franca planted three-quarters of an acre of Tristars in the Catskills, using a garden-variety rototiller to turn the soil. Rick's partner from Cornell set off on his own with more aggressive plans: wooing an investor, signing a contract with Sloan's grocery store, planting fourteen acres of Tristars, and even taking out an ad in the *New York Times.* Two other one-acre patches sprang up, one on Long Island, the other near Philadelphia. But these last two locations proved too hot for a strawberry whose critical ancestor had roots in rocky, high-altitude, mineral-rich soil. And the fourteen-acre patch went bust on account of three straight weeks of rain. Rick and Franca's undercapitalized but balanced approach—he cut firewood and furniture-grade walnut while she worked nights as a nurse—enabled their washed-out Tristar operation to survive until another year. They also harvested seven acres of traditional June strawberries six hours west of New York City, on rented land near York, Pennsylvania. When the June berries were coming in heavily, they ran them into New York City four or five days a week, initiating an exhausting cycle of picking, packing, and racing through interstate darkness, six hours each way, trying to keep awake with ginseng and caffeine and slaps to the face. "You have to be a glorified truck driver to deliver superb product," says Franca, who knows, too, that you need to know a little something about the mineral content of the soil those berries are growing in. With so many hours on the road, they often picked in the dark, with miner's lights strapped to their foreheads. On the way to New York City one morning, in the old '66 Chevy pickup they named Ralph after Ralph "straight to the moon" Kramden, Rick fell asleep at the wheel and they both woke up when the truck ricocheted off a bridge culvert. Back out onto the highway Ralph bounced, not missing a beat. Old Ralph knew the way. For the rest of that trip, at least, Rick managed to stay awake.

The June berries were a hit, but the Tristars blew people away. Rick and Franca moved the whole Mountain Sweet Berry operation to Cooks Falls in the Catskills, where they grew more and more of the strawberry whose intoxicating sweetness was a tribute to a unique mountain *terroir*. They grew blackberries and raspberries, too, and started foraging for tiny wild blueberries. In their mineral-sweetened soil, they grew fava beans and melt-in-the-mouth peas. They caught mountain-stream trout and bushwhacked for wild watercress, fiddleheads, and ramps. In honor of the exquisite mountain berries they brought to market, Danny Meyer held a special event at Union Square Cafe, "Berries and Beaujolais," in which different berries were paired with wines. Spurred on by the bottomless demand for their products, the indefatigable young pair convinced neighbors to turn over their loamy backyards to them. They paid more than ten times the going rental rate for that land. They mowed those neighbors' lawns and plowed their snow and traded them smoked trout. Seeing what a killing the young farmers appeared to be making, some of those neighbors started their own growing operations, only to learn, soon enough, that all the goodies that make a chef go haywire require tons more physical labor than most entrepreneurs are willing to put in.

"I didn't move all the way from Sicily so my daughter could struggle the way I did," Franca's father scolded her. He had assumed this would be a passing fresh-out-of-college fancy for the idealistic pair. When they'd had their fill of droughts and deluges, Rick would become a biochemist and Franca would turn to nursing, the profession for which she had trained. Instead, they hunkered down through hard times and continued to break fresh ground for the palates of New Yorkers. So it only made sense that when an aspiring potato in need of a farmer arrived in Manhattan, Rick Bishop would be the one to give it an audition. The tawdry fingerling potatoes arrived in three suitcases, seed stock that Joel Patraker, who would eventually become Greenmarket's assistant director, had brought back from a trip to California, where he'd met Rex and Susan Mongold, a pair of daring potato farmers. Purple, pink, and waxy yellow, sausage shaped and nubby, anything but uniform in size, fingerling potatoes were closer to the Andean mother of all spuds than anything available at the grocery store. Like the mountain-spawned Tristar strawberry, the high-altitude potato was well suited to the soil of a Catskill farmer with a little patience and ingenuity. Not surprisingly, David Bouley was one customer who was already familiar with fingerling potatoes, having cooked with them in Joel Robuchon's kitchen during his French tour. The first time he glimpsed the Mountain Sweet Berry truck loaded with those mind-blowingly buttery-without-needing-butter potatoes, Bouley responded with the classic chef's line: "I want all of it."

"Except he really did buy all of it," says Rick. Smitten with everything Mountain Sweet had on offer, Bouley started visiting the farm regularly, walking the fields, sampling peas, berries, even the different varieties of watercress. He preferred the more peppery and frilly leaved variety of cress. Bouley was buying thirty flats of Tristar strawberries a week and even started fronting Rick money so he could buy the expensive fingerling seed stock in spring. With Joel Robuchon and a *New York Times* reporter, Bouley flew by chartered jet to the Catskills in order to visit Mountain Sweet Berry Farm for a high-profile potato tasting. Wayne Nish, who had recently opened his restaurant, March, started sorting through Rick's Ruby Crescents and Russian Bananas for the tiniest, fingernail-sized fingerlings. Up until then, the bulk of the fingernails and marbles slipped through the harvesting machinery and stayed in the field. But not anymore. The rapport between chef and farmer opened the walk-ins of New York City restaurants to tender vegetables of a hitherto unimaginable petiteness. Besides mesclun greens and fingernail potatoes, there were inch-long zucchini, silver-dollar-sized pattypan squash, baby spinach, baby arugula, pencil-thin carrots, *haricots verts* and *haricots jaunes*. By the mid-1990s, the bar would be lowered even further when the Chef's Garden in Ohio started FedExing microgreens—sprigs of arugula, radish, mizuna, and even celery—whose roots might have spent less than a week in the soil before harvest.

All of these tiny and obscure vegetables made for more work all around. Back when I used to deliver on Saturday mornings, I would arrive in New York City at 6:00 a.m. to find a few joggers and dog walkers making their rounds. Here and there a huddle of black-clad party animals, reluctant to call it a night, would be exchanging pecks on the cheek as a cab pulled up. Otherwise, the entire city appeared to be asleep. All but the bakers and the fishmongers and, of course, the workers in the prep kitchens of restaurants like Daniel, Gotham Bar and Grill, and Gramercy Tavern, where onions were being chop chop chopped into infinitesimal dice, fava beans were popped out of their shells and peeled individually, cherry tomatoes and grapes were painstakingly divested of their skins. By midmorning at Aureole, there would be a shortage of counter space so that I had to twist and turn with my bulky boxes through a gauntlet of young, focused externs with cutting boards balanced on their knees as their knives turned out perfect cubes of melon or squash.

Repetition is what earns the stars; endlessly, flawlessly executed repetition. "You have to pick those skinny French beans every single day," says Alvina Frey, a Bergen County, New Jersey, farmer who was present at Fifty-ninth Street on Greenmarket's first day. Alvina brought lima beans from the start, limas so silky and fresh and perfectly handpicked, she made converts of hundreds of New Yorkers who thought being a grown-up meant never again having to shove another mealy lima into their mouths. With a little coaxing from chefs, Alvina started growing *haricots verts* and baby zucchini. She grew more and more beans as the years wore on, and bean lovers of all stripes showed up earlier and earlier at her stand because the more she grew, it seemed, the faster she sold out. "I never went home with anything but beaten-up beans," she says, "the ones that got picked through too many times." As word of Alvina's beans spread to the best kitchens in New York City, she expanded to the point where she was planting five or six acres of limas, *haricots verts*, fava beans, and yellow wax beans, planting them every two weeks so that she had a continuous supply up to the frost.

The art of picking had been bred in Alvina at an early age. For a month and a half during strawberry season, Alvina had picked berries early in the morning before going to school. She picked with her brother and sister and cousins. After school, they picked again until dark. The farm near Mahwah, New Jersey, started in the late 1800s by her grandmother, a German immigrant, encompassed 125 acres at its height. Her father would take a load of whatever they'd spent the day picking to the wholesale market at Paterson. If he didn't sell out by dark, he would sleep over in the cab of the truck and start selling again when the 2:00 a.m. buyers came around. When the truck was empty, he went back to the farm to pick and load up and do it all over again. Six days a week he went to Paterson. When strawberries were finished, Alvina moved on to zucchini, cucumbers, peaches. Then came tomatoes and lima beans.

"We picked more stones than anything," Alvina recalls. Walking alongside the metal V-shaped stone boat that was pulled over the field by horses, they gathered up stones of all sizes and piled them into the stone boat. Every spring, when it came time to plow again, a whole new crop of stones would appear. They built houses with fieldstone. Alvina's grandmother had built the barn with fieldstone. All of the plowing and cultivating was accomplished with horses, too. Alvina's uncle could work magic with those horses. They whinnied at his approach. He was so good with those horses, in fact, that he kept right on working with them into the 1960s. "The story was that my uncle couldn't drive a tractor in reverse," laughs Alvina, who would go out into the field at lunch to bring the horses in for their oats and hay. "The horses ate other things, too. They'd get into the tomato patch and till you caught up with them all these tomatoes would be tramped down and half eaten and there would be horse slobber all over those beautiful plump red tomatoes."

The farm started to shrink after Alvina's father died in the 1950s. Alvina was faced with a career choice. At the age of thirty-eight, she had farmed all her life. "I could play the piano," she says. "But there was no money in that. So I took this tractor, this old Farmall H, and started to plow with it. The Farmall H scared the daylights out of me because it had this tricycle front wheel, and every time I hit one of those stones with the plow, the tractor nearly tipped over. After all those years collecting stones, there were as many as when we started." The Farmall H scared her so much that she and her first husband tried to switch back to horses.

They bought a horse that was as big as a Clydesdale, but nobody could handle horses the way her uncle once did. By the time her first husband had died and she'd married again, Chad's Farm, as the farm was named, after her first husband, had upgraded to a John Deere with four solid wheels and an automatic reset plow that gave way to those stones.

There were 37 of the original 125 acres left when Alvina started coming to Greenmarket in 1976. Harvesting six acres of beans, a fair number of them the tedious, highly prized *haricots verts*, was no small accomplishment. Alvina did it with the help of one other man, Leopoldo, a Mexican with sun-toughened skin like hers. By the time Alvina's second husband died, Chad's Farm was down to 16 acres, the parcel across the road from the mud-brown stone barn her grandmother had built in the late 1800s. Leopoldo was still trying his best to keep pace with Alvina when she retired in 1999 at the age of sixty-eight. Without her, the quality of *haricots verts* in New York City went into a tailspin from which it has only recently begun to recover, thanks mainly to the planting efforts of farmers like Rick Bishop and Franca Tantillo.

From Paradise Jelly on Underhill Avenue to a ton of tomatoes at Union Square Greenmarket. After my third season growing tomatoes, we started looking seriously for a farm we could call our own. My wife, born and raised in Queens, was feverish to move out of the subpar middle-of-nowhere log farmhouse we rented. The shoestring irrigation system, the constant shuttling back and forth between the rented house and Eckerton, the occasional flare-ups with Eckerton's co-owners were wearing me thin. We would get our hearts set on a farm going up for auction, but we were no match for developers and multimillionaires who wanted to buy up land and sit on it like it was a high-value CD. There was the occasional unsold eight-to-ten-acre oddball parcel some eager-to-move-on developer was willing to sell cheap, an alfalfa-green tabula rasa amid the dozen eight-acre estates that had already been carved out of the land some Dietrich or Dunkleberger had sold off along with his cows, always with some prehistoric rust-eaten relic, a disc harrow or a manure spreader, half buried in its mud. I could have managed with ten acres, but I had enough foresight to know that all it would take to shut me down were the well-financed objections of *one* of those neighbors. After plunking down three-quarters of a million for his eight-acre piece of God's country, your prosperous "gentleman farmer" is not likely to cherish the grunt of a tractor in the hours before he wakes. Or the crow of a rooster. And when he sits out on his shaded deck, a perfect swath of manicured green surrounding him, the sight of peasants bending over to pick beans or taking a break in the shade of a tree may not have for him the same artistic allure it once did, say, for Brueghel the Elder or Jean-François Millet.

Anyhow, I wanted a farm that had not already been chopped up. I wanted what old Milt Miller had once had. The bank barn with the milking parlor. The henhouse and the weather vane. The slender, durable outhouse. I wanted a farm that no zoning board could ever tell me was not a farm because it did not contain enough acreage. As it turned out, the only thirty- to sixty-acre farms we could afford back then featured homes in poorer shape than the one we rented. Leaky roofs, gaping holes in the floors, water-damaged ceilings, wallpaper peeling off the walls, shot furnaces. Barns in the process of caving in. The living conditions of the late-twentieth-century farm family. Given the mortgage costs of the land, we would not be able to undertake renovations on these homes anytime soon. There was the added complication of my attachment to the land I had grown up on. Part of me just wanted to keep on farming Eckerton, no matter how precarious the drill. And Jill, it turned out, simply did not want to live in the country. The mud I tracked into the house made her ache for civilization. Two and a half years into our search, out of desperation, we sprang for a little Cape Cod in Kutztown, where I had attended high school. We were still landless, but the house was in livable shape and I had managed to rent an extra four acres adjacent to Eckerton. We bought the house in 2001, in the middle of summer, at a time when I was so busy, it took us three months to move in. Even then, we were only able to make the move because of the work interruption caused by the terrorist attacks on the World Trade Center, which closed down New York City for two days, leaving me with a packing shed full of stranded tomatoes and a team of sixty-hour-a-week pickers with time on their hands. On September 12, 2001, we loaded clothing and furniture onto my produce truck and hauled them to the new house. I continued renting the old log farmhouse, since the greenhouse and tomato-packing shed were critical to my operation.

But I still had a farm in my sights. Stretched even thinner between *three* locations now—home, greenhouse, and growing field—I kept at my chosen trade with the avidity of the proverbially optimistic child who, confronted with a pile of horse dung, eagerly digs and digs under the assumption that there must be a horse in there somewhere. Yes, there must be a farm in there somewhere. To save up more money, I started growing year round, harvesting tiny expensive microgreens in the greenhouse, burning gobs of greenhouse gas in January, cutting down millions of gawky, long-legged, two-week-old arugula sprigs. In the coldest months, I even toted local Pennsylvania mushrooms to New York City along with my restaurant deliveries. It was in the early spring, while delivering microgreens and mushrooms in a Subaru station wagon, that I got nailed with three parking tickets in an hour. I was coming out of Payard Patisserie and Bistro on the Upper East Side when I saw the officer pulling up to write my third ticket. I pretended not to notice the officer, jumped in the Subaru, and pulled away. Smart move. The officer came sirening after and threw my ticket at me through the driver's-side window. He stopped just shy of adding additional charges and forcing me to appear before a judge. Which was a lucky thing for me. On a day in which I had delivered $650 of product whose price didn't even cover the cost of seed and labor, I was already reeling from $405 in parking fines. After a couple of winters of trying to sell microgreens and mushrooms, it became clear that tomatoes were the only product that worked for me.

For an aspiring writer reduced to farming for his bread, the next best thing to an adoring reading public is, I suppose, an adoring eating public. My relationships with many of the chefs and customers who come to my stand go back to the first year I came to market. Bill Telepan, whose unmistakable good-natured laugh arrives at my stand a few steps before he does, is one of those chefs. So is Philippe Bertineau, who shows up a moment after Bill. At this point, I have been selling tomatoes nonstop for three and a half hours. Sweat and fumy humidity are blurring my vision, and I am running low on product. But I assure Philippe that I will have his order ready when he is through shopping the other stands, so he wanders off for Franca's strawberries.

"What ever happened to those *haricots verts*?" asks Bill. Every year, in an effort to make up for a tiny fraction of Alvina Frey's legendary output, I plant a patch of *haricots verts*. This year's patch is choked with weeds and unlikely to bear fruit, which is good news in a way because now I don't have to pick them. As I am explaining this to Bill, Colin Alevras from the Tasting Room arrives with bags of Emerite pole beans and Mexican watermelons from Honey Hollow Farm. Colin is notorious for gleaning rarities from farmers—the four or five persimmons Keith Stewart brings each year from his hardy northern tree, John Gorzynski's Gilfeather turnips and crisp dahlia bulbs. He stashes his treasure beneath the back of the truck and heads off for more.

"Oh well," says Bill, referring to the doomed *haricots verts*, reminding me again how lucky I am to be able to get away with messing up as much as I do. It would be an easy thing for a chef to give me the heave-ho and order from one of those price sheets that get faxed continually by purveyors who will deliver to the door twice on the same day. *Haricots verts* from Guatemala, picked by workers who earn less in a day than my workers earn in an hour, come in a colorful labeled box and cost substantially less than mine. From all sides, the competition in freshness edges closer. USDA organic standards have enabled more middlemen than ever to put on a pair of bib overalls and do a brisk trade in organic produce. High-end food retailers like Whole Foods and Trader Joe's have recently placed stores across Fourteenth Street from Union Square Greenmarket. The anticipated arrival of Whole Foods was accompanied by murmurings and doomsday predictions among farmers and food commentators. All the Whole Foods people had to do was peel away the cellophane wrappers and gussy up their produce to make it look like it was grown locally and not in California or Mexico, then charge a nickel less than what farmers across the street were charging. We would all be going home with ripe tomatoes to feed the hogs. But I have noticed the opposite effect. While Whole Foods appears to thrive across the street, my sales have increased since they moved in. In fact, Whole Foods is one of my customers. What started out as a dozen or so farmers willing to take their chances amid spent syringes on the edge of a park that, in its time, might have served as the naturally seedy backdrop of the 1970s movie *Taxi Driver*, has evolved into a culinary mecca, complete with restaurants and gourmet grocery stores and even a very proper Englishman who plunks down amid all the vegetable stands on the steamiest of Saturday afternoons to demonstrate the clever potato peeler he sells briskly at five dollars a pop. "You cahhhhn't buy these anywhere else and they're made in Switzerland," he repeats as ribbons of carrot accumulate about his feet.

The tide that raises all ships. Morse Pitts's pea shoots, edible flowers, and mustard greens; Ron Binaghi's tomatoes, dill, thyme, and rosemary; Keith Stewart's Rocambole garlic, Sun Gold cherry tomatoes, and red-core Chantenay carrots; Ted Blew's bacon, chile peppers, and heirloom tomatoes; Sycamore Farm's same-day corn;

Vince D'Attolico's middle-of-winter garlic shoots; John Gorzynski's salsify, burdock, and turnips; Bill Maxwell's shell beans and sweet bell peppers; Alex Paffenroth's orange, purple, white, and yellow carrots; Chip Kent's quinces and Baldwin apples; Samascott Orchards' Newtown Pippin apples; Honey Hollow's foraged chanterelles, boletes, and hen-of-the-woods mushrooms; David Graves's New York City rooftop honey; Cherry Lane's asparagus, lima beans, okra, and Jersey tomatoes; Alvina Frey's beans; Guy Jones's greens; Rick Bishop's fingerling potatoes and wild arugula; Franca Tantillo's peas and day-neutral strawberries. Rick and Franca's marriage didn't survive all of those years of exhaustion and insanity. Few marriages could. They are two separate and highly respected farms now, Rick's Mountain Sweet Farm and Franca's Berried Treasures.

I have noticed a pattern among the chefs who continue to buy from me and the other Greenmarket farmers. So many of them worked at one time or another for either Daniel Boulud or David Bouley. When David Bouley set off to study Renaissance art in Paris, could he have foreseen that the celebrated restaurant he would one day open would serve as a kind of high-pressure talent studio, not unlike the studios Vasari describes in his *Lives of the Artists*? The studio where a young Michelangelo got his nose broken in a fistfight, for instance. A jealous rival, says Vasari. These days, the chefs are painting all of the Sistine Chapels. Kurt Gutenbrunner, Rocco DiSpirito, Dan Barber, Dave Pasternack, and Eric Ripert all worked in Bouley's kitchen early on. So did Galen Zamarra, Shea Gallante, Alex Ureña, and Cornelius Gallagher. Cornelius also worked for Daniel Boulud, as did Thomas Keller, Andrew Carmellini, Alex Lee, François Payard, Bill Telepan, David Chang, Mike Anthony, Johnny Iuzzini, Philippe Bertineau, Harold Moore, and Colin Alevras.

Bouley, Boulud. Outside New York City culinary circles, folks tend to fuzz these two similar-sounding names into a single restaurant empire. Besides crossing paths numerous times as they worked the same French kitchens in the nouvelle cuisine 1970s, both put in time at Le Cirque in New York City. But there are major differences between them. Boulud is uptown, Bouley downtown. David Bouley's American path to culinary prominence, with its detour through the Sorbonne, recalls the trajectory of the first modern promoter of American cuisine, James Beard, who had set off for England in pursuit of voice lessons to further an acting career, only to find himself enthusiastically sampling the Italian restaurants of London before moving on to Parisian fare. There were numerous factors that made Beard adept in any kitchen, the years spent by his mother's side, for one, picking and putting up huckleberries, blackberries, and strawberries, or gathering Dungeness crabs and razor clams on the coast of Oregon, just so they could be broiled or sautéed the same evening. "What a job it is to find a restaurant . . . where the pleasures of regional food are still respected," Beard wrote back in the early 1960s.

Similarly, David Bouley's appetite was whetted by the years he'd enthusiastically spent on his grandparents' seaside farm in Rhode Island. His grandparents had emigrated from France, where they had run a small, tidy farm and bakery. Dinner in the Rhode Island farmhouse often featured some combination of rabbit; celery root; yard chickens; leeks; French Breakfast radishes; skate, hake, calamari, and haddock fresh from the ocean; and homemade chèvre. Bouley learned early on how the flavor of a farm-raised rabbit differed from the flavor of a hare or even a wild rabbit, because he hunted, too. And in high school, he spent his summers fishing on the day boats at Chatham, Massachusetts. The term "Chatham day-boat fish" entered New York City's culinary lexicon when, years later, the same David Bouley started sending vans to Chatham, wait staff at the helm, to pick up the morning's fresh catch. Bouley's continuing preference for fresh seafood from the source of his youth recalls James Beard's enduring partiality for the Dungeness crab. Chatham cod is even on the menu at Evolution, the restaurant that Bouley opened way down in South Beach, Miami.

Daniel Boulud took the route great French chefs have always taken. Raised on a farm—like Escoffier, like Alain Ducasse—he set off at the age of fourteen to undergo his first kitchen apprenticeship, the initial stage in a humbling and well-rounded education that would eventually earn him the title of chef. At the age of fourteen, Daniel Boulud was learning in a Michelin two-star kitchen how to stuff truffles and foie gras into pheasants like the ones he'd hunted back on the farm. Early in the morning, he was at the market in Lyon, competing with the likes of Paul Bocuse, Georges Blanc, and the Troisgros brothers for the freshest fruits, vegetables, cheeses, and fish.

For the record, Michelangelo was fourteen years old when he served his first apprenticeship with Domenico Ghirlandaio. When he finally arrived in the United States at the age of twenty-seven, a talented chef with an impressive résumé, Daniel Boulud proved himself a versatile and open-minded immigrant, embracing the ingredients he found in the States the way he had been trained to embrace local ingredients in France. He took the enormous Idaho potato and wrapped slices of it around sea bass to create one of his signature dishes, paupiette of sea bass. His application of French technique to the standardized bent of American cuisine even had a humorous self-effacing side to it that reminds me of my great-grandmother's love of white bread. The now-famous DB Bistro Moderne hamburger, for instance, a generous piece of sirloin stuffed, like those pheasants of yore, with truffles and fois gras, costs substantially more than its McDonald's brethren. And on the cover of his cookbook *Chef Daniel Boulud: Cooking in New York City*, he poses with a hot dog in hand.

It was a willingness to abandon some of the treasured transatlantic ingredients of France in favor of an un-Mediterranean Mid-Atlantic *terroir* that made the world-class kitchens of Bouley and Boulud into ideal apprenticeships for the wave of talented chefs with whom I started doing business when I first came to Green-market ten years ago. I often think of the dishes dreamed up by Alex Lee, the former chef de cuisine and executive chef at Restaurant Daniel, dishes I would often get a taste of because Alex was so excited to show me what could be done with my produce. In one memorable instance, Alex cut the tomatoes I brought into nine perfect one-and-a-half-inch squares of different colors—pink squares, white squares, brown, green, yellow, and red squares—and assembled them together into one single square that resembled the side of a large Rubik's cube. Atop this multicolored square he sprinkled Ligurian olive oil, cracked pepper, and Iranian gold osetra caviar. Mondrian to the eye. And to the tongue: musky voluptuousness of caviar inking its perfume over the musky, midsummer voluptuousness of tomatoes. By selecting the individual squares one at a time and popping them into your mouth, you could taste the nuances of sweetness and acidity: hard to believe how different those nine distinct colors could taste.

Union Square Park was not named after the winning side in the Civil War, in spite of the statue of Abraham Lincoln and the enthusiastically attended war rally held in the park in 1861. Created in the early 1800s, the park got its name from its location at the "union" of two venerable city thoroughfares, Broadway and the Bowery. At the time the park was built, a brief carriage ride up Broadway could have brought a culinary-minded urbanite into sight of a cornfield or a patch of lettuce, although development pressure on towns like Yorkville, Chelsea, and Murray Hill must have been comparable to the pressures on Bergen County, New Jersey, forty years ago: lavish estates and dense housing sending farmers deeper into the hinterlands, across the Hudson into Jersey, or the East River into Brooklyn or Queens, as far north as the Bronx, where John Gorzynski's grandfather farmed beneath the present-day Whitestone Bridge. The father of Ken Migliorelli, another Union Square farmer, also farmed in the Bronx until 1970, when he moved to Dutchess County, New York. "They never tear down a house to put in a farm," Ken Migliorelli is fond of saying.

Pick up Route 17 North in Bergen County and you cross the New York state line into Orange County, where more Greenmarket farmers are located than in any other region. Keith Stewart grows his prized garlic in Orange County. Morse Pitts and Guy Jones grow their superb greens there. Orange County's "black dirt" region, once known as the onion-growing capital of the world, produces the great majority of those succulent radishes, beets, carrots, turnips, and other root crops that turn up on Greenmarket display tables. More than any county, perhaps, Orange deserves the title "breadbasket of New York City."

Two hundred years ago, Orange County was frontier. We have a clear picture of this corner of the frontier from a book called *Letters from an American Farmer*, written by a French veteran of the French and Indian War, Michel-Guillaume-Saint-Jean de Crèvecoeur. Crèvecoeur's name is often attached to the epithet "the farmer from Pennsylvania," perhaps because of a foray down the Susquehanna River that he wrote about, perhaps because of his enthusiastic endorsement of the Quaker pacifist William Penn, whose ideas about sweat equity and religious tolerance helped populate the sylvan region I grew up in with hardworking English, Welsh, Lutheran Germans, Dutch Quakers, French Huguenots, Mennonites, and Amish. After the French and Indian War, Crèvecoeur married an Englishwoman and purchased his farm, Pine Hill, a few miles from the present-day Orange County seat, Goshen. He then set about clearing the land and planting it with corn, squash, cabbage, wheat, and "pompion," which is how the French pronounced the Native American word for pumpkin, *pompom*. He raised cattle and hogs, too, enough to feed his family. And for the seven years he lived at Pine Hill, he wrote about the experience for his civilized European friends. "I have composed many a good sermon as I followed my plough," he boasts.

Some of what Crèvecoeur writes about is the same day-to-day stuff I encounter in my fields: fat, mild, harmless blacksnakes; deer that will eat most anything you plant unless they are effectively fenced out; apple trees that, like ours at Eckerton, produced fruit every two years in the organic-because-there-was-no-alternative colonial period. At the same time, I can only gasp at the level of industry he describes:

> *I am but a feller of trees, a cultivator of lands, the most honourable title an American can have. I have no exploits, no discoveries, no inventions to boast of; I have cleared about 370 acres of land, some for the plough, some for the scythe, and this has occupied many years of my life.*

Many years of his life? Seven, to be exact. In seven years, without the aid of a tractor or a chiropractor, Crèvecoeur cleared 370 acres, or one acre every seven days, and proceeded to work those acres as farmland. It helped tremendously, I suppose, that even a slavery-opposed northerner like Crèvecoeur owned some slaves. African Americans must have felled a good number of those trees. Surely, the age Crèvecoeur writes about was hardier than the age to which I belong.

What jumps out at the reader of *Letters from an American Farmer* is what a personal paradise Pine Hill was for the writer, one that could not last. When intimations of another war started to brew, the decorated veteran of previous battles wanted only to continue tending to his orchards and his pompion, with his baby balanced on his plow and his wife sitting on the edge of the field with her knitting. He is the picture of Odysseus resisting the trip to Troy. Forced to choose sides, Crèvecoeur considered living

among the native Indians but decided against this option because
he could not think of a single instance in which a European who
went to live with Indians elected to become a European again.
But his Tory wife and his favorable views toward the Crown (a
Frenchman!) did not cast him in an ideal light among his patriot
neighbors. The last of his letters, "Distresses of a Frontier Man,"
describes the pacifist fence sitter tormented by fears of vengeful
patriot neighbors and unfriendly Indians, his nerves jangled by
every late-night noise, every midnight growl of the dog: "I fly from
one erratic thought to another, and my mind, irritated by these ac-
rimonious reflections, is ready sometimes to lead me to dangerous
extremes of violence." Forced to act at last, Crèvecoeur fled Pine
Hill, manuscript in hand, winding up in New York City, where he
was promptly arrested by a British garrison on suspicion of being
a patriot.

Unwilling to take up arms and join either side, Crèvecoeur
could not stay in New York City nor could he return to his wife,
who was eventually killed by Indians, although his children were
miraculously spared and spirited off to Boston. Deprived of axe
and plow, Crèvecoeur had a nervous breakdown but eventually
recovered enough to set sail for France, where *Letters from an
American Farmer* was published in 1782, a year after Rousseau's
Confessions came out. Sedulously romantic in its depiction of frontier life among native Indians and poisonous snakes, the book was
an immediate success. But his portraits of Europeans of all nations bushwhacking their way to an earnest living in a country
composed primarily of farmers on equal footing—the burgeoning
American "middle class" of independent freeholders—places *Letters from an American Farmer* as the cornerstone of all subsequent
literature about the peculiarly American character. "Whence the
difference arises I know not," Crèvecoeur writes, "but out of twelve
families of emigrants of each country, generally seven Scotch will

succeed, nine German, and four Irish." About the poorly performing Irish, he goes on to say, "They love to drink and to quarrel;
they are litigious and soon take to the gun, which is the ruin of
everything; they seem beside to labour under a greater degree of
ignorance in husbandry than the others . . . their potatoes, which
are easily raised, are perhaps an inducement to laziness."

Crèvecoeur, who was not above introducing the couch-potato-
inducing spud to Normandy, does not offer up statistics about
French farmers in America, presumably because his sampling was
insufficient. Nor does he discuss the Poles, who didn't farm Orange
County in statistically significant numbers until the late 1800s.
What is today known as the highly fertile—and flammable—
"black dirt" of Orange County was all swamp and ponds in Crèvecoeur's time, a shallow 5,500-acre pond, really, with the northward
flowing Wallkill River as its backbone, a shallow pond whose inky
surface concealed rot and debris and preserved mastodon bones,
thousands of years of organic sediment accumulated since the last
ice age receded. Who knew that beneath this pond surface lay
twenty-foot-thick layers of tar-black, carbon-rich topsoil? A whole
bunch of Polish immigrants from New York City did, and so did a
smattering of those dependable "nine in twelve" Germans, whiskey-
swilling "four in twelve" Irish, and some unrated Italians, all of
whom preferred the plow to the New York City sweatshop, laying
claim to the cheap swampland with scraped-together savings and
sweat equity. *You drain it and it's yours, pal.* With an industry that
must have rivaled Crèvecoeur's, the forebears of the onion-growing
dynasties of the twentieth century drained the great shallow pond
that surrounded Orange County towns like Pine Island.

While there has always been murmuring among farmers and
customers that the vegetables stacked up at some of the Greenmarket stands are suspiciously indistinguishable from the well-traveled
stuff one finds at Hunts Point wholesale market in the Bronx, there

is no disputing where Alex Paffenroth's carrots are grown. Those one-and-a-half-foot-long yellow, white, purple, and orange carrots would sink their roots clear to China if Alex's black dirt were any deeper. In addition, he grows purple, white, golden, and red beets; red, white, and purple-tinted turnips; nineteen varieties of potato; burdock; parsley root; celery root; salsify; parsnips.

Alex is a fifth-generation black-dirt farmer who grew up luke-warm to the future carved out for him in an onion field. In 1969, he was stationed at Fort Hood in Texas, preparing to ship off for Vietnam, when word came that his father had died and he had to go home for more than just a funeral: onion harvest was just a few months off. For the next decade and a half, Alex grew hybrid yellow globe onions the way his father, grandfather, and great-grandfather had before him. But in the late 1980s, his crop was butchered by a hailstorm. Unwilling to accept the loss at first, he tried to salvage what he could of the dented and cracked onions, only to dig himself deeper into debt because his harvested crop was worth next to nothing. He had to sell off some of his acres and rent out others. Five other onion farmers in his "Little York" corner of the black-dirt region went under on account of the same hailstorm, but Alex hung in there and eventually accepted some advice about diversifying from his father-in-law. "Diversify" is an understate-ment when you consider what Alex went on to do. These days, he plants every one of his seventy-two acres with those otherworldly varieties, planting in succession to ensure a constant season-long supply, double and triple cropping many of those acres with short-season vegetables like radishes. Red radishes, pink radishes, white radishes, black radishes. Red and white French Breakfast radishes. Even the watermelon radish—green on the outside, pink on the inside—that chefs never seem to get enough of these days. If he still plants ten acres of traditional globe onions, he also grows red, yel-low, white, and striped cipollini onions; three kinds of pearl onion;

slender long purplish Tropea onions; four varieties of shallots; three acres of leeks. Wednesday and Saturday mornings, Alex arrives at market with hundreds of already filled bags labeled with the names of restaurants like Gramercy Tavern, Jean-Georges, Union Square Cafe, and Telepan. Week after week, he comes through for these restaurants, the way Alvina Frey once came through with *haricots verts*. Alex Paffenroth is one of the most organized farmers I have ever met.

Ironically, the prestigious black dirt is itself partly responsible for Orange County's declining market share in the international onion trade. The fudge-soft muck can't support industrial-sized equipment of the kind large-scale growers elsewhere drive over their fields, which explains the lettuces, radishes, sweet corn, peppers, and tomatoes brought to various New York City Greenmarkets by farmers who once grew nothing but yellow globe onions: Osczepinskis, Glebockis, Glowaczewskis, Morgiewiczs, Rogowskis. Moreover, a leaning-tower-of-Pisa syndrome prohibits the construction of homes on the black dirt, ensuring that it will stay farmland for the foreseeable future. Free of development pressure, an acre of black dirt still sells for a nominal $2,500.

But Orange County's rock-strewn "brown dirt"—the type of ground Crèvecoeur and his slaves cleared—is a different story. The county's once-thriving dairy farms have been disappearing for years. Morse Pitts, whose fields of impeccable greens near Montgomery stand up like a brave but technologically overwhelmed army beside encroaching smokestacks and large industrial buildings, has been searching in vain for an affordable new location, one within reasonable travel distance from his stand at Union Square. "Everything I'm looking at is a million dollars or more," rues Morse. Where Manhattan farmland stood some two hundred years ago, where Bergen County was in the 1960s, is about where Orange County's brown dirt stands today. Keith Stewart, who bought his farm twenty years ago, says flatly that he could not have bought it in 2006. "The unavoidable truth," he writes in his book, "is that no young would-be farmer, unless endowed with a trust fund or some independent income stream, could afford to buy our place and try his or her hand at vegetable growing as I did back in 1986." Keith has finally managed to obtain a conservation easement for his farm since he and his wife do not have heirs to pass the farm on to and he is approaching retirement age. He would like to ensure that his farm stays a farm, but he also makes the very important point that the increased value of a farmer's land is a kind of 401(k) plan, since the profits from farming in themselves can rarely carry a farmer through retirement (or even semiretirement, since most farmers find it hard to go completely cold turkey). Too often, though, conservation easement payments to farmers do not bridge the gap between the value of the preserved land and the amount a young, prospective farmer could pay for the land when it goes on the market stripped of its development potential. A country home with a permanent view is something a Wall Street broker might value as much as a farmer.

In spite of the positive impact of Greenmarket and other open-air markets throughout the United States, skyrocketing real estate values continue to nudge smaller produce farms farther away from metropolitan areas like New York City. This is an undeniable and ongoing trend, one that may or may not be effectively addressed in time, since it never manifests itself as an immediate crisis, the way a war does. Or a bridge collapse. Orange County is today a different kind of frontier from the one Crèvecoeur described. The county will either hold on to some farmland or it won't. Once you get more than three hours from New York City, the pool of farmers willing to risk falling asleep at the wheel on the way home from a marathon Greenmarket session begins to dwindle significantly.

Black dirt or brown, it can be a grueling business, keeping a city like New York supplied with vegetables picked the day before on land that is situated farther and farther away from Union Square. You need to surround yourself with a crew who are willing to work as hard as they worked in Crèvecoeur's tree-felling days, or those immigrants who drained the black dirt. A crew who are willing to keep right on picking in the hundred-degree heat. And for modest pay. Chances are good that, as in Crèvecoeur's day, you need immigrants. Mexicans, Oajacetas, Michoacáners, Guatemalans. Keith Stewart pulls it off each year with a team of energetic interns culled from a well-organized wintertime search of college campuses. Like Keith, Alex Paffenroth is approaching retirement age without an heir to carry on his unique operation. I asked Alex where all of the restaurants are going to get their white carrots, Tropea onions, and peppermint-striped beets when he stops coming to Union Square. He thought for a moment and then said, with a laugh that expressed both humility and pride, "Who's gonna do what I do?"

"On or about December 1, 1910," Virginia Woolf remarked in the early part of the last century, "human nature changed." The way I see it, human nature must have changed numerous times since Crèvecoeur and his "freeholding" neighbors gleefully cleared the forests of Orange County. But in the early part of *this* century, the day that changed everything—human nature, everything—is easier to pinpoint than Virginia Woolf's December 1. The first plane flew directly over Union Square on a Tuesday, a day when the farmers were not set up. I was in the field picking tomatoes to bring to market the following day. But a number of my regular customers were in the park, relaxing, having a cigarette. The sound of the plane, so near to the ground as it screamed ahead at five hundred miles an hour, caused all eyes to turn skyward and follow it as it headed downtown.

"The landing gear wasn't down," Gloria told us six days later, when we finally made it in to Monday market. "That's how I knew something was wrong." Most of the farmers who were set up at the

World Trade Center Greenmarket the morning of September 11 had had to flee on foot, leaving their trucks and wares to be buried in rubble. We missed Wednesday market because the city had closed all its entrances. When Toby went down to Union Square on September 12 to see if any of the farmers had somehow managed to cross over onto the island on a day that fell at the peak of harvest, she found a desolate open park space in which only one familiar figure was to be seen: Natalie, with two unsold pictures in her hand, perplexed, lower lip jutting out, fuming, "Where did everybody go?" On Friday, I had managed to get in and deliver to some restaurants. But the only hearty appetites to be found within twenty-five miles of Ground Zero were those of the firemen and volunteers who were pouring into New York City to help look for bodies and clear debris. It would be a couple of months before anybody felt like going out to eat again. I was up to my ears in tomatoes, too, a bumper crop pouring off my vines, unable to sell out for the first time ever.

But it was unthinkable to be thinking about myself at a time like this. "I stayed home for three days," said the tall strong hippie girl who worked at my stand that first Monday back. "I processed it and now I'm okay with it." But not everyone was okay with it. Not yet, anyway. Some of our customers were just coming out after being shut in for five days. All of them seemed relieved to find this little corner of their universe still in place in the aftermath of the attack. "Thank you for coming," they told us over and over again, as if they'd feared we would abandon them and their wounded city. For my part, I had feared *they* would abandon me and my tomatoes. Instead, I saw customers I hadn't noticed in months because I was always working the back of the truck. Rosh Hashanah was coming up, so we had a very busy Monday, even if I didn't have the restaurants to unburden me of my whole load. One man who was notorious for showing up in the afternoon after the last tomato had been sold stood with mouth agape, looking at all of the bright tomatoes still on display, unable to speak. "Thank you for coming," he finally said.

There was no way I could possibly unload so many tomatoes without my usual restaurant sales, so I started giving away as many as I could to the suddenly underemployed chefs who were cooking for all of those hungry volunteers. Daniel Boulud was cranking out meals on a barge in New York Harbor, and David Bouley was running a busy cafeteria just off Ground Zero, where the digging and the search for bodies was going on round the clock. Every kitchen throughout New York City was making sandwiches for firemen. By the following Wednesday, I would be bursting at the seams with tomatoes, so I drove the truck down to within a few blocks of Ground Zero and unloaded everything I had on it.

But on that first Monday back, there was comfort and solace to be found amid those stacked-up Greenmarket vegetables. The solid and reassuring presence of autumn's bounty, the opportunity for good, honest commerce, helped me and my customers get through a very difficult period. "Thank you for coming," they repeated as they handed over their money and I gave them tomatoes. Before the day was over, I had to crawl into the back of the truck and cry.

Soon after 9/11, the country slipped into a recession and interest rates plummeted to thirty-year lows. Anybody with money to invest, it seemed, was putting it in the only thing guaranteed to make money: real estate. Almost overnight, land values doubled. The farm that a few years earlier seemed a little bit out of reach at $500,000 was now going for close to a million. Slowly, something began to sink in for me. All those years of living frugal as a squirrel, of running as fast as I could, with my heart pounding, trying to catch up to this pulling-out train, this farm I wanted to buy ever since I got a late start in farming. This was the story of my life, really. I was the same kid who was always racing off down the hill at Eckerton to catch the school bus because I got out of bed with no time to spare. This time around, I had to finally stop at the foot of the mountain, gulping for air, watching as the train went *shug-gashuggashugga* into the hills without me.

My farm was out of reach. For the first time in years, I could ease off and have a look at what a decade of farming had made me into. All those years of dragging my mother and her boyfriend into the field, my father, my father's girlfriend, my wife, my friends. I didn't want a wife or friends or a mother. I wanted chattels. I wanted people willing to help me pick at any and all hours. And now that we lived in town with our two daughters, there was no chance I could ever again trick the woman I married into coming out into the field. She had done her time. And I had become a marginalized human being, surrounded by a squad of Mexicans who said *sí* to every question I asked but resorted to their native Purépecha language when they wanted privacy. Without a barn to put my equipment in, I would have to watch my tractor and my disc and my plow and my transplanter accumulate rust as the years wore on. Dissolution and decay. I became angry, every bit as angry as my father used to get when a jury ruled against the little guy he'd put everything he had into defending. Or when a client whose ass he kept out of jail for the umpteenth time didn't have the dignity to cough up a retainer or pound a few nails in return. When I looked into the mirror, I could see that I was starting to look more and more like my father.

But nothing infuriated me more than the opinion of the local farmers who came upon my truck patch and took note of the weeds growing among my tomatoes and onions and radishes, farmers whose approval I had been trying to win since my father moved me to Eckerton when I was six years old. *So you think you want to be a farmer?* they asked me over and over again, asking the question without even a hint of malicious intent. What I was doing could never register in their book as farming, no matter how much money I could make at it, no matter how many palates I could please. I might as well have been some wild naked banshee, a forebear of Crèvecoeur's poorly performing "four in twelve" Irish, racing hell-bent out of the woods with knife raised high, trying against all reason to scare the daylights out of a phalanx of shiny-shielded, well-positioned Romans.

There are farms on either side of Eckerton, Milt Miller's old farm being one of them, where they regularly spread city sewage on their sloped ground. For months at a time the country breezes reek so badly you'd just as well stay inside. And there are farms along the interstate that put up billboards to help pay their real-estate taxes. *Why don't you pull aside those billboard and sludge farmers and condescend to them with your question?*

So you think you want to be a farmer? But there was no going back to work in an office for me, no cleaning the dirt out from under my fingernails and rejoining civilization. I was too far out ever to come back. I thought I had set out in life to become the next Saul Bellow or the next Thomas Wolfe. But what I had become was the next Milt Miller, a landless farmer, asocial, grumbling to myself, all bloated up with stomach-quaking anger that could erupt at any moment, raw, invective-laced, divorce-leaning, to-hell-with-the-rest-of-the-world anger, a landless farmer playing at farming on Eckerton Hill. I was playing at being Milt Miller himself although I was doing things he never would have done. I behaved badly, tracked mud into the house, the semisuburban fortress my wife had erected around our beautiful sweet daughters, just to remind her what my business was. I even revised the history of our unsuccessful farm search. *Why didn't we buy the farm back when we could afford it? We could have put a blue tarp over those damned leaky roofs, the way they do to those bungalows down by the creek. I would have lived in a yurt, for crissakes. I would have lived in a tent the way my father used to.* My father, again, the Eagle Scout for life, sleeping out in a tent every night, with the beagle lying next to him, strapping on his hiking boots to go into Allentown and argue his cases. *Go ahead, judge, criticize my shoes. See if I give a shit.*

And then, just as quickly, the anger would subside. I would be plowing a patch of ground on Eckerton Hill, the smell of dank earth all around me, or pulling weeds in the corn while some mockingbird in the tree entertained me with his endless repertoire, his no-repeat Thursday. Or I would be driving over a weedy patch of the field when suddenly the fragrance of wild strawberries would envelope me. Down off the tractor I would leap, to stain my knees red, my lips, my fingers.

With the familiar curves of her hummocks and valleys, Eckerton could soothe me just as quickly as she could drive me to the most insane fits of anger. I love her. I love her not . . .

To get to the old Pelz farm, the farm where Alvina Frey grew up picking strawberries and tomatoes, you take a right at the Dunkin' Donuts along Route 17. I had trouble getting there recently because the first Dunkin' Donuts I turned at was the wrong one. The second Dunkin' Donuts proved not to be the right one, either. I kept getting back onto Route 17, driving south for five or six miles, or north for three miles, then pulling off on the ramps that slingshotted me across an overpass and back into the opposite lane. I was on the verge of giving up when I finally got Alvina on the cell phone and she directed me to the correct Dunkin' Donuts. I wanted to visit Alvina because she had been so generous with advice and seed recommendations back when I was starting out at Greenmarket. And because in John McPhee's wonderful long essay about Greenmarket's first year, "Giving Good Weight," an essay I can never tire of reading, he closes with a picture of a forty-six-year-old Alvina. "People . . . sense when they linger close around Alvina Frey," McPhee wrote, "that she is—perhaps a little more than anyone else here—what the Greenmarket is all about."

McPhee was writing before Alvina developed her reputation for beans. Crèvecoeur would probably have commented upon Alvina's German ancestry. Behind every one of those "nine in twelve" Germans stood wives who "vie with their husbands, and often share with them the most severe toils of the field, which they understand better." Alvina's grandmother, Alwine Pelz, had cleared the land, built the stone barn, and dug the well after emigrating from Saxony in the late 1800s. At seventy-six, Alvina has outlived two husbands but has no plans to marry again. Although she has retired from Greenmarket, where chefs continue to grumble over the discontinuation of her beans, she still plants half an acre with limas, tomatoes, and the little cucumbers she calls pickles. Her half-acre patch sits on top of a hill among ramshackle implement sheds. She and her fellow bean picker, Leopoldo, work that half-acre patch, along with Frank Short, a childhood friend. Alvina still sells limas and tomatoes from her patch to the Saddle River Inn, to the same chef, Hans Egg, whom she sold to before she started going to Greenmarket thirty years ago.

Frank and Alvina can remember a time when the Shorts and the Pelzes owned all of the surrounding land. In winter, when there were no strawberries or tomatoes to pick, they would go sledding down the same road where today the chromium splendor of BMWs, Volvos, and Jaguars makes a perilous adventure out of just walking across.

Times change. But for Alvina's half-acre patch, there is no tillable ground left of either the Short or the Pelz farms. "I loved picking," Alvina says behind the wheel of her car as she takes me on a tour of the old farm. "You're free to think whatever you want to think. Your hands know what to do while in your mind you are wherever you want to be. There are not a lot of jobs that give you that kind of freedom."

My sense of the original farm's boundaries are fuzzy, but every office park we drive past, every cul-de-sac we pull into harbors some memory for Alvina. "That Minolta parking lot," she says, "is where my father liked to plant his late tomatoes. The frost always came last to that patch. There were years when we picked tomatoes into November. Boy was I glad when the frost would finally come." We pull a U-turn and backtrack past office parks before making a left onto a road that bifurcates the twenty-one-acre parcel that was the second to last to be sold off. Half-acre lots of large homes whose stylish, diagonal-wood-empaneled sides will resonate "late 1970s rustic contemporary" into the foreseeable future. "I've never come back here since we sold this," Alvina says serenely. "These are lovely homes."

"Oh!" says Alvina after we cross the busy highway where she used to go sledding, into another development. "This swamp down here. Once, I got the Farmall H stuck in this swamp. Ohhhh!" I can imagine the mishap from the look on her face: a day or two of pulling with chains and trying to shove pieces of wood under the tires to give them traction. The Farmall H that she had tried to trade in for horses. Shoving wood under the wheels and pushing and tugging while so much work piled up in the meantime, ground to be plowed and peas to be picked, while that old Farmall H merrily spit out rooster tails of mud.

"Now these stones on the edge of the swamp," she says. "They haven't moved since we sold this land. Will you just look at those stones? This is still Bergen County, but Rockland County is more like it."

"Stones" hardly describes what I'm looking at. "Rocks" doesn't do them justice, either. Alvina's stones are big round boulders, four times the size of a basketball, all of them sitting randomly where they sat when the land went into development, like bocce balls left behind by a race of Titans interrupted in the middle of a game.

"Well, look at that," Alvina says with gleeful surprise. "There's a stone somebody rolled into their yard. Good to see someone made use of the stones."

Back out onto the sledding road, we stop at the old barn that Alvina's grandmother had built of slightly smaller stones. Repointed and sharpened up, its wide doors replaced, today the barn houses the Mahwah Historical Society. A plaque next to the door reads:

The Pelz family presents this plaque to Alvina Pelz,
granddaughter of Franz and Alwine Pelz,
who farmed the family land
for 60 years.

Alvina Pelz. The name of the girl who picked all of those strawberries before and after school, the name that with a few small alterations would be the same as the name of the grandmother who built the stone barn and started a farm more than one hundred years ago.

Directly across the street from the barn sits the last sixteen-acre patch where Alvina picked her crisp, succulent beans until eight years ago. After her retirement, developers wasted no time rotating the patch permanently out of beans. The soil that once yielded such fabulous limas has since spawned mansions, terra-cotta roofs, elaborate fountains. I am reminded that we are the richest nation on earth. And while a fair number of people in New York City ruefully recall the *haricots verts* that once grew in this Beverly Hillsian cul-de-sac, the unavoidable truth is that people have got to live someplace.

For sure, people have got to live someplace.

Acknowledgments

A HUGE THANK-YOU to all of the people who read these pieces and read them again: my mother and longtime editor, author Sharon Sheehe Stark, who has always given me an honest critique and encouraged me to keep writing; Gerry Howard, my editor at Broadway Books, who singled out the pages that were nearest to my heart and pushed me to keep at it when the tomatoes wouldn't let up outside; Irene Skolnick, my agent, whose enthusiasm didn't flag when mine did; Toby Arons, who offered insights both literary and culinary; Bill Bascom, my mother's charming and intelligent boyfriend; and James Weaver, fellow farmer and storyteller extraordinaire.

Thanks, too, to Wayne Miller, who put in field hours of the kind I did in the early years so that I could be free to sit in a farmhouse and fidget over what it was I was going to write. Since there could not have been a story without the farm, I am indebted to a number of people whose practical knowledge and freely offered time were critical to getting the farm off the ground and keeping one cantankerous old tractor and a lot of rusty equipment up and running. So thanks to Daryl Smith, Kim Goldman, and Ted and Kelly LaMastra. The farm would have collapsed of its own exhaustion if not for the tenacity and cunning of many individuals, including Bonnie Mauger, Heidi Secord, Enrique Solis, Ignacio and Natalya Bautista, Joe Bowman, Eric de Jesus, Beth Duby, Lee Weigle, Ernest Kohler, Deb Trabosh, and Pedro Salvador.

Nor would the farm have survived its first tumultuous year without the chefs, restaurateurs, and kitchen staff who took an interest in my products and often gave me something to eat. To name everyone individually would easily take up five pages, and I'm sure I would still leave out some names since it is the end of another growing season and I am very forgetful. Naming all of the customers who stopped regularly at the stand over the years would take up an additional five pages. Thank you to everyone.

I am especially grateful to seven talented farmers who shared their stories with me and/or showed me around their farms: Ron Binaghi Jr., Guy Jones, Rick Bishop, Franca Tantillo, Alvina Frey, Alex Paffenroth, and Keith Stewart. Four individuals were critical to seeing to it that my voice found an audience: editors Paulette Licitra and Peter Selgin at Alimentum accepted a story after a fourteen-year drought and invited me to read in New York City; chef Dave Pasternack provided invaluable literary-agency services in exchange for some scrapple; author Kate Christensen steered me toward a wonderful editor.

The whole New York City metropolitan area is indebted to Barry Benepe and Bob Lewis for setting up New York City's Greenmarket.

Finally, thanks to my father, who first brought me to Eckerton; to my wife, Jill, who has hung in there from the start; and to my beautiful girls, Charlotte and Gwendolyn, who never fail to inspire me.